Arctic Life
Challenge to Survive

Design by Dolores Kacsuta Parks
Typeset in Baskerville by Hoechstetter Printing Company, Inc.,
Pittsburgh, Pennsylvania
Printing by Geyer Printing Company, Inc.,
Pittsburgh, Pennsylvania

Library of Congress Catalog Card Number: 82-73756
ISBN: 0-911239-02-2

Manufactured in the United States of America
© 1983, The Board of Trustees, Carnegie Institute,
Pittsburgh, Pennsylvania

Front Cover:
*At Umingmaktuk in Canada's Northwest
Territories,* inuksuit *are outlined against the
midnight sun. Constructed from rocks and
stones and placed in a converging-row
formation, the* inuksuit *channel caribou
toward waiting hunters.*

Back Cover:
*A young girl gathers seagull eggs on a cliff
overlooking Bathurst Inlet in Canada's
Northwest Territories.*

Arctic Life
Challenge to Survive

Martina Magenau Jacobs and James B. Richardson III, Editors

John Frechione, Ruth Anne Matinko, and Claudia N. Medoff, Editorial Assistants

The Board of Trustees, Carnegie Institute, Pittsburgh, Pennsylvania

*George W. Wyckoff Jr. on a Carnegie Museum
of Natural History expedition to the Central
Canadian Arctic.*

Dedication

George W. Wyckoff Jr. was one of those rare individuals whose insatiable curiosity about life led to intense involvement in a variety of subject areas and to mastery of several skills. Not only did he maintain a successful business career, but he was also accomplished in aviation, cinematography, and athletics. George also actively pursued an interest in the natural world and lent his steadfast support to institutions and organizations devoted to natural history and the environment. Carnegie Institute is fortunate to have had George serve as a Term Member of the Carnegie Museum of Natural History Committee from 1968 through 1973.

George's support of Carnegie Museum of Natural History was far more than passive. His adventurous spirit led him to participate in several field expeditions. In the spring of 1972, George accompanied an expedition led by Dr. J. Kenneth Doutt to the Clyde River region of the Central Canadian Arctic. Ambitious as always, George served as cinematographer for the expedition, documenting on film the everyday life of an Inuit family who were following a way of life reminiscent of their forebears. From this footage, a fine documentary film was ultimately produced.

Throughout his stay in the Arctic, George often expressed his admiration for the Inuit and their ability to adapt to challenging environmental conditions. He repeatedly expressed his hope that the field work and filming might lead to an exhibition at Carnegie Museum of Natural History that would convey the fascinating and ever-changing world of the Inuit.

Now, eight years after his untimely death, the institution which he staunchly supported can fulfill that vision. The permanent exhibition "Polar World: Wyckoff Hall of Arctic Life" and the complementary publication, *Arctic Life: Challenge to Survive*, commemorate George Wyckoff's efforts to present the Inuit—their patience, ingenuity, and achievements in response to harsh environmental conditions. These are fitting tributes to this man who possessed tireless energy, personal warmth, and a zest for knowledge and life itself. I am deeply honored to so dedicate this volume.

Arthur M. Scully Jr.
The Board of Trustees,
Carnegie Institute
Carnegie Museum of Natural
History Committee
December 1983

Contents

Foreword

This catalog is a companion publication to the permanent exhibit "Polar World: Wyckoff Hall of Arctic Life" that opened at Carnegie Museum of Natural History on December 10, 1983. The collection of essays both complements and supplements the basic themes expressed in the three-dimensional displays. The primary purpose of the exhibit is to highlight the story of the successful, often ingenious, adaptations of the Inuit to one of the most rigorous and challenging environments in the world. It is a story which has been unfolding for over 4,500 years in the North American Arctic.

Both the Polar World exhibit and this book were inspired by the late George W. Wyckoff Jr. In 1972 he traveled to the Clyde River area of Baffin Island and filmed the everyday activities of a small group of Inuit who still lived primarily by hunting. Wyckoff, a staunch supporter of Carnegie Museum of Natural History, envisioned this expedition as the groundwork for a future major museum exhibit.

Successful completion of this publication has been a complex collaborative effort. Primary acknowledgment goes to the nine essay authors, each a recognized expert in a particular discipline, for their valuable contributions.

The production of the catalog drew upon the talents of dozens of individuals in several departments of Carnegie Museum of Natural History, Carnegie Institute, with general coordination and administrative supervision by Assistant Director Timothy Parks.

Dr. James B. Richardson III, Chief Curator of Anthropology, and Dr. Martina Magenau Jacobs, Program Specialist for Publications within the Division of Education, were most instrumental in organizing and editing this volume. Dr. Richardson organized the content, arranged for the participation of the essay authors, and oversaw scientific editing. He was assisted by two other members of the Section of Anthropology: Dr. John Frechione, Project Coordinator for the Polar World exhibit, and Claudia N. Medoff, Collection Manager, were deeply involved in scientific editing, in the securing of photographs and other materials for both the exhibit and the catalog, and in preparing captions for photographs and illustrations.

Dr. Jacobs edited the essays, coordinated their review, and managed the overall production of the book. She was given invaluable assistance by Ruth Anne Matinko, also Program Specialist for Publications. The painstaking work of proofreading and general research was performed ably by Dr. Elizabeth Mertz, professional docent in the division. Division of Education Secretary Denean Y. Fox processed all the manuscripts.

Special acknowledgment must go to the talented staff of the Division of Exhibits, under the direction of Chairman Clifford J. Morrow Jr.: James R. Senior (Assistant Chairman), Nancy J. Perkins (Scientific Illustrator), Gail S. Richards (Museum Artist), and Christopher Malczewski (Graphic Artist) prepared many of the superb illustrations which appear in this volume. Museum Photographer Vincent J. Abromitis successfully completed the enormous task of preparing photographic material for use both in the exhibit and for this catalog.

Dolores Kacsuta Parks translated the numerous visual and written elements into a cohesive and coherent whole. Serving as art director, graphic designer, and illustrator, Ms. Parks designed and supervised the production of the catalog. A special note of thanks also goes to Geyer Printing Company, not only for excellent work in printing this volume, but also for its steadfast support and interest in this project over the past two years.

Several of the artifacts illustrated in these essays were generously loaned for the exhibit by the American Museum of Natural History; National Museum of Man, National Museums of Canada; Field Museum of Natural History; and The University Museum, University of Pennsylvania. These, along with many objects from the permanent collection of Carnegie Museum of Natural History, were photographed by Stan Franzos. We also acknowledge the important work of Conservator Joan S. Gardner of the Section of Anthropology, who prepared the artifacts for both exhibit and photographic uses.

Many individuals and institutions have generously supplied photographs for this catalog. They are acknowledged on page 206.

The greatest thanks goes to the Wyckoff Memorial Exhibit Steering Committee which, under the leadership of Arthur M. Scully Jr., worked diligently for over eight years securing the necessary financial resources and providing invaluable advice and assistance which have made the exhibition and this publication possible. Over a dozen Pittsburgh foundations, corporations, and trusts, and more than 200 individuals contributed generously to bring to completion this fitting tribute to George W. Wyckoff Jr.

We offer very special thanks to the National Endowment for the Humanities for its generous grant which specifically supported the production of this publication as well as many other key interpretive elements within the permanent exhibit.

It has been my pleasure to witness the completion of the Polar World exhibit and companion catalog, initiated under the direction of former director, Craig C. Black, and to make this innovative and sensitive view of the Inuit and their world available in Pittsburgh.

Robert M. West, Director
Carnegie Museum of Natural History,
Carnegie Institute
December 1983

USSR

Bering Sea
Coast

Chukchi
Peninsula

Chukchi Sea

Point Hope

Bering Strait

Icy Cape

Point Barrow
Barrow

Arctic Ocean

Saint Lawrence
Island

King
Island

*Kotzebue
Sound*

Kotzebue

Queen Elizabeth Islands

Seward
Peninsula

Norton Sound

Nome

Bering Sea

Saint Michael

Holy Cross

Beaufort Sea

Banks Island

Parry Channel

Sachs Harbour

Prin
of W

Bethel

Kuskokwin River

ALASKA

Yukon River

Tuktoyaktuk

Mackenzie
River
Delta

Inuvik

Amundsen Gulf

Holman
Island

Victoria Island

District of M

Bristol Bay

Nushagak

Nushagak River

Anchorage

*Prince William
Sound*

*Mackenzie
River*

Coppermine

*Cambridge
Bay*

Willia

Alaska Peninsula

Coronation Gulf

*Coppermine
River*

*Queen
Maud Gulf*

Kodiak
Island

Kayak Island

Great Bear Lake

N O R T H W E

YUKON TERRITORY

St. Elias
Mountains

Whitehorse

District of Mackenzie

E

Cross Sound

Juneau

Yellowknife

Dist

Bake

Sitka

Great Slave Lake

Barren Grounds
Region

Fort Smith

BRITISH COLUMBIA

*Lake
Athabaska*

Chu

ALBERTA

Edmonton

SASKATCHEWAN

MANIT

Pacific Ocean

Victoria

Regina

Winnip

U N I T E D   S T A T E S

Pearyland Region

Iceland

Alert

Ellesmere
Island

Thule

GREENLAND

Baffin Bay

Angmagssalik

Bylot Island
Pond Inlet

ARCTIC CIRCLE

Clyde
River

Nuuk

Pelly
Bay

BAFFIN ISLAND

Davis Strait

Pangnirtung

Melville
Peninsula

Cumberland Sound

Repulse
Bay

T E R R I T O R I E S

Foxe Peninsula

Frobisher Bay

Cape Dorset

Markham Bay

Lake Harbour

tin

Southampton
Island

Hudson Strait

Chesterfield
Inlet

Rankin Inlet

Saglouc

Ivujivik

Ungava Bay

Labrador Sea

no Point

UNGAVA
PENINSULA

Cape Smith

George
River

Povungnituk

Fort Chimo

Hudson Bay

Port Harrison

LABRADOR

Belcher Islands

Strait of
Belle Isle

NEWFOUNDLAND

QUEBEC

St. John's

River

James Bay

ONTARIO

Quebec

Montreal

Atlantic Ocean

Ottawa

Great Lakes

Toronto

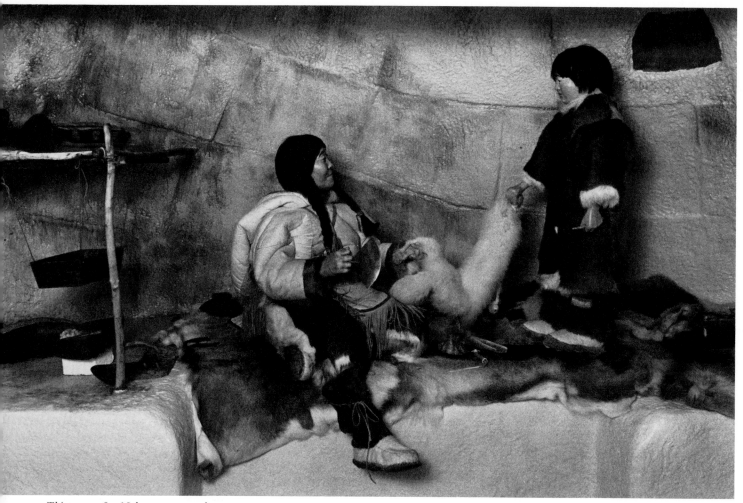

This scene of a 19th century snowhouse interior is included in Carnegie Museum of Natural History's "Polar World: Wyckoff Hall of Arctic Life" exhibit. A woman and child can be seen on the sleeping platform where they are preparing a fox skin for use.

Introduction

James B. Richardson III, Section of Anthropology,
Carnegie Museum of Natural History, Pittsburgh, Pennsylvania

. . . [T]hese proud people have survived in this harsh environment for . . . thousands of years . . . and developed a system of survival based on the different animals of the region that is unparalleled in the history of man. (George W. Wyckoff Jr., *Diary*, April 1972)

In April 1972, after two years of planning, George W. Wyckoff Jr., left Pittsburgh for Baffin Island. He travelled to this remote corner of the world to study the Clyde River Inuit and to capture on film Peungitoo, the last hunter in this region to live solely off the bounty of the Arctic. Accompanying him was Dr. Kenneth Doutt, then curator of Carnegie Museum of Natural History's Section of Mammals and an experienced Arctic researcher.

Their research was the first stage in the development of a permanent exhibit devoted to Inuit adaptations to the arctic environment and its resources. At the time of their study, the Inuit were moving into permanent settlements and abandoning their traditional way of life. George Wyckoff was, therefore, witness to a major change in Inuit culture. He was deeply concerned that the Inuit's movement into permanent settlements would have a negative effect upon a culture which had been an integral part of the arctic landscape for thousands of years.

This concern led George Wyckoff to encourage scientific research on Inuit culture. He was instrumental in obtaining funding from the Rachelwood Foundation to support anthropological research on the Inuit. George W. Wenzel's doctoral research on the Clyde River Inuit, conducted through McGill University, and Samuel Robinson's master's thesis on the influence of American whalers on the Hudson Bay Eskimos, conducted through McMaster University, were made possible by this support.

Carnegie Museum of Natural History has, likewise, been a major contributor to the body of scientific knowledge concerning many aspects of the Arctic. Since 1901, over 48 expeditions have been conducted by the Museum to collect scientific information and specimens on arctic flora, fauna, geology, paleontology, and anthropology.

"Polar World: Wyckoff Hall of Arctic Life" represents the culmination of these varied research programs. The exhibit hall also pays tribute to George Wyckoff's deep-seated concern and compassion for the people of Arctic Canada. It was George Wyckoff's understanding of cultural change as inevitable and irreversible that in 1978 led Dr. James B. Richardson III and Ms. P. Lynn Denton of the Section of Anthropology to begin developing the exhibit, with cultural change as its central theme. The exhibit hall presents the entire panorama of 4,500 years of Eskimo culture. The articles in this catalog, written by leading authorities, supplement the exhibit by offering a more in-depth discussion of Inuit culture, past and present, and the arctic environment.

The native inhabitants of the Canadian Arctic are increasingly using the term *Inuit* as a self-designation in place of the term *Eskimo*. In Inuktitut, the native language of the Canadian Arctic, *Inuit* means "The People." The widespread use of this term throughout the Canadian Arctic emphasizes the cultural unity of these people as they confront the modern world.

Pictured here is Peungitoo of Clyde River (Baffin Island, Canada), 1972. While on a Carnegie Museum of Natural History expedition to the Arctic George W. Wyckoff Jr. lived with Peungitoo and his family in their camp.

Eskimo is from a term originally used by the Cree Indians to refer to the Inuit. Although it has been widely adopted by Europeans, the original Cree word *Askimawak* means "eaters of raw flesh" and is considered derogatory by many Inuit. Thus, since 1950 the term Inuit has superseded the term Eskimo. *Inuit* is now the official designation used by the Canadian government. In this catalog and in the exhibit, *Inuit* is generally used with reference to the native inhabitants of Arctic Canada after 1900, whereas *Eskimo* is used as a designation for the period prior to 1900.

4,500 Years of Eskimo Cultural Change

Generally, cultural change is the result of responses made to two major forces. The first is the continually changing environment upon which cultural groups are dependent for their livelihood and to which they must adapt. Secondly, changes in cultural systems are due to contacts with other indigenous groups and with cultures from outside the local region. Throughout its 4,500 years, Eskimo culture has continuously developed as adaptations were made to changing environmental conditions and to contacts with other cultures.

The first section of the exhibit, entitled "Top of the World," sets the environmental scene. The articles by Mary R. Dawson, Frederick H. Utech, and Joseph F. Merritt discuss the Arctic's variation in flora, fauna, and geography. As the arctic environment and its natural resources have varied from region to region, so, too, has Eskimo culture, scattered throughout the arctic vastness, shown diversity in its adaptations. This diversity is reflected in the numerous subcultural or tribal divisions which have arisen within Eskimo society: the Copper, Iglulik, Netsilik, Caribou, Polar, and Baffinland Eskimos.

The Alaskan region was first occupied by man prior to 20,000 years ago. Some 4,500 years ago, as people moved into the Canadian Arctic, they adapted their way of life and their technology to a basically maritime environment. The second section of the exhibit, "The People

Arrive," illustrates through artifacts and graphics the process of technological development that allowed these early arctic dwellers to become successful maritime hunters. As noted in Robert McGhee's article, the first 4,000 years of cultural adaptation to the Canadian Arctic have been revealed through archaeological research at sites where these maritime hunters lived. Spreading from Alaska to Greenland, the earliest arctic inhabitants, the Pre-Dorset peoples, were well-equipped to survive in the Arctic. They had the harpoon and the bow and arrow for hunting, and housing and clothing suitable to protect themselves from the rigors of the environment.

As these early inhabitants continued their successful adjustment to a changing environment and the resources therein, the second age of Eskimo culture was attained by the Dorset peoples. During the Dorset period, lamps of soapstone appeared. There is a suspicion on the part of archaeologists that the use of lamps for cooking and heating indicates the invention of the snowhouse, the most spectacular adaptation of any of the world's hunters and gatherers to the problem of living and surviving in the snowy Arctic. As various harpoon types became the main hunting weapon of the Dorset, the bow and arrow were dropped from the tool inventory. Evidence of bone runners coupled with little evidence of dogs or dog harnesses suggests that the Dorset used sleds that were pulled by man. There is also some evidence that the kayak made its appearance at this time, thus affording the Dorset the basic technology that we all associate with Eskimos. These items, the snowhouse, sled, and kayak, allowed the Dorset to extend greatly the geographic range of their sea-mammal hunting to open water and out onto the ice.

Approximately 2,500 years ago, with a cooler arctic climate and sea ice covering larger areas for longer periods, sea-mammal populations increased. The Dorset were able to cluster together in larger groups for longer periods, and at this time Dorset art reached its florescence. Dorset art was probably produced

for hunting purposes, as an aid in magically luring the animals within range of their harpoons.

In Alaska, the ancestors of the modern Inuit, who had become accomplished whale hunters, began to migrate eastward as the climate became warmer, and the whales they depended upon became more dispersed. Between A.D. 900-1200, Thule people moved rapidly from Alaska to Greenland in pursuit of the behemoths. Their homes, constructed of whale bone, are found throughout the Arctic. With the Thule's expansion, one of the greatest long-distance migrations known for the prehistoric New World, Dorset culture disappeared throughout most of the Arctic. The Dorset were either assimilated into Thule culture or died out due to competition for resources—but not before their inventions of the snowhouse and sled became a crucial part of Thule culture. Along with the snowhouse and sled, the kayak, umiak, and all other technology associated with the historic Canadian Eskimos were utilized by the Thule.

During the period of Thule expansion into Canada and Greenland, Vikings also settled in Greenland. By A.D. 1500, Viking populations died out because of a deteriorating climate, political problems on the European mainland, and, possibly, pressure from the Thule. The Viking-Thule interaction is an excellent example of a society based upon agriculture, herding, and metallurgy that came in contact with a hunting society and yet left no lasting impact upon that culture.

The Thule were constantly shifting their settlements and hunting territories because of climatic fluctuations. After A.D. 1200, as the climate became colder, they abandoned much of the High Arctic and pushed southward along the Labrador coast. Shifts in animal resources brought about by climatic changes are the key to our understanding of the adaptations that took place within Eskimo culture during the prehistoric period. Significant changes in resource distribution resulted in cultural readjustments.

Only 5,000 or so Thule lived

The whaling ship Morning Star *of New Bedford, Massachusetts is pictured while enroute to the Arctic. The* Morning Star *remained in the Hudson Bay region during the winter of 1864-1865. The wintering-over of whaling ships provided the first sustained contact between Westerners and Canadian Eskimos and resulted in many changes in Eskimo culture.*

throughout the 2-million-square kilometers (772,000 square miles) of the Canadian Arctic. This translates into 1 person per 400 square kilometers (1 person per 154 square miles). Thule population was, thus, at an optimum level for the limited resources that were available. With a greater number of resources available, the Alaskan Eskimos, in contrast, attained a higher population density.

External Cultural Contact and Change

The impact of European culture was a major factor in the disappearance of many indigenous Arctic populations. Those cultures that did not vanish because of massive European intrusion made adjustments that allowed them to continue as viable cultures. In the Canadian Arctic, after A.D. 1700, environmental changes and resource shifts were no longer the major factors in the alteration of Eskimo culture. Continued European contact over the last 300 years has had a massive effect upon Eskimo culture and has resulted in significant changes.

The third section of the exhibit, "Cultures Touch," begins with the first important stage in European contact. In their search for a Northwest Passage, the early European explorers left behind the wreckage of many of their ships. Even though Eskimos used the wood, metal, and other items on board the ships as raw materials, early explorers did not have a major impact upon Eskimo culture. Since explorers were only in the Arctic because of their search for the elusive Northwest Passage and a trade route to Asia, no permanent trade or settlements were established. As James W. VanStone notes in his article, the increased number of ships searching for the explorer Franklin between 1848 and 1857 brought more continuous contact with the Eskimos.

The first sustained contact between Eskimos and Europeans began in the 1860s when the American whaling industry moved into Hudson Bay in search of the oil-bearing bowhead whale. The fourth section of the exhibit, "A Lasting Impact," points out that intensive whale hunting by

New England whalers brought about this sustained contact. Until about 1915, whaleships voyaged to Hudson Bay and wintered over at specific spots in order to take advantage of spring whaling. The wintering-over whalers became dependent upon the Eskimos for meat supplies and clothing to see them through the long arctic winter. In return, the whalers provided the Eskimos with whale boats, guns, and a wide range of other trade goods.

The Eskimos located their winter settlements to take advantage of these frozen-in trading stations. Ultimately, Eskimos were incorporated as part of the whaleboat crews and trained to capture whales with European harpoons and harpoon guns.

As VanStone notes in his article, without the Eskimos, New England whalers would have found it difficult, if not impossible, to remain in the Arctic during the winter. The sustained interaction between the two cultures brought powerful and fundamental changes to many aspects of Eskimo culture. The Eskimos depended upon the whalers for guns, ammunition, and other trade goods. The location of the Eskimos' winter camps was altered to take advantage of these "floating settlements."

With the demise of whaling, the Hudson's Bay Company and other groups established posts in the Arctic for the purpose of trading European goods for animal furs. Royal Canadian Mounted Police posts and religious missions were also established at this time. The resulting contact with the Eskimos from these land-based settlements extended the range of European impact throughout much of the Arctic. Legal authority and religious indoctrination, in addition to trading relationships, thus became pervasive forces in a rapidly changing Eskimo culture.

In "Polar World," the period between 1700 and 1900 is given prominence through the use of four dioramas and other materials contained in the section called "Yesterday's People." This section is devoted to what many persons consider to be traditional Eskimo culture. David Damas describes

this period in his chapter "The Traditional Culture of the Central Eskimo."

Thus, within the short span of some 200 years, most Eskimos within the Canadian Arctic have experienced unrelenting and accelerating change brought about by European domination. Yet, it is important to note that lack of contact can also have a major effect upon a culture. Because of an increasingly colder climate after A.D. 1200, the Polar Eskimos of Northwestern Greenland were cut off from contact with all other Thule groups. Most Thule moved southward, but the Polar Eskimos were trapped in a small area by massive ice sheets and glaciers. During their period of isolation, the Polar Eskimos lost three crucial items of technology: the kayak, fishing spear, and bow and arrow. Thus, sea mammals, fish, and caribou were no longer within reach of these people. Until they were contacted by Captain John Ross in 1818, the remaining 200 Polar Eskimos considered themselves the only inhabitants of the earth. Not until 1860, when the shaman Kritag of Northern Baffin Island led his people on a four-year journey northward to join the Polar Eskimos, was their survival assured by the reintroduction of these three crucial items of Eskimo technology.

In contrast, the Caribou Eskimos demonstrate adaptability to new resources and areas opened up as a direct result of European contact. Originally users of the kayak and umiak for sea-mammal hunting along the west coast of Hudson Bay, the Caribou Eskimos moved inland. Here, they occupied the region which had recently (around 1800) been abandoned by Chipewayan Indians whose population had been decimated by disease. With guns and traps adopted in place of the bow and arrow, these Eskimos were able to take advantage of the caribou and the fur trade. The Caribou Eskimos were much closer to the sources of trade at Hudson's Bay Company posts and were able to capitalize on new resources and adapt their culture to a new mode of subsistence in a different environmental zone.

With the disappearance of whaling

in 1915, the commercial trapping of such fur-bearing animals as Arctic fox became the economic mainstay of Inuit trade with Europeans. The fur market collapsed in the 1930s and it was not until after World War II that the Inuit developed a new exportable resource which could be exchanged for European goods.

After 1900, the number of Anglican and Roman Catholic missions increased, and trading companies and Canadian governmental units were clustered together at many of these same locations. For the first time, the potential for the establishment of permanent Inuit communities was realized.

Through the 1950s there was increasing movement of Inuit to permanent settlements where they found employment with various governmental agencies. The Canadian government also established medical stations and, finally, schools for the Inuit at these locations. In 1948, James Houston, a Canadian artist, encouraged the Inuit to make soapstone and ivory carvings for sale to Europeans. This spectacular development of a major artistic tradition soon became the economic mainstay of many Inuit communities.

By 1960, the Inuit began to organize cooperatives in order to gain control over their own economic base. This economic self-determination resulted in the Inuit's producing and marketing their own products which soon included printmaking, appliqué, embroidery, and a wide range of other craft products. As Nelson H. H. Graburn has stated in his article, graphic arts became big business, with the Inuit cooperative at Cape Dorset, for example, selling over $1 million worth of graphics in a year. The section of the exhibit entitled "A Mirror of Change: Eskimo/Inuit Art" shows a range of the art forms that have enabled the Inuit to become more self-sufficient and less dependent upon the Canadian government for support.

The Inuit have established a number of organizations to represent their interests. One such organization, the Inuit Tapirisat of Canada, was founded in 1971 to represent Inuit economic, environmental,

A modern Inuit man and woman of Clyde River (Baffin Island, Canada) are pictured in a combination of Western and traditional dress.

and educational concerns to the Canadian government. Through various organizations, the Inuit are gaining control over their culture and the land and its resources that for thousands of years they had managed successfully.

By the 1970s, most Inuit had settled in permanent towns. To the *qallunaat* (white men), the exterior appearance of Inuit towns, three-wheeled Hondas, boats with inboard and outboard motors, movie theaters, schools, televisions, and myriad other store-bought items initially suggests that the Inuit are becoming incorporated and submerged into Canadian national culture. The Inuit have incorporated much of Western culture over the past 100 years and have shifted their economic system away from dependence upon the land to an economic system intimately linked with that of Canada.

Because of the adaptive nature of their culture, the Inuit have been able to restructure their society to meet successfully the forces of change during a period in time when hundreds of the world's cultures have disappeared. The final section of the Exhibit, "Today's People," portrays the last 80 years of cultural development and places emphasis on the changes in Inuit society as the people continue to adapt to external cultural forces. In her article, Minnie Aodla Freeman discusses some of the forces affecting contemporary Inuit life.

It is clear that the Inuit are firmly in control of their own destiny. As George W. Wyckoff Jr., has stated, Inuit culture will continue to thrive as the society best adapted to live in the Arctic. Richard G. Condon notes in his article, the highly successful art industry and the Inuit's involvement in many government and private programs such as the search for Arctic energy sources are once again promoting economic independence.

Time changes and the world goes on. The Eskimos that survive the sudden changes in their civilization and culture will contribute much to their southern neighbors. They have great aptitude and ingenuity, and a patience and understanding rarely seen outside their world. (George W. Wyckoff Jr., "Peungitoo of Baffin Island." Carnegie Magazine, Oct. 1972, p. 346.)

Reading List

Bruemmer, Fred. "The Polar Eskimos." *The Beaver*, Outfit 309:4 (1979), 24-33.

Clark, Brenda. *The Development of Caribou Eskimo Culture.* Archaeological Survey of Canada Paper, No. 59. Mercury Series. Ottawa: National Museums of Canada, 1977.

Martin, Kenneth R. "Life and Death at Marble Island." *The Beaver*, Outfit 309:4 (1979), 48-56.

Robinson, Samuel. "The Influence of the American Whaling Industry on the Aivilingmiut, 1860-1919." M.A. Thesis, McMaster University, 1973.

Ross, W. Gilles. *Whaling and Eskimos: Hudson Bay 1860-1915.* National Museum of Man, Publications in Ethnology, No. 10. Ottawa: National Museums of Canada, 1975.

Taylor, J. Garth. *Labrador Eskimo Settlements of the Contact Period.* National Museum of Man, Publications in Ethnology, No. 9. Ottawa: National Museums of Canada, 1974.

Wentzel, George W. *Clyde Inuit Adaptations and Ecology: The Organization of Subsistence.* National Museum of Man, Canadian Ethnology Service Paper, No. 77. Ottawa: National Museums of Canada, 1981.

Wyckoff, George W., Jr. "Peungitoo of Baffin Island." *Carnegie Magazine,* 46 (1972), 331-346.

Zaslow, Morris, ed. *A Century of Canada's Arctic Islands: 1880-1980.* Proc. of the 23rd Symposium of the Royal Society of Canada. Ottawa: Royal Society of Canada, 1981.

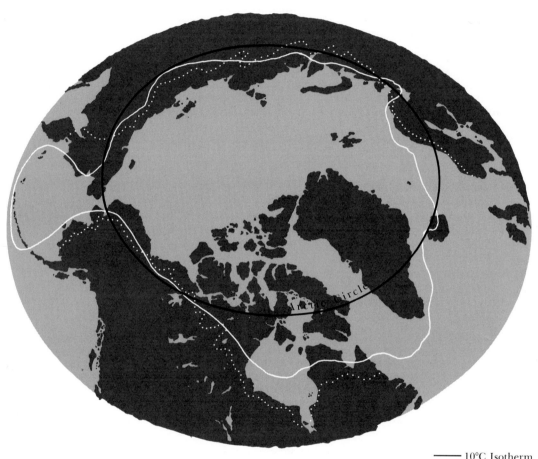

—— 10°C Isotherm
· · · · · Tree Line

Polar View of the Earth. *Features of Arctic geography that are illustrated include: (a) the Arctic Circle at 66°33' north latitude (the southern boundary of the characteristically Arctic light regime), (b) the 10°C isotherm, and (c) the northward limit of trees (which roughly coincides with the 10°C isotherm).*

Adapted from Polar Regions Atlas, *p. 4.*

Arctic Environments: The Physical Setting

Mary R. Dawson, Section of Vertebrate Paleontology,
Carnegie Museum of Natural History, Pittsburgh, Pennsylvania

Introduction

The history and patterns of development of the Inuit are inextricably interwoven with the extreme and demanding physical conditions under which these people live. Over the centuries, the adaptations of the Inuit, and of the other living organisms of Arctic regions, have been molded by the harsh Arctic environment. This environment features basically a cold climate, having long, dark winters alternating with short, light summers. Such a climatic regime leads to the development of ice on open waters for long periods of the year, to land-based glaciers and ice caps, and to permafrost, or frozen ground, which plays a crucial role in modifying the surface of the ground.

Polar life, including that of the Inuit, cannot be understood unless the environmental parameters of the northern polar regions are taken into account. The physical conditions within these regions will be considered in this chapter. First, the relationship of a polar global position to climate and seasons will be explored. Following this, the climate itself and Arctic atmospheric conditions will be discussed. Finally, the geomorphology of regions occupied by the Inuit will be described, especially as it relates to ice and the tundra. This discussion of Arctic environments will focus upon the North American Arctic, with only occasional mention of conditions in Arctic regions of Eurasia.

Before entering into these matters, however, it should be established what the term *Arctic* means in a discussion of the environmental conditions under which the Inuit live. In the popular imagination, the term Arctic brings first to mind cold, followed perhaps by thoughts of snow and ice, darkness and wind. All these features are indeed associated with Arctic life for at least part of the year, but the term Arctic should be more precisely defined. Actually, there are several ways to define Arctic. Perhaps the simplest definition is a purely geographic one, the Arctic being the region north of the Arctic Circle, which girdles the Earth at 66°33' north latitude. The Arctic Circle is not itself a geographic feature, of course, but it does delimit an important characteristic of polar regions. North of 66°33' north latitude the sun does not rise on at least one day of the year and does not set on at least one day of the year. This characteristic will be more fully described below. Here it is sufficient to give this as one definition of the Arctic. Though simple and precise, this definition does not clearly set apart those northern geographic regions of the Earth with a rather uniform set of cold climatic conditions. In order to do so, a different definition, based on temperature, is required. On this basis the Arctic is defined as the area where the average temperature for the warmest month (July) is below 10°C (50°F). The 10° isotherm (a line climatologists use to join places having the same air temperature) delimits quite effectively the Arctic as a climatic zone. One of the important features of this isotherm is that it follows roughly the northward limit of trees, thus marking the biologic boundary between the treeless northern tundra and the more southerly, tree or shrub covered taiga. It is significant also, of course, that this isotherm more or less sets apart the more northerly regions occupied by the Inuit from the more southerly regions occupied by the American Indians. Other definitions of Arctic are possible, based on distribution of permafrost or on extent of the sea ice, but it is the definition of Arctic based on temperature that will be followed here.

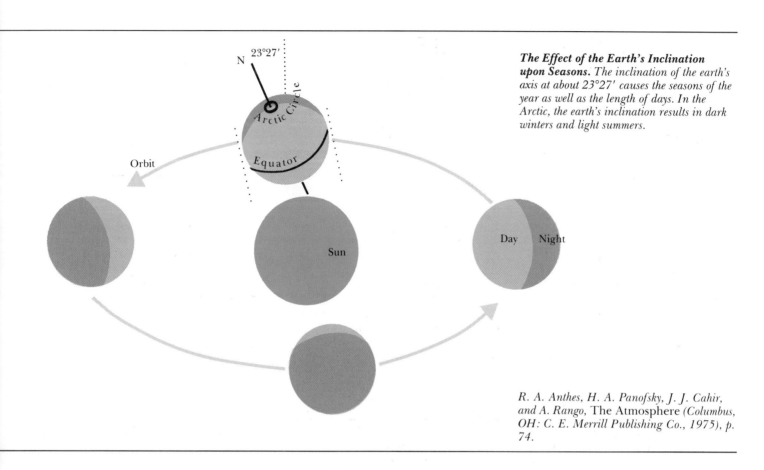

The Effect of the Earth's Inclination upon Seasons. *The inclination of the earth's axis at about 23°27' causes the seasons of the year as well as the length of days. In the Arctic, the earth's inclination results in dark winters and light summers.*

R. A. Anthes, H. A. Panofsky, J. J. Cahir, and A. Rango, The Atmosphere *(Columbus, OH: C. E. Merrill Publishing Co., 1975), p. 74.*

Distinction between Solar Rays Reaching the Arctic and those Reaching Lower Latitudes. *At northern latitudes the sun's rays strike the earth's surface at a wider angle than farther south. They pass through a thicker layer of atmosphere and are spread over a larger surface area. As a result, the sun is "weak" at higher latitudes, delivering less energy per unit area than at lower latitudes.*

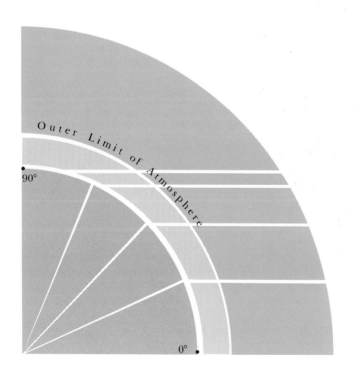

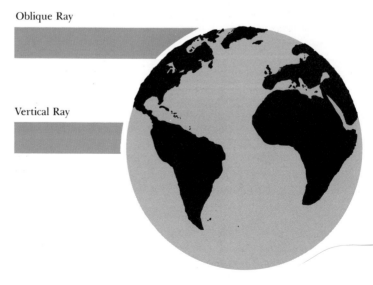

Adapted from Trewartha, An Introduction to Climate, *p. 12.*

Geography of North Polar Regions: Why the Poles are Cold

Two features of the Earth's position relative to incoming radiation from the sun are tied directly to the cold temperatures that characterize polar regions today. First, there is the angle at which the sun's rays strike the higher latitudes of the Earth. The intensity of solar radiation depends on the angle at which a ray of sunlight, all of which are the same in intensity, is received on a portion of the curved Earth. At higher latitudes of the Earth, a solar ray is received at a higher angle, the oblique ray is spread over a greater area after passing through a thicker layer of atmosphere, and thus delivers less energy per unit area than a ray striking more vertically and passing through less atmosphere. As a result, the sun is "weaker" at high latitudes than it is low latitudes.

The second major feature of the Earth's position on which temperature depends is the length of day when solar energy is received or the length of day compared with length of night. Here the position of the Earth as it orbits the sun is of greatest importance. The Earth rotates on its axis, the ends of which are the north and south geographic poles, at the rate of once approximately every twenty-four hours. During this interval, places on the Earth's surface are alternately toward and away from the sun, resulting in light and darkness. In its orbit around the sun, the Earth takes one year. Because the Earth's axis is tilted at an angle of about 23°27′ from a line vertical to the plane of the Earth's orbit, the northern and southern hemispheres receive different amounts of radiation at different times in the course of the year. It is this peculiarity of the Earth that leads to the distinct seasons that are so much a part of life for the Earth's inhabitants. The year is divided into seasons marked by two equinoxes ("equal nights") on about March 21 and September 23, and two solstices ("sun stands still") on about December 22 and June 22. From the autumnal equinox until the vernal equinox the northern hemisphere experiences nights longer than days.

The effect becomes more pronounced at higher latitudes. Thus, after the autumnal equinox continuous darkness reaches more and more of the Arctic until finally, at the time of the winter solstice, all the area within the Arctic Circle experiences twenty-four hours of darkness. The process then reverses, and light gradually returns toward the north. By the vernal equinox, the Arctic is again light for twelve hours and length of day increases until the summer solstice, when the entire area within the Arctic Circle has twenty-four hours of daylight. The extreme of light conditions is, of course, reached at the pole itself, where there is a six-month interval of light and a six-month interval of darkness. The effect is modified as distance south from the pole increases, but long intervals of darkness during the winter are always featured in northern regions.

Comparison of Yearly Ranges of Temperature and Precipitation at Selected Stations from Pittsburgh, Pennsylvania, U.S.A. to Alert, Ellesmere Island, Canada. *This chart demonstrates the rigorous climatic conditions within Arctic regions.*

Location			Elevation (meters above sea level)	Average Daily Temperature (°C)								Extreme Max. (°C)		Precipitation (centimeters)				
				January		April		July		October								
				max.	min.	max.	min.	max.	min.	max.	min.			Jan.	April	July	Oct.	Avg./Year
Pittsburgh, PA	40°27′N	80°00′W	228	4.4	-3.9	17.2	5.5	29.4	18.3	18.3	7.2	39.4	-28.9	7.1	8.6	9.1	6.4	93.7
Frobisher Bay, NWT	63°45′N	68°33′W	34	-22.8	-30.6	-8.9	-18.3	11.6	3.9	-1.7	-7.8	24.4	-45.0	1.8	2.0	3.8	2.8	33.8
Resolute, NWT	74°43′N	94°59′W	67	-28.9	-36.1	-18.3	-8.9	7.2	1.7	-11.7	-17.8	16.1	-51.7	0.3	0.5	2.3	1.3	14.0
Alert, NWT	82°31′N	62°20′W	29	-28.3	-33.9	-22.2	-27.8	6.6	2.2	-16.7	-21.7	19.4	-47.2	0.5	0.8	1.3	2.3	16.0

Adapted from J. A. Ruffner and F. E. Bair, eds. The Weather Almanac *(Detroit, MI: Gale Research Co., 1981), pp. 306-307.*

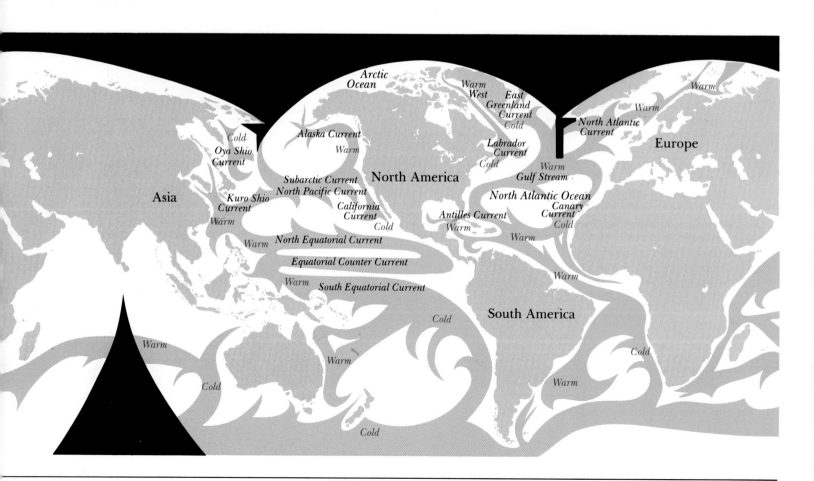

Ocean Currents in the Arctic. *Polar climates may be influenced by ocean currents. Relatively warm currents, for example, moderate climatic conditions around the Bering Strait and Norwegian and Barents seas.*

Adapted from Robert Barton, The Oceans *(N.Y.: Facts on File, 1980), pp. 44-45.*

Arctic Climates and Atmospheric Conditions

Low temperatures characterize the climate of Arctic regions. Winters are long and bitterly cold, summers short and cool, resulting in a low mean-annual-temperature for the region. The cool temperatures are directly related to paucity of solar radiation, as mentioned above. Added to this is the effect of the high reflective property, or albedo, of the ice and snow that cover much of the Arctic. Between 80 and 90 percent of the radiation reaching the Arctic's cover of ice and snow is reflected, resulting in heat loss back into the atmosphere. This reflective property is an important factor in determining the overall heat budget of polar regions under their cover of ice and snow. Further, much of the heat energy of solar radiation is expended in melting the snow and evaporating melt water, so little heat is available to warm the land surface and the air.

Arctic climates have been subdivided on the basis of warmest month (July) isotherms into tundra climates and icecap climates. The tundra climate occurs between the 10°C (50°F) and 0°C (32°F) warmest month isotherms. The icecap climate features average temperatures below freezing for all months; vegetation does not grow in this region. Characteristically these Arctic climates show low daily ranges of temperature, especially when there is continuous day or night. In North American Arctic regions, temperatures drop sharply at the end of the summer, which occurs by the end of August in the far north and in September near the tree line. December, January, February, and early March are typically very cold. January, for example, shows temperatures averaging between -20°C (-4°F) and -40°C (-40°F). Cold temperatures also occur farther south, in subarctic regions of interior Canada and northeastern Siberia. Some Siberian stations show January average temperatures of -60°C (-76°F), a low that also has been recorded on the Greenland icecap. As the sun's radiation returns to northern latitudes in the spring, the tundra warms and melting of snow and ice begins. Mean temperatures are above freezing for between two and four months, although snow may fall and frost may occur at any time even during these warmest months. It is during this brief warm interval when the tundra's plant and animal inhabitants spring into activity in a short but beautiful flourish.

An important factor influencing temperature in some Arctic regions is the presence of open water and the poleward flow of warm ocean currents. Thus, Arctic climates may be subdivided also into polar marine and polar continental. Polar marine climates, featuring open water and warm currents that are influential in warming winter temperatures, occur around the Norwegian-Barents seas, along Baffin Bay, and into the Bering Strait. As welcome as the ameliorating effect of open water on climate may be, it also leads to fogs, which may last for days, hindering greatly visibility for travel, hunting, and other activities. The Canadian Arctic islands and eastern Arctic mainland have a polar continental climate, influenced by the frozen Arctic Sea and the associated pack ice.

An Arctic high pressure system tends to dominate the north in the spring. The intense cold of the winter is usually associated with cyclonically controlled airstreams. Winds may be high at any time of the year. The windchill, which is a measure of the cooling effect of wind at different temperatures, may make life very difficult in the winter, when high winds are often coupled with intense cold.

Chart Illustrating Wind Chill Factor.
Low temperatures plus winds combine in determining the wind chill factor. This chart shows how the wind markedly augments the effect of low temperatures upon exposed plants, people, and other animals.

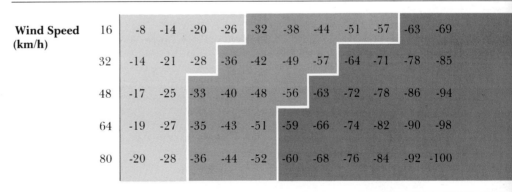

Local Temperature (°C)		0°	-5°	-10°	-15°	-20°	-25°	-30°	-35°	-40°	-45°	-50°

Wind Chill Equivalent Temperature (°C)

Wind Speed (km/h)												
	16	-8	-14	-20	-26	-32	-38	-44	-51	-57	-63	-69
	32	-14	-21	-28	-36	-42	-49	-57	-64	-71	-78	-85
	48	-17	-25	-33	-40	-48	-56	-63	-72	-78	-86	-94
	64	-19	-27	-35	-43	-51	-59	-66	-74	-82	-90	-98
	80	-20	-28	-36	-44	-52	-60	-68	-76	-84	-92	-100

Little danger for properly clothed persons
Considerable danger from freezing to exposed flesh
Very great danger from freezing to exposed flesh.

Adapted from Polar Regions Atlas, *p. 9.*

Since Arctic regions are typified by presence of ice and snow, they may be thought of as areas having high rates of precipitation. This is actually not the case. Total yearly precipitation is usually low, a feature related to the low moisture-carrying capacity of cold air. It should be noted, however, that measurement of rain and snow fall is made difficult in many stations by the blowing of the wind. Precipitation in the summer and autumn falls as both rain and wet snow. Winter snow is typically rather light, especially in regions with a polar continental climate. North of Hudson Bay, relatively heavy snow falls are associated with strong, northwesterly winds. The winter snow is usually dry, forming a compact layer. Wind sweeps some tundra areas clear of snow, whereas deep drifts accumulate in other places. It also strongly affects the size and shape of snow particles, producing many varieties. The Inuit have several dozen words for these various kinds of snow, including, of course, one for the dry, compact snow used to construct snow houses. The insulating properties of snow, with its layers of trapped air, are important not only to the Inuit with their snow houses but also to other Arctic life. Snow forms a blanket on the earth, holding in warmth of the earth and keeping out cold air. This cover protects plants and small animals in and on the earth. Larger animals, such as polar bears, wolves, foxes, and sled dogs, may burrow into drifts or simply allow a snow blanket to cover them as they lie on the surface.

Arctic climates have not always been so cold and forbidding. Evidence from fossils shows that in the early Cenozoic, in the interval between about 45 and 60 million years ago, temperate climate plants and animals flourished in Arctic regions. The Earth's climatic cooling later in the Cenozoic led to the development of extensive continental and mountain glaciers that advanced and retreated across parts of the northern hemisphere between about 1 million and 10 thousand years ago. Ever since the last major retreat of the glaciers, climatic history has not been one of steady warming of the Earth's climate. Paleontological and geological evidence shows, for example, a warm interval, the *climatic optimum*, between 4,000 and 6,000 years ago. In historic times temperature oscillations have been recorded. Climate records from Iceland document warming trends for the northern hemisphere around 1000 and 1100 A.D., another warm interval in the 1400s, and a distinct cooling between 1550 and 1850 A.D. The causes of these climatic fluctuations are unclear, but surely they have affected the floral and faunal events of the Arctic, including the history of the adaptable people who have populated Arctic regions.

Atmospheric conditions in polar regions produce a variety of interesting optical effects. Perhaps the best known of these are the auroras. The *aurora borealis* creates spectacular wavering curtains and bands of light, often colored, that appear in the night sky of northern latitudes. These glorious, and often bright, displays, occur most frequently in a belt around 23° south of the magnetic pole. Thus, they are well known to Arctic inhabitants. The light comes from energy released by atmospheric gases that are bombarded by charged particles, which enter the atmosphere, move and descend along lines of magnetic force.

Other conditions of the air lead to the appearance of mirages. In the Arctic, mirages are often associated with temperature inversions in which the air near a cooler land, ice or water surface is more dense than that at higher elevations. The result of these density differences is the downward bending of light rays so that a distant object appears higher than its true position. This phenomenon, called looming, may assist Arctic travelers by enabling them to see objects over the curve of the Earth's surface.

A somewhat more complicated mirage, the *fata morgana*, also results from temperature inversion, though one with greater variation in air density. Here, the mirage produces the appearance of elaborate towers, walls, or cliffs. It was probably this type of mirage that led various early polar explorers to "see" land masses where none really exist. For example, the British explorer, Sir John Ross, seeking the Northwest Passage in 1818, apparently saw such a mirage, in Lancaster Sound, for he turned back after finding his way blocked by "mountains." Later explorers never found these "mountains." Robert Peary, during his attempt in 1906 to reach the North Pole, saw a mountainous land, which he called Crocker Land. A later explorer, Donald MacMillen, attempted to find this land. Although he and his party did see a mirage, Crocker Land itself proved to be only an illusion.

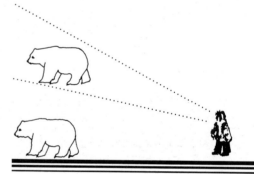

Illustration of Looming, an Optical Illusion Characteristic of Arctic Regions. Cooler, denser air near the earth's surface causes light rays to bend downward. This type of optical illusion enables people to see objects that are below the horizon.

The awesome, weathered cliffs of Prince
Leopold Island form good nesting ground for
many sea birds. Prince Leopold Island lies off
the north coast of Somerset Island in the
Eastern Canadian Arctic.

Early in the summer, Bylot Island remains a
land of snow and glaciers. The large glacier,
seen between the mountain ranges in the distance, flows into Eclipse Sound (foreground).

Other optical peculiarities encountered in the Arctic are related to reflections. Different surfaces, whether dark or light, have different reflective abilities; these surfaces will, in turn, be reflected from the cloud cover or even the sky. Thus, there may be a "sky map" of the surface of the ground. This sky map is useful to those traveling in the north. The sky's reflection called an "ice blink" shows that sea ice lies ahead, whereas a "water sky" reveals breaks in the ice or open water. Another reflected peculiarity is a whiteout, which occurs because of multiple reflections from snow and ice that eliminate shadows and even the line of the horizon. Without these visual clues, orientation becomes very difficult, people may lose their balance, stumble over unseen obstacles, and fall off undetectable heights. Another hazard of Arctic reflections is snow blindness, an inflammation of the eye's conjunctiva that may produce considerable discomfort and sensitivity to light. It is caused by the reflection of ultraviolet light off the snow. Fortunately, the condition is of short duration and may be prevented by appropriate shields to the eyes.

The Frozen North: Ice and Tundra
Arctic regions of the world consist basically of an ice covered sea surrounded by land, with breaks between the continents for the North Atlantic Ocean and the Bering Strait. Nearly two-thirds of the Arctic region is covered by the Arctic Ocean. The North American lands fringing that ocean are varied in nature. In part, they are underlain by igneous rocks of the Canadian shield, in part by plains covered by glacial and other flat-bedded sediments, and in part by folded mountains. Permanent ice covers nearly two-fifths of these surfaces. The great ice cap of Greenland and smaller caps of Ellesmere, Baffin, and Devon islands in the eastern Canadian Arctic Archipelago are typical of these vast reservoirs of cold and water. Glaciers also occur, especially in mountainous terrain, where they advance and retreat with climatic fluctuations. In the past glaciers were more extensive. Since the weight of the glacial ice has been removed, the land-level is rising, a phenomenon called glacial "rebound." This has raised some beaches 150 to 300 meters (495 to 990 feet) above sea level. These raised beaches may form a conspicuous feature. Their relatively even surfaces are frequently used as summer roads by Arctic travelers. In northern Canada, the rebound continues at a rate of up to one meter (3.3 feet) per century.

Ice caps and glaciers have a strong influence on local temperatures and winds, but are inhospitable to most life. The sea ice, on the other hand, plays a leading role in the composition and conduct of Arctic life. Sea ice is composed of both fast ice, which is floating but attached to land, and pack ice, which is drifting and unattached to land. In the spring the fast ice shrinks and as the summer progresses nearly all of it melts. In contrast, only about half the Arctic pack ice thaws during the summer before starting its yearly expansion again in the autumn. As the pack expands, it merges with new fast ice and drift ice, and incorporates within itself drifting icebergs. The pack ice is not static but changes constantly as breaks, called leads, open and close, and the pack moves within the Arctic Basin. Where pack ice meets fast ice, complex pressure ridges of jammed blocks tend to develop. These often build to several meters above sea level and are even thicker below. Sea ice forms when the surface waters cool to about -2°C (28.4°F). It thickens as water that has flowed to its surface from underneath freezes in turn.

The Arctic pack ice is not a desolate, lifeless zone. Plankton tends to thrive below the ice. Higher invertebrate animals and fish follow the rich growths of plankton and attract walruses, seals, whales, and sea birds. Polar bears hunt from the pack and Arctic foxes are frequently found scavenging the kills of the bears. Hunting for seals, walruses, polar bears, foxes, and whales from the pack ice is important for the Inuit, for whom the ice is a winter highway. Travel on the ice may be hazardous, however, due to the changeable, uncertain nature of the pack. This is especially true in the spring when the ice surface becomes slushy, the leads widen, and the ice becomes unsuitable as a place for hunting and travel. Ice floes may break away and icebergs calve from glaciers, join the pack and move south into open waters.

In the summer, some melting occurs on the Ellesmere Island ice cap, resulting in ponds on the ice and waterfalls from the margins.

During the summer the ice in Eclipse Sound between Baffin and Bylot islands retreats from land. This view of Eclipse Sound was taken at midnight.

This view of Eclipse Sound, photographed on a summer day, shows a storm approaching from the north.

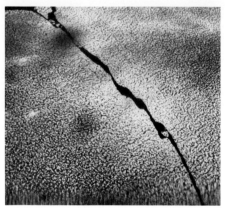

Early in the summer the edge of the Bylot Island ice cap is awash with melting water cascading onto the tundra. The melt water merges into the Aktineq Creek seen in the foreground.

Icebergs, such as this one off Axel Heiberg Island in the Eastern Canadian Arctic, result from calving, or breaking off, of glaciers where they meet the sea.

Leads, irregular cracks in the sea ice, make the ice a treacherous surface for summer travel. The ice pictured here borders Ellesmere Island in the Eastern Canadian Arctic.

Permafrost, or perennially frozen ground, underlies most Arctic land surfaces as a continuous zone. It is usually found within the -8°C (17.8°F) mean annual air temperature isotherm. Permafrost extends as a discontinuous layer even farther south, roughly within the 0°C (32°F) isotherm. Both bedrock and sediments are incorporated in the frozen layer, which has been measured to a depth of 500 meters (1,640 feet) in Canada and still deeper, to 1,500 meters (4,992 feet), in Siberia. Overlying the permafrost is an active zone, which thaws in summer and refreezes in winter. The thickness of this zone, which varies from about one-half to five meters (1.6 feet to 16.5 feet), depends on both the substrate and the warmth and length of the summer thaw. Tundra surfaces underlain by permafrost are characteristically poorly drained, as underground movement of water is inhibited, and surface ponds are common. The tundra above permafrost tends to weather, following freezing and thawing, into patterned ground, which is characterized by surfaces formed into polygons and other shapes as a result of sorting by size of soil sediments. These polygons vary from less than half a meter to over 100 meters (1.6 to 328 feet) in diameter. On slopes, the water-logged active layers of soil are susceptible to solifluction, a process in which the soil flows downhill, disrupting vegetation and causing difficulties to travelers. As a result of all these features, including soil mounds and polygons, solifluction, and the generally water-logged surface, the tundra in summer forms a generally poor surface for overland transport. Arctic soils are characteristically shallow and poor in nutrients due to the slowing effect of the cold on processes of soil formation and organic decomposition.

Ice Caps and Permafrost Regions of the Arctic. Arctic climates and soil conditions are strongly influenced by the presence of ice caps and permafrost, or permanently frozen ground.

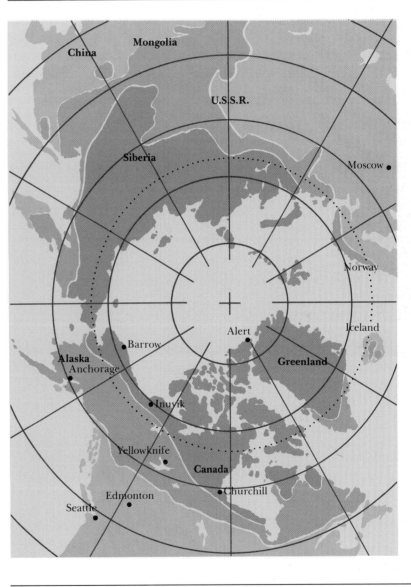

Permafrost Zones   ■ Continuous   ■ Discontinuous

Adapted from Polar Regions Atlas, *p. 15.*

This aerial view of the tundra on Ellesmere Island shows the polygons (foreground) that form in response to the freezing and thawing of the ground.

Summary

North polar environments can hardly be described as hospitable to life, especially from the perspective of inhabitants of the world's temperate regions. However, these environments, even with their cold, darkness, ice and snow, support plants and animals that have adapted to these conditions. The summers are brief, but bring the beautiful flowering of the tundra and flourishing both of the north's permanent animal inhabitants and of its migratory ones. Winters are long and bitterly cold, frequently greatly taxing the survival abilities of Arctic inhabitants. Surviving through the centuries under these environmental conditions has led to the marvelous physical adaptations of today's Arctic inhabitants as well as to the remarkable cultural adaptations of the Inuit.

Reading List

Polar Regions Atlas. Washington, D.C.: Central Intelligence Agency, 1978.

Greenler, R. *Rainbows, Halos and Glories.* Cambridge: Cambridge University Press, 1980.

Trewartha, G. T. *An Introduction to Climate.* NY: McGraw-Hill, 1968.

When a seal (shown in the distance) rests on the ice, it is seldom far from the hole through which it can easily slip back into the water. This winter scene was photographed off Axel Heiberg Island in the Eastern Canadian Arctic.

Glaciers, moving and abrading the ground,
flow in tongue-like lobes across mountainous
parts of Axel Heiberg Island in the Eastern
Canadian Arctic.

Arctic willow, Salix *sp., Salicaceae (Willow Family).*

Arctic Plant Life

Frederick H. Utech, Section of Botany,
Carnegie Museum of Natural History, Pittsburgh, Pennsylvania

Introduction

Travelers should always be botanists, according to Charles Darwin, for it is the plants that everywhere give character to the landscape. In the Arctic, however, vegetation does not assert itself and one must search, sometimes on the sides of rocks or even under snow, to investigate the flora. Plant species of the Arctic, although limited in number, do, nonetheless, exhibit interesting adaptations to this harsh environment.

The North American Arctic zone includes all of the treeless mainland and islands lying north of the transcontinental coniferous forest. The absence of trees is, in fact, the most striking single feature of this area. The name *tundra*, referring to the barren landscape, is derived from the Finnish word *tundren* meaning "treeless rolling plain."

The tree line, which forms the southern boundary of the Arctic, is not a straight line; it roughly corresponds with the line demarking the area in which the average temperature during the warmest month is 10C (50F).

The total number of plant species within the Arctic, is a little under 900. This number is small when contrasted with more southern latitudes. In Pennsylvania, for example, there are 1,800 plant species, whereas the number increases to 3,400 in the Carolinas, 5,400 in Texas, and 9,000 in Panama.

The Arctic zone can be divided into four rather distinct phytogeographic (vegetational) regions. These include the arctic portions of Alaska and the Yukon, the arctic portions of the Northwest Territories and the Ungava Peninsula, the islands of the Arctic Archipelago, and Greenland.

Of these four regions, the arctic portions of Alaska and the Yukon possess the most interesting and varied vascular plant flora (604 species). The main reason for this relative abundance is that this area was largely unglaciated during the Pleistocene ice age and was previously connected to the rich flora of eastern Asia by the Bering Land Bridge. Furthermore, both Alaska and the Yukon are connected by mountain ranges with the rest of western North America. Following the Pleistocene ice age, this massive mountain system provided migration routes and a wide range of habitats (both in elevation and latitude) for alpine and arctic species. During the ice age these plants survived in protected mountain habitats. Today the western mountains, Alaska, and the Yukon are rich in local endemics and isolated species; their presence is indicative of the great age and stability of that flora.

Even though it is the largest of the four regions, the arctic portions of the Northwest Territories and Ungava Peninsula have a very uniform flora (651 species). Several reasons account for such uniformity. In the past, the various advances of the massive continental glacier leveled existing mountains and eliminated potential habitats. At present, the dry climate of this interior plateau also contributes to the uniformity of the flora.

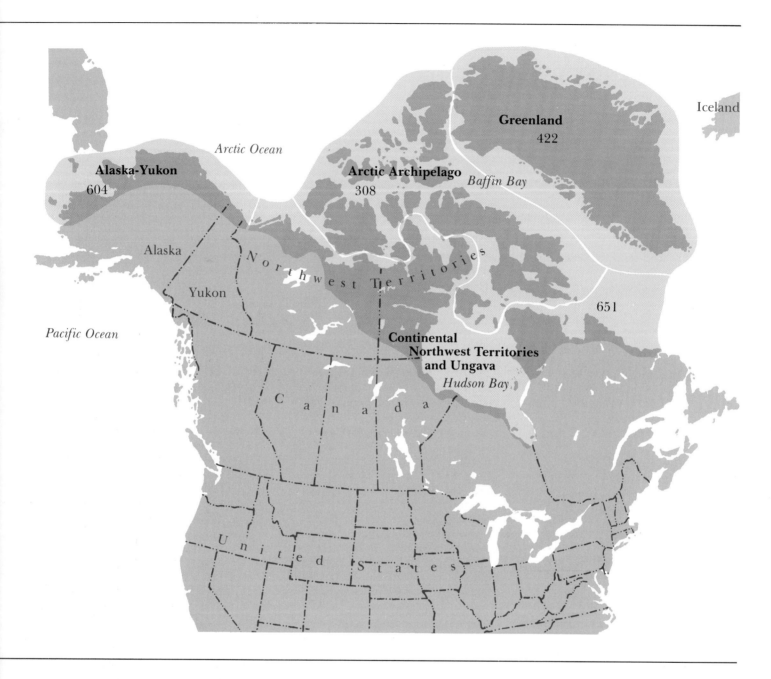

Labels on map:

Arctic Ocean

Iceland

Greenland
422

Alaska-Yukon
604

Arctic Archipelago
308

Baffin Bay

Alaska

Northwest Territories

Yukon

Pacific Ocean

**Continental
Northwest Territories
and Ungava**

651

Hudson Bay

Canada

United States

**Four Phytogeographic Regions of the
North American Arctic Zone.** *The phytogeographic regions are as follows: (a) Alaska-
Yukon, (b) Continental Northwest Territories
and Ungava, (c) Arctic Archipelago, and (d)
Greenland. The number of plant species in
each region is indicated. The total number of
species in the Arctic Zone is 894.*

Adapted from Porsild, 1955, p. 36.

In comparison to the flora of Alaska, the Yukon, and other parts of the North American continent, the flora of the Northwest Territories and Ungava Peninsula region is very young. Its comparative youth is indicated by many unstable plant communities and by the fact that less than a dozen plant species are unique to the region. It is also significant that comparatively few species from Asiatic or western mountain centers have had time to cross the Mackenzie Valley and establish themselves in the region.

The total number of plant species recorded for the arctic portions of the Northwest Territories and Ungava Peninsula is artifically high. Included in this number are plants which should properly be associated with the transitional boreal forest communities common to zones farther south. It is not clear whether these plants are now invading the Arctic zone, due to an amelioration of the climate, or if they are lingering survivors from a former, milder, climatic period.

The vascular flora of the Arctic Archipelago (308 species) is even poorer. This is understandable considering the present cold climate. Many of the region's endemics belong to largely parthenogenic (asexual) genera. Such parthenogenic genera as *Antennaria* (pussy-toes), *Hieracium* (hawk-weeds), and *Taraxacum* (dandelions) are able to form seeds without fertilization. Because of this modification to the reproductive system, minor mutants or variations may be perpetuated, and, if treated as separate species, inflate the number of species within the region. Although these parthenogenic "species" are counted as endemics, they are probably all of relatively recent origin. There has been a lack of botanical collecting in the region, and a relatively high number of endemics and curious distributional patterns makes further botanical exploration here highly desirable.

Although the flora of Greenland, the easternmost of the four regions, has been studied longer and more intensively than that of the rest of the Arctic, it still presents some very puzzling and unexplained problems in plant geography. Considering the vast extent of the Greenland coastline, the number of identified species (422) is not large. Furthermore, the small number of endemic or isolated species suggests that it, too, has a relatively young flora.

Pleistocene Glaciation and the Arctic Flora

The effects of the advances and retreats of Pleistocene ice sheets on arctic plant distribution and vegetational associations have been profound. During the maximum advance of the ice sheets, the Ungava Peninsula and all of the continental Northwest Territories (except a narrow fringe east of the Mackenzie Delta) were covered by a great ice sheet. This massive continental glacier extended southwards into the United States as far as the present-day Ohio and Missouri Rivers. Interestingly, some of the northern portion of the Arctic Archipelago may have escaped glaciation. Likewise, part of Alaska and the central Yukon were unglaciated, except for local glaciers in the high mountains.

In unglaciated areas, called *refugia*, plants survived the glacial period which destroyed plant communities and individual species in the ice-covered continental areas. Following the melting of the Pleistocene glaciers, the present arctic and sub-arctic floras migrated and recolonized the available landscape. Colonization extends to the very borders of the present-day ice caps.

Significant portions of the Arctic Archipelago and all of central Greenland are covered today by thick ice. In Greenland, only a coastal fringe, varying in width from a few kilometers to 240 kilometers (150 miles), is free from ice. The conditions prevailing today in Greenland must be similar to those that existed near the edges of the Pleistocene ice sheet. The glacial history of Greenland is still imperfectly known, but it is certain that there were several successive advances and retreats of the ice front which resulted in the narrowing and broadening of the ice-free coastal fringe and in the changing colonization patterns of plants. The fact that arctic plants grow in such close association with the ice front is an example of the successful environmental testing and selecting that has been operating for millions of years.

Arctic Conditions Affecting Plant Growth

Although the Arctic tundra is marked by an absence of trees, several woody plants do grow in this region. Dwarf willows, ground birches, heather, and various kinds of berry bushes are among the tundra's low and stunted woody plants. They characteristically grow laterally and are generally restricted to places where protecting snow cover is assured during the winter.

Because of the severe climate (long, cold, dark winters alternating with short, cool, light summers) and short growing season (about 60 days), arctic plants have a very slow growth rate. Many species require years before they flower and fruit for the first time. This is especially true of woody plants. No less than 300 annual rings have been counted in the Lapland rhododendron (*Rhododendron lapponicum* [L.] Wahlenb.), the creeping stems of which are no thicker than a thumb.

The short growing season is counter-balanced by the period of continuous daylight which characterizes Arctic summers. Plants are thus exposed to almost perpetual sunlight during the six-month summer. Many arctic species are "long-day" plants; when they are transplanted or grown from seed in lower latitudes, they flower poorly or not at all. On the other hand, "short-day" plants native to temperate or tropical countries do not flower or reproduce well if grown in greenhouses in the Arctic's continuous daylight.

Precipitation in the Arctic is about the same as in the Sahara Desert. It usually averages under 25 centimeters (10 inches) a year near the Arctic Circle and as little as 4.5 centimeters (.75 inches) in High Arctic areas such as Ellesmere Island. Contrary to popular belief, winter snowfall is light and frequent gales, which often reach hurricane velocity, sweep the snow off the level ground. Plants are, thus, exposed to the detrimental drying effects of the wind.

Rainfall is very light during the growing season. Indeed, most of the Arctic would be a lifeless desert if it were not for the fact that the soil remains perpetually frozen several centimeters below the surface, thereby holding the surface water within reach of shallow plant roots.

The short growing season, low amounts of precipitation, and other factors have a more marked, limiting effect on plant life than does the cold temperature. In fact, certain factors counteract the cold temperature and consequently prolong the growing season. These factors, continuous sunlight and the absorption of heat by dark-colored soils, increase the temperature of the soil surface and air immediately surrounding the plants by as much as 10 to 20C. While temperatures a meter (3.3 feet) above ground may be several degrees below freezing, near the ground or within the plant cushion the increased temperatures are high enough for photosynthesis to occur.

In many ways, arctic plant life is identical with that found in alpine regions. Several forms of plant life and many species are common to both the Arctic zone and to mountain peaks more than a thousand kilometers to the south. The principal physical difference is in the length of the growing season. But this is actually more apparent than real, because in the high mountains the accumulation of snow is often so great that the length of the effective growing season after the snow melts closely approaches that observed in the Arctic.

Within the Arctic, the subsoil is permanently frozen, often to great depths. This condition is referred to as *permafrost*. The annual thaw varies with the soil's texture: in sand and gravel, permafrost may be found at 2.5 meters (8 feet); in wet, peaty soil, it may appear only a few centimeters below the surface.

Owing to poor drainage and poor aeration (both due in part to the low temperatures), arctic and subarctic soil are generally acidic. Slowly decomposing granitic bedrock also is acidic. Because of this, organic decay

Draba alpina *L., Cruciferae (Mustard Family).*

by bacteria and fungi is extremely slow, with a consequent deficiency of nitrogen as well as other necessary plant nutrients. In a few places where nitrogen and phosphate are recycled, such as bird cliffs, musk-ox meadows, areas with skeletal remains, and refuse heaps near human habitation, many arctic plants respond with lush and luxuriant growth. Such enriched local areas often have an interesting micro-flora; both ubiquitous and rare species can be found in these locales. These "oases" in the arctic desert are visible at some distance and are often particularly rewarding to the botanical explorer.

Adaptations of Arctic Plants

Most arctic flowering plants have similar growth forms. They are small perennials with shallow, regenerating buds, reduced stems and leaf surfaces, and large, showy flowers adapted to quick pollination. Over 40 percent of the arctic plants come from five plant families: the grasses (*Poaceae*), the sedges (*Cyperaceae*), the mustards (*Cruciferae*), the roses (*Rosaceae*), and the composites (*Asteraceae*).

Fireweed or Broad-leaved Willow-herb,
Epilobium latifolium *L., Onagraceae*
(Evening Primrose Family).

Mountain Avens, Dryas integrifolia *M.
Vahl, Rosaceae (Rose Family). This is the
official flower of the Northwest Territories.*

That perennials, and not annual plants, are characteristic of the Arctic is a result of adaptation to the short growing season. The short summers do not provide adequate time for most annual species to complete a life cycle of seed production. The failure of a single seed crop would, of course, exterminate an annual species in a local region. Although perennials produce seeds, they can also survive through other reproductive means. Seed production in the Arctic may be high, but the number of seedlings surviving to maturity is low. Many species require years of development from the germination of their seeds to their first flowering.

Under ideal conditions, the products of photosynthesis may be equally divided between asexual growth, which ensures the physical presence of a plant, and sexual reproduction which, through seed production, results in descendents with new combinations of characteristics. But if limiting factors or conditions are imposed, vegetative growth becomes the major priority for the use of the plant's resources. Hence, vegetative propagation through perennial root and rhizome systems is widespread and is highly conservative of a plant's integrity. These plant populations exhibit little genetic or morphological variation. Plants just keep growing, forming large clones of themselves.

Evolution among arctic plants, thus, has been slow. Annuals, on the other hand, characteristic of deserts, modify their complete genetic and morphological make-up each year through sexually produced seeds. For this reason, evolutionary change among desert plants has been high.

A remarkably high percentage of arctic vascular plants are polyploid compared to those in deserts and other plant communities. The polyploid condition is common within the plant kingdom, but rare within the animal kingdom. Humans and most other animals are diploids; that is, they have two of each chromosome, one from each parent. In polyploids, each chromosome is replicated more than two times. With each chromosome represented by many copies, polyploids are less susceptible to mutation and change. High amounts of ultraviolet radiation, known to induce mutation, are characteristic of arctic summers. Polyploids, therefore, may undergo mutations but rarely express them because of the multiple sets of chromosomes. This mechanism promotes uniformity in flora in a region of the world where the environment is uniformly harsh.

Many arctic plants are adapted to live in dry environments. Such plants have small, often leathery, leaves and densely matted hairs covering the leaves and stem; these features reduce water loss during periods of prolonged drought. The plants' low, compact, cushiony growth form serves to reduce heat loss as well as to resist desiccation and mechanical abrasion caused by arctic winds and drifting snow. The wintering buds of many arctic plants are located just above or below the soil surface. Here, the dead leaves of former years protect the buds from low temperatures and desiccation.

Climbing plants, plants that sting or are poisonous, and plants which are protected by spines or thorns are not found in the Arctic. The implication is that such adaptations are not needed.

As in deserts, spring comes with a rush in the Arctic. Many arctic species (in common with desert plants also adapted to a growing season with limited available water) require only a short time to break their winter dormancy, come to bloom, mature their fruits, and prepare again for winter. Most arctic plants require only a month to complete this cycle. A special adaptation is the ability of many arctic plants to freeze solid at almost any stage of growth and, upon thawing, continue to grow as if nothing had happened.

While seeds may not be needed for survival, the flowers of many arctic plants are indeed showy. In addition to white, the primary colors of red, blue, and yellow are common among arctic flowers. Along with these visible colors, many flowers also have patterns visible only in the ultraviolet spectrum; these ultraviolet patterns serve as nectar guides for insects. Bees, in particular, can see these ultraviolet patterns which aid insect nectar-gathering and plant pollination activities. The same ultraviolet radiation which can induce detrimental mutations is, in this case, benefical to plant pollination.

Nectar production is high among arctic plants. Although many arctic insects clearly depend on nectar and pollen from flowering plants for their survival, these same plants, with highly adapted means of vegetative reproduction, may have little or no need for the insects.

Plant Migration and Dispersal

An important factor affecting arctic plant migration is that solid ice bridges form not only over lakes and rivers but, in many parts of the Arctic, also over considerable expanses of sea, particularly straits and sounds separating islands. Each winter, high winds and drifting snow level rough spots on the sea ice and the land surface; these smooth areas greatly facilitate the dispersal of seeds. The wind blows seeds from many arctic plants over considerable distances; the frozen conditions allow seeds to cross bodies of water that would otherwise be barriers to migration. A high percentage of arctic plants have relatively small, light-weight seeds ideally equipped for such wind dispersal.

Seeds of wind-dispersed plants may often be observed in the drifting snow. The seed capsules do not mature and open until after the snow covers the ground. Such plants commonly produce stiff and erect fruiting stalks which protrude through the shallow winter snow.

During the winter, large snowdrifts accumulate on the lee side of large rocks or moraines. In the spring, when the snow melts, large deposits of loess (wind-transported dust) mixed with plant remains, including seeds, may be seen. Such accumulations of enriched soil become ideal sites for plant colonization.

Rivers and streams provide another important means of plant dispersal. Each spring during the snow melt-down and ice break-up, the north-ward flowing arctic rivers are loaded with driftwood and flotsam. The flotsam is, in part, composed of plant remains and seeds which have accumulated on the ice of lakes and rivers during winter. Ocean currents are also responsible for the dispersal of many seashore plants at this time.

Long distance dispersal by resident and migratory birds is a major factor in plant colonization. Seeds or other plant material capable of vegetative reproduction may be carried or passed by birds to new locales. Ptarmigans, ravens, sea gulls, and geese, for example, eat the red and black berries of *Empetrum*, *Rubus*, and *Vaccinium* and, thus, disperse the seeds. Many aquatic plants found in the High Arctic are unable to reproduce by seeds, yet they are found distributed over a remarkably wide range. Transport by birds may be the key to their wide-spread dispersal.

Arctic mammals also aid in the dispersal of plants. The omnipresent ground squirrels, as well as voles and lemmings, feed on and store seeds of a number of plant species. These animals also inadvertently carry seeds which adhere to their fur. Certain plant species can be found around ground squirrel burrows and the dens of foxes and wolves.

Because animals traveling in search of food and shelter move from one ecologically equivalent area to another, animal migration is always preceded by plant migration.

Labrador Tea, Ledum decumbens *(Ait.) Lodd., Ericaceae (Heath Family).*

The Arctic Flora in Relation to Man

With the paucity of plant life, few plants native to the Arctic are of direct importance to man. The major source of subsistence for the Inuit (the contemporary designation for Eskimos of the Central Canadian Arctic) has been hunting, with plants representing a small portion of their diet. In the High Arctic, some green and red marine algae (dulce or sea-lettuce) have been eaten in times of scarcity. In Greenland, succulent young stalks of angelica (*Archangelica officinalis* L.) and the leaves of mountain sorrel or scurvy-grass (*Oxyria digyna* [L.] Hill) are used. The latter is very common through-out the Arctic and may be eaten raw as a salad, cooked as a pot-herb, or stewed as rhubarb. Leaves of the prickly saxifrage (*Saxifraga tricuspidata* Rottb.) and labrador-tea (*Ledum decumbens* [Ait.] Lodd.) have been used for brewing tea. Bistort (*Polygonum viviparum* L.) has a pecan-sized, starchy, and slightly astringent rhizome which may be eaten raw but is highly prized when cooked. Tubers of the Eskimo potato (*Claytonia tuberosa* Pall.) were commonly eaten and preserved in seal oil, the universal Inuit preservative. Several kinds of berries, including crowberry (*Empetrum nigrum* L.), cloud berry or baked-apple (*Rubus chamaemorus* L.), and bog-bilberry (*Vaccinium uliginosum* L.) have been eaten by Inuit.

None of the woody plant species are large enough for use in construction. Wood has traditionally been gathered as driftwood or through trade. Heather, various berry bushes, stunted willows, alders, and dwarf birches were used by the Inuit as fuel for cooking. White heather (*Cassiope tetragona* [L.] D. Don), common throughout the Arctic, is so rich in resin that it will burn even when moderately wet. Nearly all of the larger species of lichens, partic-ularly species of *Cladonia* and *Cetraria*, are highly flammable when dry and may also be used as fuel. Raw peat, particularly heath turf, and partly decomposed sphagnum moss are available nearly everywhere in the Arctic and in Greenland and provide an important source of fuel.

In the Canadian Arctic, lyme grass (*Elymus arenarius* L. spp. *mollis* [Trin.] [Hultén]) was carefully woven and shaped into socks. In Greenland, the soft, hairy spike and broad flat leaves were used as a disposable insulating "boot hay." Lyme grass baskets with soapstone handles have been used throughout the Hudson Bay area.

Indirectly, the arctic vegetation is of great importance to man because nearly all sedges, grasses, fructicose lichens, and many herbaceous and woody plants furnish food for the large herds of grazing animals. Furthermore, seeds, winter buds, and roots of many species are eaten by birds and small rodents which, in turn, constitute the food of some of the fur-bearing mammals. Like-wise, the comparatively rich marine plant life furnishes food for the sea mammals so important in the economy of the Inuit.

Reading List

Arnason, T., R.J. Hebda, and T. Johns. "Use of plants for food and medicine by native peoples of Eastern Canada." *Canadian Journal of Botany*, 59 (1981), 2189-2325.

Flint, R.F. *Glacial and Pleistocene Geology.* NY: John Wiley & Sons, Inc., 1957.

Flint, R.F. *Glacial and Quaternary Geology.* NY: John Wiley & Sons, Inc., 1971.

Ford, R.I. "Ethnobotany in North America: An historical phytogeographical perspective." *Canadian Journal of Botany*, 59 (1981), 2178-2188.

Geiger, R. *The Climate Near the Ground.* Trans. M.N. Stewart et al. Cambridge, MA: Harvard University Press, 1950.

Gribbin, J., ed. *Climatic Change.* Cambridge, England: Cambridge University Press, 1978.

Hultén, E. *The Amphi-Atlantic Plants and their Phyto-geographical Connections.* Kungliga Svenska Vetenskakademiens Handlingar, Fjarde Serien, Band 7, Nr. 1:1-340, 1958.

Hultén, E. *The Circumpolar Plants. I. Vascular Cryptogams. Conifers, Mono-cotyledons.* Kungliga Svenska Vetenskakademiens Handlingar, Fjarde Serien, Band 8, Nr. 5:1-279, 1962.

Hultén, E. *Flora of Alaska and Neighboring Territories: A Manual of the Flowering Plants.* Stanford, CA: Stanford University Press, 1968.

Hultén, E. *Outline of the History of Arctic and Boreal Biota During the Quaternary Period: Their Evolution During and After the Glacial Period as Indicated by the Equiformal Progressive Areas of Present Plant Species.* 1937 Stockholm Edition rpt. Lehre, W. Germany: Verlag von J. Cramer, 1972.

McGrath, J.W. *Dyes from Lichens and Plants.* Toronto: Van Nostrand Reinhold Ltd., 1977.

Polunin, N. "Pteridophyta and Spermato-phyta." In *Botany of the Canadian Eastern Arctic.* National Museums of Canada Bulletin, No. 92. Ottawa: National Museums of Canada, 1940, pp. 1-408. (Also Biological Series, No. 24.)

Polunin, N. "Vegetation and Ecology." In *Botany of the Canadian Eastern Arctic.* National Museums of Canada Bulletin, No. 104. Ottawa: National Museums of Canada, 1948, pp. 1-304. (Also Biological Series, No. 32.)

Polunin, N. *Circumpolar Arctic Flora.* Oxford: Clarendon Press, 1959.

Porsild, A.E. *Vascular Plants of the Western Canadian Arctic Archipelago.* National Museums of Canada Bulletin, No. 135. Ottawa: National Museums of Canada, 1955, pp. 1-226.

Porsild, A.E. *Illustrated Flora of the Canadian Arctic Archipelago.* National Museums of Canada Bulletin, No. 146. Ottawa: National Museums of Canada, 1957, pp. 1-209.

Porsild, A.E., and W.J. Cody. *Vascular Plants of Continental Northwest Territories, Canada.* Ottawa: National Museums of Canada, 1980.

Scoggan, H.J. "General Survey." In *The Flora of Canada.* National Museum of Natural Sciences Publications in Botany, No. 7 (1). Ottawa: National Museums of Canada, 1978, pp. 1-89.

Taylor, R.L., and R.A. Ludwig. *The Evolution of Canada's Flora.* Toronto: University of Toronto Press, 1966.

Wright, H.E., Jr., and D.G. Frey, eds. *The Quaternary of the United States.* Princeton: Princeton University Press, 1965.

Caribou (Rangifer tarandus) *undertake annual migrations between their winter quarters in the taiga forests to the south and their summer grazing area on the tundra. This migration may cover a distance of 1,600 kilometers (1,000 miles).*

Animals of the Arctic

Joseph F. Merritt, Powdermill Nature Reserve,
Carnegie Museum of Natural History, Pittsburgh, Pennsylvania

Introduction

The extreme cold is a pervasive, selective force in the arctic tundra of North America. This cold, coupled with a short growing season, lack of food, and paucity of precipitation, presents plants and animals with a harsh environment. The ways in which plants cope with such extremes is discussed in "Plants of the Arctic." Here, we will discuss the adaptations of the animals that enable their survival.

While many animal species have disappeared from the Arctic since the end of the Pleistocene, about 10,000 years ago, there are numerous survivors. These animals have evolved various means of surviving and reproducing in the hostile arctic tundra. Two of these strategies, avoidance and tolerance, permit animals with limited long-distance mobility to adapt. A third method of dealing with the cold winters is to leave. Birds, for example, have evolved the ability to migrate, enabling them to overwinter in milder climates to the south.

Arctic Life and Pleistocene Glaciation

About 30,000 years ago, during the last glacial event of the Pleistocene Epoch, tremendous masses of ice covered much of the arctic tundra in Canada and large expanses of Europe and Asia. Ice-covered lands were nearly lifeless; the movement of animals and plants was limited to ice-free areas called *refugia* in parts of Asia and much of temperate America.

Small areas near the Mackenzie Delta, Banks Island, parts of Northern Ellesmere Island, and Greenland escaped glaciation and provided a habitat for life. More southerly parts of the great continents were buried under a massive sheet of ice. Immediately south of the ice sheet, a narrow, sinuous belt of land also supported a tundra-like vegetation. Plants and animals confined to these refugia faced environmental selection that, as is true in the Canadian Arctic today, favored tundra adaptation.

Another refugium was a land bridge called *Beringia*. With the formation of northern and southern ice caps, the level of the oceans was lowered by over 100 meters (330 feet), and a continental shelf bridging Siberia and Alaska—Beringia— was exposed. A grassy and sedgy, tundra-like vegetation covered this dry land bridge that, ultimately, allowed plants and animals to move between Asia and Alaska. Massive glaciers isolated this refugium from the major part of America.

About 10,000 years ago, as continental ice caps melted, the encroaching waters submerged Beringia, forming what is today the Bering Strait. With the submergence of this land bridge, animals in Alaska with Asiatic origins became cut off from Asia. With the melting of ice sheets, vast regions of Northern Eurasia and America also became exposed for resettlement.

Evolution seldom met this environmental change by "inventing" new species to colonize these new lands. Rather than the evolution of new species, the biological transition from 10,000 years ago to the present has been usually marked by many extinctions and the expansion of the geographic ranges of populations earlier restricted to refugia by the glaciers.

Post-Pleistocene Extinctions

Shortly after the end of glaciation, rapid extinction of many species of large mammals of the northern hemisphere occurred. Within 3,000 years, huge mammoths, large bison, horses, and some 95 percent of the large mammals occupying North America met their demise. In addition to these large herbivores, predators such as large sabre-tooth cats, dire wolves, and short-faced bears also ceased to exist rather suddenly. Clearly, something was occurring during these first millenia following the melting of the continental ice caps.

With the possible exception of the extinction of dinosaurs at the end of the Cretaceous Period, no other natural catastrophe has elicited as many causal hypotheses as the Pleistocene extinctions. One hypothesis that has won popular acceptance is referred to as the Overkill Hypothesis. Proponents of this hypothesis argue that paleo-Indians may have been responsible for the extermination of the mammoths and other large herbivores in North America.

Although attractive to many, the Overkill Hypothesis has not received general acceptance among vertebrate paleontologists, many of whom favor hypotheses based upon environmental change. According to these hypotheses, climatological changes are believed to have influenced vegetation patterns in North America. Altered vegetation patterns, consequently, influenced the food resources of mammals.

Because this chapter focuses upon today's arctic fauna, those wishing to delve further into the topic of Pleistocene extinctions should refer to the bibliography at the end of this chapter. We will now turn our attention to the survivors of this natural catastrophe and the strategies they have evolved to cope with the harsh arctic environment of today.

The Permafrost Zone

Even though the average precipitation on the arctic tundra is only about 20 centimeters (8 inches) per year, its outward appearance bears little resemblance to deserts as we perceive them. The tundra is cold and covered with a layer of permafrost, a frozen layer found between 12.5 centimeters (5 inches) and 3 meters (10 feet) below the surface. Because cold air cannot easily absorb water vapor, the land retains its meager water. The permafrost prevents normal drainage. Unlike other deserts, the tundra, thus, holds on to its water in the form of lakes and swampy ground, permitting a lush growth of arctic plants.

Permafrost is one of the most important factors in the ecology of the North Lands. The moisture retained by the permafrost, although important to plants, can create hardships for small mammals. Voles, lemmings, and shrews which search for food in the matted vegetation between the permafrost and the surface may become wet. Even though the fur of small mammals is a good insulator when dry, wet fur may cause death.

In addition to restricting the penetration of water, permafrost also restricts the growth of plant roots and the burrowing activities of small mammals. The distribution of many small mammals as well as certain insects with a burrowing larval stage is, in fact, regulated by the permafrost. Fossorial (burrowing) mammals such as moles and gophers are, thus, notably absent from permafrost areas.

When possible, the burrow systems of other small mammals are confined to well-drained areas. The hibernation sites of the arctic ground squirrel, for example, are determined by the permafrost zone. This squirrel is somewhat of an anomaly in that it is a true hibernator successfully existing in an environment notably unsuited for hibernators. Ground squirrels construct their burrow systems, especially their hibernacula (winter quarters) in areas where the permafrost line lies well below them. If this were not the case, seasonal thawing could cause flooding of nest sites.

The Arctic Winter

Winter is indeed the "acid test" for polar animals. For eight to nine months of the year, arctic animals must cope with the climate extremes of winter. Only large mammals such as the arctic hare, fox, wolf, caribou, and musk-oxen are metabolically able to withstand the extremes of cold encountered on the surface of the snow. Smaller mammals have such a small body mass with respect to their heat-dissipating body surface (and comparatively inefficient fur) that their metabolism cannot maintain normal body temperature if subjected to extreme cold for prolonged periods of time. Because the fur coat of small mammals must be relatively short and light for agile movement, it, likewise, provides poor insulation. Survival of small mammals during winter months is, thus, made possible only by behaviorial adaptations that cause them to seek shelter under the tundra snowcover in elaborate burrow systems and nests.

Here in the Arctic, where the average temperature may reach minus 32C (minus 25F) and lower, the survival of small animals rests heavily on the unique insulation abilites of snow. On the ground surface, below only 25 centimeters (10 inches) of snow, there is little temperature fluctuation. Even when the surface temperature reaches a minus 45C (minus 50F), the subnivean environment (the zone between the snow and soil surfaces) remains near zero. At this level, small mammals such as shrews, lemmings, voles, and weasels survive under the snow in nests that are dark, quiet, and moist. Little light or sound penetrate the snowcover; the air is calm and essentially saturated with moisture. In this subnivean environment, the small mammals are warmed by the summer heat trapped in the earth's surface.

To lemmings, the structure of the snowpack is just as important as its depth. Gases are not readily diffused through dense, wind-packed snow. Scientists have shown that a build-up of carbon dioxide in the subnivean environment at different times of the year may be due to high population densities of lemmings. Further, snow chimneys, tunnels dug by lemmings from the ground to the snow's surface, are frequent when lemming populations are high. These chimneys may act as "ventilator

The collared lemming (Dicrostonyx torquatus) *is a major food source for arctic predators. This small, prolific rodent undergoes cyclic population explosions: Every three to four years its numbers tend to increase and then suddenly decline.*

shafts" to relieve the subnivean environment of carbon dioxide.

Lemming tracks are often seen in fresh snow around the chimneys. Sometimes the tracks can be traced to another chimney, indicating that the lemming returned to the subnivean environment. In other cases the tracks may lead to a dead lemming or the scene of predation by a fox or owl. There are always risks associated with ventures above the snow.

Lemmings are well-adapted to life in snowy regions. Their elongated third and fourth toes serve as powerful digging claws and enable them to tunnel through the snow. A horny pad also develops on the bottom of these toes during winter months and lasts through the winter. When spring arrives, the pad loosens and is sloughed off. In addition to lemmings' unique adaptation for winter digging, the collared lemming develops a white winter coat. These adaptations make lemmings one of the best-adapted small mammals living in the Arctic.

The king eider (Somateria spectabilis), *shown here, and the common eider* (Somateria mollissima) *are large ducks that regularly winter in the ice-free waters of the Arctic. Their heavy layer of down provides excellent insulation. Inuit use eider skins for clothing and robes. Icelandic farmers harvest eiderdown from the lining of the birds' nests.*

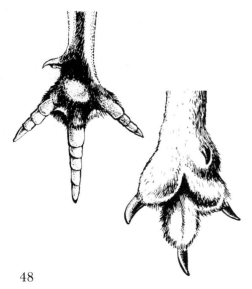

Left to right:
Comparison of the Feet of the Ptarmigan (Lagopus spp.) **in Summer and Winter.** *Unlike most birds, the ptarmigan grows feathers on its toes during winter to serve as "snowshoes" and aid in heat conservation during this harsh time.*

Some animals insulated with fur, fat, or feathers also take shelter. The ptarmigan, a bird that overwinters in the Arctic, finds shelter from the elements by digging tunnels into snowbanks where it stays protected from the cold sometimes for days at a time. The few overwintering birds such as the ptarmigan, snowy owl, and the raven have heavy layers of fat beneath the skin or long, dense feathers. Ptarmigan and snowy owls even have feathers on their ankles and toes. The feathered toes of the ptarmigan act as snowshoes, preventing these rather chunky birds from breaking through the snow crust while walking.

Large arctic mammals such as the musk-ox, caribou, and wolf have long, dense fur as well as heavy layers of fat beneath the skin. The musk-ox, in particular, is equipped with an immense cloak of coarse guard hairs, over 30 centimeters (1 foot) in length, and an underfur of thick, dense, silky wool called *qiviut*. The hairs of the musk-ox are thicker at the tip than at the root so that they form an almost airtight coat. In addition to insulating fur, the musk-ox is large enough to carry huge reserves of fat, which are employed as an energy source during the cold winter months. Short, stubby legs are attached to the musk-ox's very compact body; it stands only 1 meter (3 feet) high, though it is 2.5 meters (7 feet) long. The neck is thick, the tail very short, and the ears hidden in the furry coat.

Although caribou lack the long guard hairs and elaborate qiviut of the musk-ox, they possess the same type of club-shaped hairs as the musk-ox. Caribou are, thus, surrounded by a continuous layer of warm air that cannot escape and provides excellent insulation.

How do marine animals keep warm in the icy arctic waters? Because thermal conductivity of water is about 20 times greater than that of air, the arctic marine animals must protect themselves from heat loss, particularly when inactive and when in cold seas. Air trapped in dry underfur, such as that of the harp and ringed seal, acts as an effective insulator. Blubber is also an important insulator.

When considering arctic animals such as whales, walruses, and seals, the importance of blubber as an effective insulator cannot be over-emphasized; in some animals, it makes up one quarter of the body weight. It varies in thickness from 5 centimeters (2 inches) in small seals to 60 centimeters (2 feet) in a bowhead whale and acts like the wet suit of a scuba diver. In some whales, blubber is also an energy reserve for migration.

On land, marine animals have a problem with overheating. One way in which marine animals control overheating is by keeping their fur moist. Another way to control heating is by sleeping; in some species sleeping reduces heat production by almost 25 percent.

In general, the amount of heat loss depends both on the amount of surface area and on the temperature difference between the body surface and the surroundings; large mammals, for example, have less heat loss than small mammals because of their large body mass relative to surface area. The arctic marine animals that survive in extremely cold water can tolerate a great drop in their skin temperature. Measurements of skin temperature have shown that it is only a degree or so above that of the surrounding water. By permitting their skin temperature to drop, these animals, which maintain an internal temperature as warm as that of man, expend very little heat outside of their fat layer and, thus, keep warm.

Similarly, many arctic land animals permit temperatures in their extremities to drop and, therefore, are able to conserve heat. For those animals that commonly stand on the ice, this strategy is essential from another standpoint. If the feet of a herring gull were as warm as its body, they would melt the ice, which might then freeze over them, trapping the animal until the spring thaw set it free. Needless to say, this is not very adaptive for survival! As a result, the extremities of such animals are actually adapted to function at a different internal temperature from that of the rest of the animal. If one were to measure the temperature of the gull's foot it would be about zero C (32F), nearly 21C (70F)

colder than the rest of its body.

The gull regulates its external body temperature through a system called countercurrent exchange. The arteries bearing warm blood toward the extremities are closely bunched or entwined with the veins carrying cold blood back to the heart. The warm blood is cooled, the cold blood is heated, and the extremities are kept cold so that they lose little heat. The nervous systems of these cold-tolerant birds are also adapted to function at temperatures where warm-climate birds would be immobilized.

Birds such as the gulls are not the only land animals that regulate the temperatures of their extremities. The leg temperature of the caribou has been found to be about 50 degrees lower than that of its body. The arctic fox has, likewise, evolved an interesting way of dealing with the trials of walking on snow while still maintaining the agility so important to their hunting ability. The fat in the arctic fox's foot has a different thermal behavior from that in the rest of its body. Its footpads are, therefore, soft and resilient, even at temperatures of minus 45C (minus 50F).

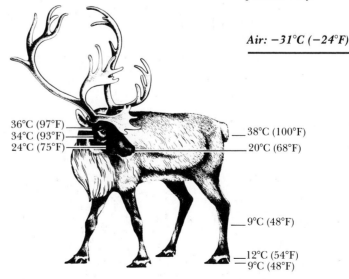

Regulation of External Body Temperature in the Caribou (Rangifer tarandus). *Temperature regulation is accomplished in part by countercurrent heat exchange. An intricate mesh-work of veins and arteries acts to keep the temperature of the legs near that of the environment so heat is not lost from the body.*

Air: −31°C (−24°F)

36°C (97°F)
34°C (93°F)
24°C (75°F)

38°C (100°F)
20°C (68°F)

9°C (48°F)

12°C (54°F)
9°C (48°F)

Compared with foxes living in more southerly regions, the arctic fox (Alopex lagopus) *has ears that are smaller, more rounded, and densely furred. The arctic fox's smaller ears reduce the amount of heat lost to the environment and thus aid in coping with the long, cold arctic winters.*

Two rules have been proposed to describe the adaptive responses of warm-blooded animals to the north-south latitudinal gradient: Bergmann's Rule and Allen's Rule. Bergmann's Rule states that warm-blooded animals of the same or related species tend to be larger in cold regions and become smaller toward the equator. This rule was accepted for a long time and has some sound physics behind it: The larger an object, the more slowly it tends to lose heat. This relationship works in terms of the surface-to-volume ratio: Many of the arctic mammals and birds tend to grow larger than their southern relatives. The northern race of the ermine in the Yukon Territory, for example, is considerably larger than the southern race living in Colorado.

Allen's Rule states that the appendages of warm-blooded animals become shorter in colder climates (northern latitudes) compared to those appendages of animals found closer to the equator. For instance, the arctic fox has small, rounded, and densely furred ears, whereas foxes living in deserts, such as the kit fox of the Southwest and fennec of North Africa, have large, elongated, and thinly furred ears. Similarly, arctic birds usually have shorter bills and legs than their southern relatives.

Allen's Rule makes a great deal of sense and is true for some species. A long nose and tail, long ears and legs tend to add unnecessarily to the body surface and would be great heat-wasters for arctic species. For a species living in hot climates, long appendages aid in the dissipation of heat.

The trouble with such "rules" is that there are too many exceptions to them. Polar bears are not globular and woolly with stubby appendages, and tropical bear species do not tend to be skinny with long appendages. Current scientific research has pointed out that external insulation in the form of feathers and hair and behavioral adaptations such as the habit of several animals huddling together in winter and construction of elaborate nests may be more important as adaptive mechanisms than changes in body size and proportion.

We have concentrated our discussion thus far on the warm-blooded animals (homeotherms) and how they cope with the arctic cold. But any visitor to the Arctic during the summer will certainly become familiar with the legions of mosquitos and blackflies. They are, indeed, well-represented, and since they do not migrate, they must cope with the long winter cold just as the homeotherms do. Some insects find refuge in the warm fur or feathers of homeotherms, but most, like the Arctic's masses of black flies and mosquitos, come to life only on a few warm days of summer.

Most arctic insects undergo a complete metamorphosis consisting of four stages of growth—egg, larva, pupa, and adult. Not unlike those in the Northeastern United States, many arctic insects, namely mosquitos, survive winter in an egg stage. The pupa stage occurs in early spring and serves as a rest period. During this time, metabolism is reduced and no food is needed.

The secret of the insect's ability to survive the extreme cold of the North is not yet solved. Scientists suspect the answer may lie in part in the insects' ability to produce an internal "antifreeze" for the winter: Insects have the ability to convert glycogen, a carbohydrate related to starches, within their bodies to glycerol, an alcohol-type substance with a highly freeze-resistant quality; this is reconverted to glycogen in the spring.

The Ears of Foxes Help to Regulate Body Heat. *The kit fox* (Vulpes macrotis) *(bottom) of the American Southwest has relatively long ears that help to dissipate heat. In contrast, the relatively short ears of the arctic fox* (Alopex lagopus) *(top) help to conserve heat. The red fox* (Vulpes vulpes) *(middle) of temperate America possesses intermediate-sized ears.*

This female rock ptarmigan (Lagopus mutus) is shown with her nest. Each year rock ptarmigan display three different plumages. In summer the male's plumage is grayish brown and the female's is a coarsely barred black and buff. In fall both sexes resemble summer females, and in winter both sexes are white.

Arctic hares (Lepus articus) *normally show seasonal changes in coat color. Hares inhabiting the Far North, however, keep their white coats year-round, even though there is no snow in mid-summer.*

The arctic ground squirrel (Spermophilis parryii) *is the sole hibernating arctic mammal. The sik-sik, as the Inuit refer to it, will sleep for almost eight months of the year, curled up in its grass-lined hibernaculum well above the permafrost zone.*

Such "antifreeze" is also employed by certain arctic fish. In general, temperatures of arctic waters below a depth of about 9 meters (30 feet) remain at approximately minus 2C (30F) all year. During summer, water near the surface remains at about 5C (40F). In winter when ice forms, the surface water temperature decreases to minus 2C (30F). Certain fish live in the deeper water in a continuous supercooled state. If they are caught and brought to the surface in winter, these fish will freeze when they contact water containing ice crystals. Those fish that live close to the surface of the water will either migrate seasonally or produce an "antifreeze" substance similar to that produced by arctic insects. As with insects, this substance lowers the freezing point of the body tissues below that of the surrounding water, thus preventing freezing.

As we have seen, animals of the arctic tundra exhibit some fascinating behavioral and physiological adaptations for dealing with the harsh winter climate. Many of these adaptations are rather subtle. Perhaps the most obvious trait defining arctic animals is their affinity for the color white. Many of the arctic mammals either remain white year-round or change to white in winter. Those that remain white year-round include the polar bear, arctic hare of the Far North, the northerly forms of caribou, and the timber wolf. A seasonal color change (dimorphism) is seen in the collared lemming, ermine, and arctic fox. Of the birds that remain in the Arctic during winter, the rock and willow ptarmigan undergo a seasonal change from a mottled brown or gray fall plumage to a white, winter color. The snowy owl maintains its white color year-round.

Why arctic animals dress in white during winter is not fully known. The color does conceal both predator and prey. It was believed to reduce the amount of heat radiating from the body. Recent experiments indicate, however, that this is apparently not true. There are many unsolved questions concerning the adaptive nature of color changes in the Arctic.

We have no clear-cut answers for such puzzles as why the brown lemming, unlike its close relative and neighbor, the collared lemming, does not have a white winter coat. How does one explain the blue color phase which sometimes occurs in the arctic fox? If whiteness is a winter adaptation which provides protection from predators, how can this sooty blue phase be considered adaptive when it provides a contrast against the white snow of winter? If this blue phase is not adaptive, then how did it evolve? If white is adaptive, then how does the blue phase survive? The picture is further complicated by the fact that in many parts of the Arctic, the fox can have no possible use for its white color because during winter it subsists upon carrion left by bears or caches of animals collected and stored up in the autumn.

A further challenge to the protective function of white coloration is provided by the arctic hare. Far northern hares keep their white coats year-round. In areas such as Ellesmere Island, which lack snow during mid-summer, the arctic hare maintains its white coat.

Hibernation in the Arctic: The *Sik-Sik*

Animal activity in the Arctic is geared to short summers and long, harsh winters. Although we may think that an ideal way to cope with winter is to sleep through it, hibernation is surprisingly uncharacteristic of arctic animals. The winter season is much too cold and too long. The only hibernator on the arctic tundra is the arctic ground squirrel or *sik-sik* as the Inuit call it. The polar bear, which most of us associate with hibernating, in fact, does no more than fall into a deep sleep. This sleep is short-lived and found only in females in a maternity den.

In late fall, the *sik-sik* puts on fat and prepares its winter burrow. Dry, sandy regions located well above the permafrost layer are chosen. The hibernaculum is padded with grass and is well stocked with a cache of assorted foods. Here, curled up in this cozy chamber, the *sik-sik* will survive for nearly eight months of the year. During this time its heartbeat drops radically from a normal rate of over 200 beats per minute to a rate of 5 to 10 per minute. The *sik-sik* will breathe only once or twice every minute, and its body temperature will drop from a normal 37C (98F) to close to freezing.

During winter the squirrel is "dead to the world" and can actually be lifted from its nest without waking. Until the weather warms in spring, the *sik-sik* gains nourishment from its accumulated fat. In the spring, the *sik-sik* emerges from its burrow lean and famished after its long hibernation. Soon after emerging, it mates and its young are born in mid-June after a 25-day gestation period. The young are highly independent from birth and gain weight rapidly; by late September they are ready to hibernate. Because of the abbreviated growing season, animals of the Arctic such as the *sik-sik* work at an accelerated pace. They must take advantage of food when it is available; there is no time to waste.

The Migrants

As we have seen, arctic animals have evolved many specialized adaptations that permit them to cope with the harsh northern winter. Many species of birds, however, do not stay in the Arctic for the winter. The mass exodus of these birds from the Arctic is probably due to their inability to procure food. Many of these migratory species tend to be principally insect-eaters and ground feeders. If they had sufficient food, in most cases, these migrants could probably survive in the Northlands during winter.

For millions of years migration has been a way of life for most arctic species of birds. During winter, only an occasional hawk, ptarmigan, raven, or owl will be encountered in the High Arctic. In the spring, however, birds return to the arctic tundra en masse and are quick to begin nesting. There is no time to waste; they will raise their young and then leave

The long-tailed jaeger (Stercorarius longicaudus) is the smallest and most graceful of the three jaeger species, all of which nest in the Arctic. Although related to gulls, as predators jaegers have evolved several anatomical and behavioral specializations. They often chase smaller birds such as terns to make them drop their prey; the jaegers then snatch the food.

The glaucous gull (Larus hyperboreus), a large, pale species, is a true arctic-dweller. It is a major predator of the eggs and young of other arctic birds, but will also eat carrion, especially dead fish and invertebrates found along the shore.

Smallest of the four loons, the red-throated loon (Gavia stellata) always nests at the water's edge. Although a superb swimmer, it is almost helpless on land. Food is obtained by diving from the surface and swimming under water.

This arctic tern (Sterna paradisaea) is sitting on a nest. Males and females are of identical size and coloration. Both sexes take turns incubating the eggs.

promptly for southern latitudes.

Migration requires much energy and may prove fatal to many. There are many advantages, however, to spending summer months in the North and winter months in the South. Possibly, the major advantage in migrating is to secure a better climate for living. Birds will fly thousands of miles in order to trade the harsh cold and long, dark nights of the North for the warmth and sunlit days of the South. But it works both ways. In the summer, birds can escape the humid heat of the South for the long, cool days of the North.

Spending summers in the Arctic has another major advantage of gastronomic importance. Although arctic summers are short, food in the form of protein-rich insects is profuse. This high-energy food is essential for meeting the needs of young, growing birds. Because of the long summer days, birds have longer "working hours" in which to gather insects. For example, at 69°N latitude, a female American robin may feed its brood about 21 hours each day. Scientists have found that the farther north a species breeds, the larger its brood. In short, larger brood size is related to the hours of daylight available to collect food and the availability of food for the brood.

There are other advantages of spending the summer in the North. In the arctic environment, there are fewer predators to interfere with the raising of young. Likewise, fewer parasites and infectious microorganisms exist in the Arctic because these organisms cannot cope with the long, cold winter and shallow, frozen soil. Lastly, scientists believe that the Far North provides more area for each breeding pair of birds, whereby the competition for food and nesting sites is reduced.

Many migrants make remarkably long journeys between arctic breeding grounds and southern wintering regions. The champion "globe trotter" and long-distance flier is the arctic tern. The name *arctic* is well earned, because its breeding range is circumpolar; its nests have been found as far north as 7.5 degrees from the North Pole.

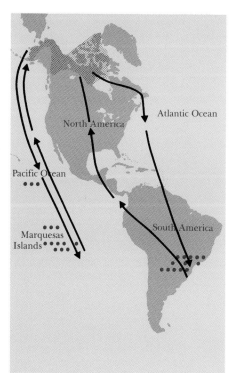

Migration Routes of the Arctic Tern (Sterna paradisaea). *Although some arctic terns nest as far south as New England, most inhabit the Far North. Members of the arctic population are among the champion long-distance fliers, departing in the early fall for the Antarctic, a distance of about 40,000 kilometers (25,000 miles) round trip. No other animal in the world enjoys as many hours of daylight.*

░░░ *Breeding Areas*
∴ *Winter Areas*
▶▶ *Migratory Routes*

Adapted from Frederick C. Lincoln, Migration of Birds *(Washington, D.C.: U.S. Government Printing Office, 1979), p. 45.*

Migration Routes of the American Golden Plover (Pluvialis dominica). *In spring, following a round-trip voyage of about 25,700 kilometers (16,000 miles), these birds will return to the Arctic and settle down on the same patch of tundra that they vacated in the fall.*

░░░ *Breeding Areas*
∴ *Winter Range*
▶▶ *Migratory Routes*

Adapted from Frederick C. Lincoln, Migration of Birds *(Washington, D.C.: U.S. Government Printing Office, 1979), p. 83.*

In the early fall, many arctic terns leave the Northlands for a three-month journey covering about 17,600 kilometers (11,000 miles). The birds cross the Atlantic Ocean to Europe following the cool, nutritious waters of the western shores. Next, they move along the coast to Africa, finally crossing the South Atlantic to Antarctica and Patagonia. Here, in the Antarctic, the birds spend the winter. Throughout their stay, the Antarctic experiences continuous sunlight.

The arctic tern's return flight to its northern breeding site in the tundra is not well known. Scientists believe that some birds move north along the east coast of South America and North America while others return by the same route employed in their southern migration.

It is estimated that arctic terns probably fly at least 40,000 kilometers (25,000 miles) each year. No other animal in the world enjoys as many hours of daylight as does the arctic tern. The sun never sets during the arctic tern's nesting season in the Arctic, and, during its sojourn in the South, daylight is also continuous.

The second place for champion world traveler must be awarded to the American golden plover. During the summer, many of these birds nest in the Canadian Arctic. In the early fall, American golden plovers fly south along the Atlantic coast to Southeastern South America. After reaching the coast of South America, the birds make a short stop and then continue overland to the pampas of Argentina where they remain from September to March. In the early spring they head north, crossing Northwestern South America and the Gulf of Mexico and continuing up the Mississippi Valley. The birds touch down in their arctic breeding grounds in June. The path of this journey takes the form of an enormous ellipse encompassing a total distance of about 25,600 kilometers (16,000 miles). In contrast, the golden plover populations of the arctic coasts of Alaska and Eastern Siberia migrate across hundreds of kilometers of open ocean to winter in the islands of the Pacific. Banding recoveries indicate that each year these birds have the amazing ability to find the same tiny Pacific island as well as the same patch of tundra.

The Arctic is also the breeding ground for a small, delicate bird called the wheatear, which may well exhibit the longest migration of any perching bird. This bird, which measures about 15 centimeters (6 inches) in length, is a Eurasian species that has extended its range into the North American Arctic. It has arrived on two fronts: a population from Eastern Siberia arrived into Alaska on the west and another from Northern Europe arrived into Greenland and Baffin Island on the east. In September, both of these American populations migrate all the way from the High Arctic to tropical Africa.

Migration Routes of the Wheatear
(Oenanthe oenanthe). *The wheatear is a medium-sized thrush that nests primarily in Eurasia. The small population that inhabits the Eastern Canadian Arctic migrates eastward to Europe and then follows a southerly route; the Alaskan population migrates by way of Asia.*

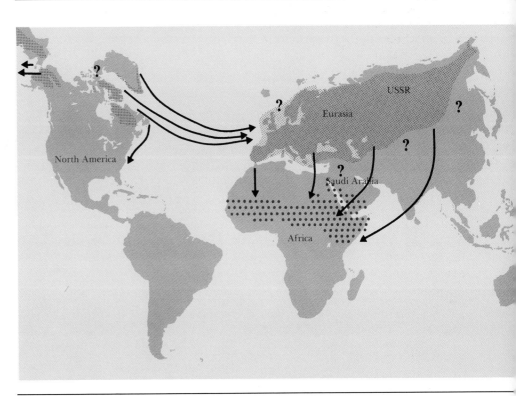

▦ *Breeding Range*
⋮ *Winter Range*
▶▶ *Migratory Routes*
? = Uncertain as to whether it reaches here

Adapted from K. H. Voous, Atlas of European Birds (N.Y.: Thomas Nelson & Sons, 1960), p. 213.

The musk-ox (Ovibos moschatus) is protected from the arctic cold by its long, shaggy overcoat and a thick, soft underwool. In May the underfur begins its annual molt and clings to the overfur as a matted layer until it gradually is torn off.

Although birds hold the record for long-distance migrations, certain mammals of the Eastern Arctic display impressive migrations. Many caribou do not spend the entire year on the tundra but rather winter in the moist, subarctic taiga forests. During winter months, caribou find protection and food in this coniferous forest region to the south.

A thick growth of reindeer moss (*Cladonia rangiferina*) carpets the region. This is not a moss, as the name implies, but rather a lichen (a partnership between fungi and algae). Reindeer moss, together with the grasses, sedges, and dwarf willows, forms the diet of the caribou of the North American tundra. The "moss" is a staple in the caribou's diet, making up about 80 to 95 percent of its winter food. About 4.5 to 9.0 kilograms (10 to 20 pounds) of "moss" may be consumed each day.

The winter distribution of caribou is strongly influenced by the character of the snow cover. Foraging is concentrated in areas where the snow is soft, light, and thin; such snow allows the caribou to dig easily and uncover the essential food below.

In spring, caribou begin to move from the taiga forests to the northern tundra. Their roundtrip migrations may sometimes cover a distance of 1,600 kilometers (1,000 miles). Migrating caribou are easy prey to the timber wolves (*Canis lupus*) which commonly follow the herds.

Caribou calves are born from May to June. During the summer in the tundra, caribou build up fat reserves for the fall rutting season and for the lean winter months to come. Mating occurs in September and the herds move south again, using age-old migration routes. By October, the caribou are back in the shelter of the taiga forest.

Although, at first glance, caribou may look a bit clumsy with their heads thrust awkwardly down and forward and with their disproportionately large feet, they are well-adapted for travel over the tundra. Their bodies are well-supported by large hooves which make them look as if they were wearing overshoes. Caribou can gallop from 48 to 64 kilometers per hour (30 to 40 miles per hour) on the tundra's snow or soft ground. They are also accomplished swimmers, able to swim 6.4 to 8.0 kilometers per hour (4 to 5 miles per hour).

Unlike the caribou, musk-oxen are more conservative. Migration takes them only a few kilometers, between valleys and hills. During summer months, musk-oxen forage in the valleys on grasses, sedges, and their preferred food, dwarf willow. In winter, when snow begins to accumulate in the valleys, the musk-oxen move to the wind-swept ridges. Here, although the vegetation is scant, they can easily gain access to it by pushing aside the thin layer of snow.

In addition to their formidable appearance, musk-oxen (Ovibos moschatus) *band together in a unique protective behavior. Males encircle females and their young and thus form a solid wall of sharp horns against marauding wolves and other predators. Unfortunately, this behavior is of little help against men with modern rifles.*

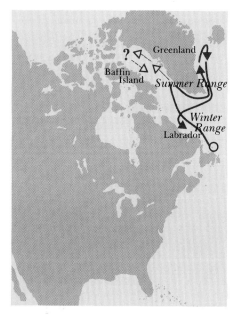
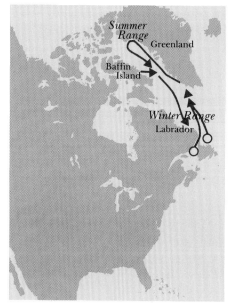
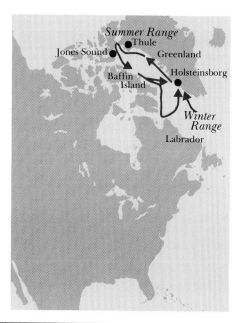

○   breeding grounds

--------- possible route

Migration Route of the Hooded Seal
(Cystophora cristata). *The hooded seal makes extensive migrations. Like the harp seal (Phoca groenlandica), it breeds in the Newfoundland area but somewhat farther out to sea and on heavier ice.*

Migration Route of the Harp Seal (Phoca groenlandica). *The harp seal's migration route is similar to that of the hooded seal (Cystophora cristata). Both seals travel Newfoundland and Baffin Bay.*

Migration Route of the Atlantic Walrus (Odobenus rosmarus). *The walrus is isolated into an Atlantic and Pacific race. The Atlantic race migrates between Labrador and Ellesmere Island.*

In addition to land animals, some marine mammals also migrate during the arctic winter. Although the narwhal, white whale (beluga), and the bowhead whale are essentially full-time arctic residents, all three species undergo short migrations or wanderings in winter to stay clear of the pack ice. During the short migrations, they remain in the arctic zone and do not pass the boundary of the warmer southern waters. During January, ice packs may momentarily break up, permitting narwhals and white whales access to a rich food supply closer to land. This reward, however, may be short-lived, because ice may quickly freeze again, blocking their exit to the open sea. When they are trapped by the ice, many whales will die because they cannot store enough oxygen for the return trip to open sea.

Today, the large bowhead whale is uncommon in the Arctic Atlantic waters. Intensive commercial whaling has made this once-abundant baleen whale almost extinct. Its present wanderings are now confined to seasonal movements along the margin of pack ice.

Some arctic seals, likewise, have extensive migration routes. The harp seal undertakes the longest migrations; during the year it travels from Newfoundland to Northern Baffin Bay, covering from 1,920 to 2,880 kilometers (1,200 to 1,800 miles). The hooded seal also makes extensive migrations.

The ringed seal is the most common High Arctic species. During winter, the ringed seal survives under pack ice by establishing breathing holes; the sharp claws on its fore-flippers are used to keep the breathing holes open. The bearded seal is another species common to the Arctic; it winters near the ice edge farther out to sea. Like the ringed seal, the bearded seal uses the claws on its foreflippers to maintain its breathing holes. Unlike the ringed seal, the bearded seal tends to winter in places where currents keep the water open or permit only a thin ice sheet to accumulate.

Walruses also undergo lengthy seasonal migrations. Their route follows fairly shallow water close to land or the ice along the Arctic coast. The walrus is isolated into two distinct geographic races: the Pacific walrus, residing in the vicinity of the Bering Sea, and the Atlantic walrus, living in the arctic waters and extending south into Hudson Bay and the Northeastern coast of the Ungava Peninsula.

The Atlantic walrus winters in Southwestern Greenland and will begin its northern movement in late April. During this trek, which takes about two-and-a-half months, the females will give birth to calves. Summer is spent in this northern region. In September, most walruses begin the southern migration along Ellesmere, Devon, and Bylot islands and along the coasts of Baffin Island. They then cross Davis Strait eastward to Greenland where they will spend the winter.

In late July, the Arctic also witnesses a fish migration that, although not long distance, is equally important and fascinating. This migration is undertaken by the arctic char, a close relative of the lake trout. The arctic char is common wherever arctic land is drained by small rivers which lead to lakes.

Arctic char living in these lakes descend to the sea in spring as the ice breaks up. Here, they gain nourishment on the abundant food. In late July, they begin to return to their native lakes to spawn. Young are hatched in fall and will remain in the lakes sometimes for three to four years before beginning the migration sequence.

The Arctic Summer
Migrating birds arrive from the South in May and settle down in the ponds to take advantage of the flush of new vegetation. Waders such as dunlins, turnstones, and plovers will feed on the legions of insect larvae. Songbirds such as the snow bunting, horned lark, pipits, sparrows, longspur, redpoll, and wheatear will feast on emerging insects, seeds, and berries. By June, the snow has usually dis-appeared and, as the days lengthen, plants begin flowering. The Arctic will now prepare for the great onslaught of migrating birds, repro-ducing lemmings, and the emergence of the infamous insects. The insect larvae which abound in the lakes and rivers will support arctic char, grayling, lake trout, and whitefish. Lemmings will serve as a valuable food source for arctic fox, snowy owls, and ermine that now have young to feed.

The profusion of insect life during the summer months is frequently mentioned in accounts of the Arctic. Because of their effects on man, the insects that have attracted most attention are the mosquitos, black-flies, deerflies, no-see-ums, and snipeflies. These insects belong to the Order Diptera that makes up about 50 percent of all species of insects on the tundra. This is in sharp contrast to the insect species found in such temperate regions of North America as Pennsylvania. Here, beetles make up half of the insect species, and dipterans account for only 20 percent of the total number.

The adjectives used to describe the abundance of dipterans in the Arctic have not been overly complimentary. When faced with the relentless irritation of mosquitos during the summer, some tourists have kiddingly suggested that they should be properly recognized by the Canadian government and possibly even replace the maple leaf as the national emblem. The journals of arctic explorers and travelers have also attested to the mosquitos' viciousness and sheer numbers on the tundra. One such account was given in 1743 by the manager of the Hudson's Bay Company at Fort Prince of Wales. According to him, the mosquitos were ". . . so thick that we have been obliged to shovel them away before we could get in at the door!" Although it is clear that mosquitos were a menace, even some 240 years ago, this man's statement represents a bit of an overstatement.

In 1911, the famous naturalist Ernest Thompson Seton was the first to undertake a quantitative assess-ment of mosquito numbers. The number of mosquitos inhabiting different localities on a northern transect of the Arctic was measured by counting the number which bit his bare hand over a five-second period. Seton reported that his "biting index" rose as he traveled north. In southern regions of Canada, five to ten mosquitos bit a specified area of his hand within the five-second period. This number rose to 15 to 20 as he moved farther north. At Great Slave Lake in Canada's Northwest Territories, Seton counted 50 to 60 mosquitos within a five-second period on his bare hand. By the time he reached Artillery Lake, somewhat farther north, 100 to 125 mosquitos were counted within the five-second period. Incidently, this experiment has not been duplicated in recent years; apparently, others are less eager to give up their own blood in the name of science! It is reassuring to know that August represents the terminus of the mosquito season. Many may pray, however, for their return, because the mosquitos are quickly supplanted by the little black fly that is far worse than the most annoying mosquito.

Insects of the Arctic are not only a nuisance to man. In the summer, caribou are tormented by two parasitic flies: the warble fly and the nostril fly. Warble flies resemble bumblebees but do not bite or sting; rather, they live a portion of their life as larval parasites of the caribou. In the early spring, warble flies will awaken from their winter sleep and the adult will search for caribou. The fly will lay eggs on the fur of the caribou's legs or underside. In about one week, the eggs will hatch and the larvae will burrow through the animal's skin. The larvae will live within the flesh, traveling under the hide to the back. In order to breathe, the larvae will cut holes in the back of the caribou's hide. The larvae may sometimes be as large as a man's thumb. After a period of several weeks, these larvae will emerge through the skin and drop to the ground. After an approximately one-month pupal stage, they hatch into adult warble flies and begin their life cycle again.

The warble flies parasitize the caribou during their northward migration in the summer. Approximately 90 percent of all caribou are infested with warble flies. This is a difficult time for the caribou. The parasitism, combined with the long journey following a hard winter, can considerably weaken them. It is interesting to note that small calves born in spring are not attacked by the warble flies. There is an apparently adaptive explanation for avoiding the caribou calves: The infestation might prove lethal, in which case, the parasite would also die.

Unbelievable as it may seem, the holes pierced in the caribou's hide by the burrowing larvae are probably less irritating than the constant buzzing of warble flies as they attempt to lay eggs on the fur. Caribou will commonly have violent, panicky reactions to this harassment; even bathing in ponds is ineffective in warding off these parasites.

It would seem that the warble fly would be a sufficient challenge for the caribou. Another parasite, however, the nostril fly, also imperils the health of these animals. About 20 percent of the caribou are infested by nostril flies. These rather large flies deposit their larvae in the nostrils of the caribou. Each caribou may possess from 10 to 40 larvae. From the nostrils, the flies move into the throat region where they spend the winter. In spring the nostril flies grow rapidly. In May, the larvae dislodge from the throat, fall to the ground, and, by June, are ready to begin the cycle again.

The Land of the Lemming

Some naturalists have referred to the Arctic as "the land of the lemming." The designation probably stems from the fact that this furry little rodent will sometimes dominate the landscape; it is, likewise, a major food source for many arctic predators.

During some arctic summers, the small, scurrying, mouse-like lemmings are common features of the tundra. The squeaking and chattering of the brown and the collared lemming may be easily heard. At such times, one may even catch a glimpse of an arctic fox, ermine, snowy owl, or rough-legged hawk pursuing one of these small animals. Such summer occurrences are common symptoms of what is referred to as a "lemming year." During a lemming year, these small rodents reach a growth peak or undergo a population explosion. During such a period, over 200 lemmings may inhabit each .4 hectare (1 acre) of tundra and may have established over 4,000 burrows.

According to legend, at the time of a population explosion, lemmings reduce their numbers by the thousands by flinging themselves into the sea. This story is not entirely true, however. Lemmings do not undergo these premeditated suicidal marches into the sea. During years of high density, lemmings will, in fact, disperse. When lemmings reach a body of water such as a river, lake, or an arm of the sea, they may attempt to cross to the other side. Although lemmings are good swimmers, many will drown.

Population explosions can be attributed to the lemming's frequent breeding and short gestation period. Breeding begins before the snow melts in spring, and a litter of from four to nine young may be produced. Sometimes lemmings will reproduce year-round, and, thus, in a good year, a female may produce from 20 to 25 offspring.

These prolific animals undergo cyclic population fluctuations; their numbers tend to rise every three to four years and then suddenly crash. Thus, while one summer may be marked by an overabundance of lemmings, as few as one lemming per every 4 hectares (10 acres) may be found during the following summer.

No one is certain why these small mammals undergo population explosions and crashes on such a predictable schedule. There are almost as many theories for this phenomenon as there are scientists working on the problem. Nevertheless, some theories are more accurate than others. One early theory espoused by Aristotle attributed the disappearance of mice to heavy rains. This theory was at variance with one espoused by early Norwegians and Inuit. The two groups believed lemmings fell from the sky because they seemed to appear suddenly in great numbers. For this reason, medieval Scandinavian peasants called lemmings "sky mice."

Early naturalists felt that the

lemmings' drastic population crashes were caused by epidemic disease or predation from birds and mammals. By the mid-20th century, scientists generally agreed that these regular and marked fluctuations in numbers could not be explained simply by factors such as disease, predation, food shortages, or sunspots.

An interesting theory that gained momentum in 1950 contended that, as the lemming population expanded, the animals suffered mounting social stress from overcrowding. This social stress upset hormonal balance (via the pituitary-adrenal-gonadal axis) and inhibited breeding, thereby causing a population crash.

Since this time, other theories have gained prominence. One currently popular theory suggests that the effects of overcrowding are not exhibited in the first generation of animals but, rather, are found in their offspring. A genetically based or hereditary mechanism for limiting the population, therefore, is implicated. According to this currently held theory, some animals would be able to tolerate high population densities, whereas others, because of genetic programming, would leave or disperse.

Scientists are still uncertain as to what causes the regular cycles of the lemming. In order to unlock this secret, many are analyzing the lemming's every move: its food, genetic composition, and behavior. Through such careful study the behavior of this animal, which forms the base of the terrestrial arctic food web, will be better understood.

Like the lemming, the snowshoe hare and its predator, the lynx, undergo regular population oscillations. These oscillations, however, occur about every ten years. The Hudson's Bay Company records of the pelts of fur-bearers which have been trapped annually since about 1800 have helped us to understand these cycles. The records show that lynx reach a population peak every nine to ten years. The snowshoe hare follows this same cycle, with its peak preceding that of the lynx by about a year or more. Since the lynx is dependent on the hare for food, it seems likely that the cycle of the predator is related to that of the prey. The story is not quite so simple, however, because the hare undergoes population cycles in areas where there are no lynx! Again, another problem for scientists.

Population cycles, be they at three-year or ten-year intervals, are unique to northern regions. Why is this so? Scientists believe it is related to the structure of the arctic ecosystem—a topic that will follow.

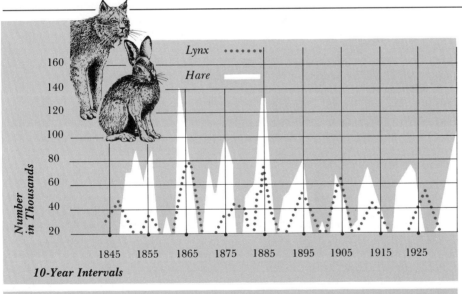

Cycles of Population Density of the Snowshoe Hare (Lepus americanus) *and the Canadian Lynx* (Felis lynx). *The figure is based on the number of pelts purchased by the Hudson's Bay Company from 1845 through 1935.*

Adapted from D. A. MacLulich, Fluctuations in the Numbers of the Varying Hare (Lepus americanus) *(University of Toronto Studies, Biological Series, No. 43, 1937), pp. 1-136.*

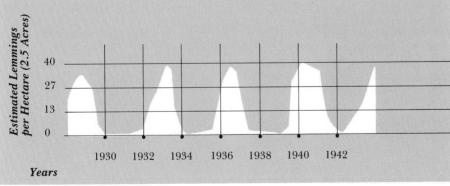

Population Density of the Brown Lemming (Lemmus sibiricus) *near Barrow, Alaska. Population peaks are commonly separated by an interval of three to four years.*

Adapted from James P. Finerty, The Population Ecology of Cycles in Small Mammals *(New Haven: Yale University Press, 1980), p. 39.*

Why So Few Kinds of Animals in the Arctic?

If one were to leave the Arctic and travel south through the temperate zone to the tropics, one would find that the number of plants and animals increased with this southern movement. For instance, of a world list of 3,200 mammals, only 23 land mammals reside north of the tree line. Similarly, while only about 19 species of breeding land birds inhabit the tundra of Northern Hudson Bay, this number increases to about 177 in Pennsylvania and to about 625 in Costa Rica. Reptiles also appear to increase in number as one moves from north to south: No snakes are found in the High Arctic, but 22 snake species occur in Canada, 26 species are found in the United States, and 293 species in Mexico. Although the total number of insects in the world is not known, we can say with some certainty that there are only about 25 species of mosquitos inhabiting the immense Northwest Territories. This figure jumps to approximately 800 to 1,000 species of mosquitos in Panama. It is clear from these distribution trends that tropical habitats support a larger number of species of animals. Nonetheless, although arctic fauna are impoverished in terms of the numbers of different kinds of animals, the large numbers found within the individual species point to a successful adaptation to the arctic environment.

Scientists have offered some reasonable explanations for the difference in number of species between the Arctic and the tropics. One attractive hypothesis deals with the amount of food available in each location. In the Arctic, there is less radiant energy for plants to utilize and fix into food for animals. Likewise, few organisms have had the time to adapt to this relatively new environment that was exposed after the retreat of the ice sheet.

Another hypothesis concerns the concept called the ecological niche. Within a habitat, an organism has a distinct, functional relationship to everything else in the environment and occupies a specific position and status, called an ecological niche.

An organism's niche might be regarded as its particular "profession" in life. While many different species can have the same habitat, only rarely, if ever, can two different species completely occupy the same ecological niche.

Since each species occupies a distinct niche, scientists believe that more species exist in the tropics because there are more available niches or that these niches are more fully occupied or, possibly, more constricted than those in the Arctic. Since these niches can be measured, there is good support for this claim. It is felt that, because there are many species in the tropics, there may be an overlap of niches which may produce competition for resources. In the Arctic, however, the number of individual animals is large because there is little competition from other species with overlapping niches. The Arctic is a harsh and exacting environment. It seems that only a few "designs" have evolved that can function well under its physically demanding climate.

Food Chains in the Arctic

Whether simple as in the Arctic or complex as in the tropics, all plant and animal communities are organized along similar economic lines. As fixers of solar energy, plants are the key to all life. Energy fixed in the tissues of plants passes to herbivores and then to carnivores. The relationships of eating and being eaten can be simplified and summarized through food chains. In real life, however, food chains are usually cross-linked with each other to form food webs. These interrelationships quickly become very complex.

The Marine Environment

The arctic waters support a host of plant and animal forms. At the base of the food chains are microscopic diatoms, collectively called phytoplankton, floating plant life. The success of all life in the arctic seas— from worms to whales—depends upon the great pastures of phytoplankton. Phytoplankton serves as a marine savanna, with algae taking the place of grass.

Production of phytoplankton in the Arctic Ocean is highest in spring and summer, when the days are long and the sun is highest in the sky. Light penetrates deep into the water, and the diatoms and other surface-living plants multiply rapidly. Although minute (millions float in a liter of water), each diatom species is neatly encased in a jewel-like external silica skeleton. Although diatoms cannot be seen with the naked eye, the deep blue-green color of arctic waters in the summer is a sign of their immense numbers.

The tiny herbivores of the sea, the zooplankton, graze on this phytoplankton. These animals, microscopic in size, include protozoans, rotifers, small crustaceans, jellyfish, arrow worms, surface-living polychaetes, and larval forms of starfish and sea urchins.

The zooplankton are drifting animals that migrate to the surface waters in spring to capture energy from the phytoplankton. They, in turn, will provide food for more-advanced species of zooplankton called copepods; each copepod is the size of a rice grain.

The food chain can be pictured as an ecological pyramid, because fewer and fewer animals are encountered at each progressive level. The larger planktonic animals that prey on the herbivores are, in turn, eaten by larger predators such as pelagic fish, squid, seals, toothed and baleen whales, and seabirds. Fish are eaten by seals, birds, and larger fish, and seals, narwhals, and beluga are consumed by killer whales. The squid feed on surface plankton and are, in turn, eaten by whales and fish. Debris (called detritus) from this feeding activity constantly rains down upon the sea bed where it nourishes clams, corals, sponges, and sea anenomes. These bottom-dwelling creatures are consumed by narwhals, walruses, bearded seals, and such deep-sea fish as cod and haddock. The northern seas are obviously capable of supporting a rich and varied marine mammal fauna. Unfortunately, it has been greatly depleted through systematic slaughter by commercial whalers, sealers, and walrus hunters.

The Arctic Marine Ecosystem. *Minute plants and animals form the base of this complex food web. Organisms in this ecosytem range in size from microscopic phytoplankton to the blue whale* (Balaenoptera musculus), *the largest animal known to man.*

Solar Energy

Polar Bear

Phytoplankton

Zooplankton

Baleen Whale

Toothed Whale

Squid

Seal

Pelagic Fish

Walrus

Wolf Fish

Cod

Starfish

Brittle Star

Haddock

Worm

Starfish

Spider Crab

Sea Urchin

Mollusc

Detritus

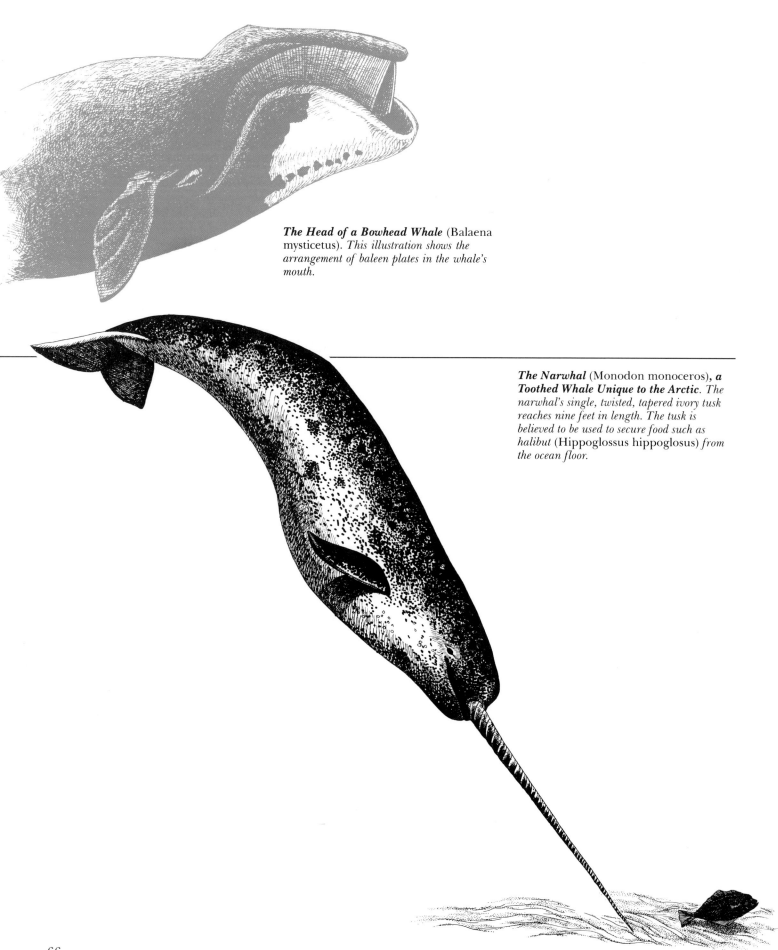

The Head of a Bowhead Whale (Balaena mysticetus). *This illustration shows the arrangement of baleen plates in the whale's mouth.*

The Narwhal (Monodon monoceros)**, a Toothed Whale Unique to the Arctic**. *The narwhal's single, twisted, tapered ivory tusk reaches nine feet in length. The tusk is believed to be used to secure food such as halibut* (Hippoglossus hippoglosus) *from the ocean floor.*

Among the common pinniped (fin-footed) mammals inhabiting the Arctic are the walrus and the harp, bearded, hooded, ringed, and harbor seals. Their diets range from shellfish, as in the walrus and bearded seal, to polar cod and capelin, as in the harp and ringed seal.

Whales of the arctic seas are grouped into two general categories: the toothed whales and the baleen whales. The toothed whales possess peglike teeth and include the sperm whale, white (or beluga) whale, narwhal, and killer whale. The baleen whales possess no teeth but have strips of whalebone, called baleen, hanging from the roof of the mouth. These strips are frayed along the edges and help to strain small organisms from the water. Common baleen whales of the eastern arctic seas include the blue (or sulphur-bottom), bowhead, finback, piked, and humpback whales.

The narwhal is a truly arctic species. This strange-looking whale has long been hunted for its single, twisted, tapered ivory tusk which resembles a very long corkscrew. The tusk, which may reach a length of 270 centimeters (9 feet), is normally found only on males. Occasionally, a narwhal will bear two tusks, but this is rare. In the Middle Ages, some people, seeing a narwhal tusk, believed it was the horn of that famous mythical beast, the unicorn.

The function of the narwhal's tusk is not fully known. The Inuit have claimed that it is used to secure halibut (a bottom-dwelling fish), a favorite food of the narwhal. Many scientists contend that the tusk represents an ornament of the male. Although the tusk may be used for play and possibly in feeding, narwhals do not seem to use the tusk for defense against other animals or for ramming boats as some stories have indicated.

Whereas the narwhal is principally a bottom-feeder, a close relative, the beluga (or white whale), prefers foraging in shallow water. During summer months, large schools of beluga whales may be found in the estuaries of large rivers that flow into Hudson Bay. Here, they capture fish such as cod and capelin.

The bowhead, a baleen whale weighing as much as 54,545 kilograms (60 tons), also exploits the sea's upper level, but by a means different from that of the beluga. Like the blue and finback whales, the bowhead is a filter feeder; as the bowhead moves with its head partly exposed through the water, plankton is skimmed from the surface. This planktonic mixture is commonly called *krill* and is food for all pelagic animals such as crustaceans, snails, and worms.

The bowhead whale may also seek food down to several hundred meters (1,000 feet) below the surface. Plankton-rich water is taken into the bowhead's large mouth. By using its enormous tongue, the mixture is strained through the plates of baleen. The plankton is retained and the water is released through the baleen plates. The strained plankton is then swallowed.

Another marine mammal that exploits the sea bottom is the huge and streamlined walrus. The walrus, which may weigh up to 1,215 kilograms (1.35 tons), will dive to depths of 90 meters (300 feet) to eat shellfish. Clams, in particular, are raked up from the bottom with the walrus' long ivory tusks. Aided by its stiff whiskers, the walrus holds the mollusks in its lips and suctions out the meat within the shells. The shells are then discarded and the animals within are swallowed.

The bearded seal also forages on the ocean floor but does not eat clams as does the walrus. It feeds mainly on large whelks, snails, shrimp, worms, sea cucumbers, and small fish.

The arctic marine environment is not always filled with so much activity. As the summer draws to a close, the sun disappears, ice forms on the water, and the remaining light is reflected away. Photosynthesis slows down, and food becomes scarce at the surface. Zooplankton will now sink to deep water to spend the long winter. Most seals and whales will migrate to more southerly areas to seek food in ice-free waters.

The Arctic Land Ecosystem. *Compared to tropical ecosystems, the Arctic ecosystem has fewer kinds of organisms making up the food web. The lemming forms the base of this ecosystem; it acts as the principal food source for many higher animals.*

Polar Bear

Seal

Sandpiper

Plover

Phalarope

Owls, Hawks, Falcons

Jaeger

Fox

Sandpiper

Plover

Phalarope

Ptarmigan

Perching Birds

Wolf

Masked Shrew

Arctic Hare

Lemmings and Voles

Arctic Ground Squirrel

Lemmings and Voles

Caribou

Mask-Ox

Lemmings and Voles

Insects

Vegetation

The Terrestrial Environment

Temperature and seasonality of food resources exert such strong limitations on arctic life that only relatively few kinds of organisms have successfully adapted to Far Northern conditions. As a consequence of this harsh, selective pressure, we see comparatively simplified food chains and food webs at the terrestrial level.

As is the case with the marine ecosystem, plants form the foundation of life: They are food for a number of animals. On the tundra, the reindeer moss, grasses, sedges, and dwarf willow form the diet of the caribou. The caribou are a major consumer of plant life. The caribou, in turn, represent the major food item in the diet of wolves and man.

The small, furry lemming forms the center of the food web for many animals in the arctic terrestrial environment. These small rodents graze on the grasses and sedges and, in turn, are prey for a variety of birds and mammals.

The arctic hare and ptarmigan are herbivorous animals that reside year-round on the tundra, feeding on low-growing plants including the leaves of the dwarf willow. During the long arctic winter and brief summer, the arctic fox, ermine, short-eared owl, snowy owl, and jaeger will survive largely on the lemming, arctic hare, and ptarmigan. In the brief summer, predators feed on the adults and the eggs of many bird species.

Fluctuations in the number of arctic fox are supposedly controlled by the abundance of its principal prey, the lemming. During winter months when a thick snow cover may protect lemmings from predators, the fox must shift food items in order to survive. During this time, the fox may follow wolves or polar bears in hopes of inheriting the remains of kills.

There is a similar correlation between lemming population fluctuations and the numbers of both short-eared and snowy owls. Snowy owls have moved south into the Northern United States for the winter, when there has been a sharp decline in the lemming population during the preceding fall. This southern movement may represent a search for an alternate food source.

Snowy owls are an important predator on the arctic tundra. In addition to consuming lemmings, they prey on such songbirds as Lapland longspurs and horned larks. The gyrfalcon, another truly arctic bird, also preys on small birds and rodents. Other birds and rodents are, likewise, important to the peregrine falcon's diet.

Like the lemming, the arctic ground squirrel, or *sik-sik*, is certainly not immune from predation pressure. The rough-legged hawk, which breeds in the Arctic, is a prinicipal predator of the *sik-sik*. Snowy owls, gyrfalcons, arctic fox, and wolves also prey on the *sik-sik*.

The marine and terrestrial ecosystems are bridged by the polar bear, a highly carnivorous animal. Called *nanuq* by the Inuit, the polar bear is a relentless enemy of the arctic seals. The polar bear has poor eyesight and its hearing is average; however, it has an acute sense of smell.

Although seals spend most of their life in the water, they are mammals and must surface about every ten minutes to breathe. During winter months, when the sea is covered with a sheet of ice, sometimes 150-centimeters (5 feet) thick, ringed seals will gnaw breathing holes through this ice. The breathing holes are commonly covered by snow which makes them invisible, but the polar bear is guided to them by its keen sense of smell.

Once the bear locates an active hole, it scrapes the snow away, crouches down beside it, and waits. Because an individual seal may have many breathing holes, this waiting period may be several days. Once the seal does emerge, the polar bear strikes the seal with a rapid blow of its huge paw, crushing its skull.

The snowy owl (Nyctea scandiaca) *breeds on the arctic tundra where it depends largely on lemmings for food. When lemming numbers are low, snowy owls will migrate south in search of food.*

The "frosted" appearance of this young snowy owl (Nyctea scandiaca) *is caused by the white natal down that clings to the tips of the dark gray second down. As the owl matures, the down will be replaced by the white and black plumage of the adult.*

Polar bears also hunt young seals born on the ice in the spring. When seal hunting is poor, the polar bear may attack foxes, baby walruses, sea birds, and even man.

The hordes of insects that inhabit the Arctic also play an essential role in the arctic food web. With the emergence of insects and the abundance of migratory birds, food chains become larger and definite food webs develop. Insects provide food for the numerous migrating birds that return to the Arctic each spring in order to breed. Larval insects are also an essential part of the diet of the small shrews that are active year-round; even during the winter they forage in the subnivean environment. Waders, such as sandpipers and plovers, will also settle to breed on the tundra in spring and summer and consume the abundant larval insects. Snow buntings, horned larks, water pipits, Lapland longspurs, and wheatears will consume both seeds and insects. These small migrants will, in turn, attract falcons that may catch them on the wing. The eggs and young of nesting birds provide food for both avian and mammalian predators.

Thus, all flora and fauna of the Arctic are woven into patterns of interdependence. Not only is there a web of interdependence of life within the sea and on the tundra, but the two food chains are interconnected by the polar bear and man.

Conclusion
In comparison with animals inhabiting other areas of the earth, arctic animals are of relatively recent origins. Concurrent with the Pleistocene glaciation, arctic animals have evolved adaptations that are finely tuned to the forbidding cold and seasonality of food resources. Present-day arctic animal life, thus, represents an evolutionary frontier. As is revealed in other chapters, the human animal has, likewise, made remarkable adaptations for survival in this hostile, exacting environment.

Reading List

Brown, J., ed. *An Arctic Ecosystem, the Coastal Tundra at Barrow, Alaska*. U.S. IBP Synthesis Series, No. 12. Stroudsburg, PA: Dowden, Hutchinson and Ross, 1980.

Bruemmer, F. *The Arctic*. NY: Quadrangle, The New York Times Book Company, 1974.

Colinvaux, P.A. "The Environment of the Bering Land Bridge," *Ecol. Monogr.* 34 (1964), 297-329.

Contu, J. *Animals of the Eastern Arctic: A Checklist in English and Inuktitut*. Rankin Inlet, NWT: Department of Education, Regional Resource Center, 1981.

Formozov, A.N. "Snow Cover as an Integral Factor of the Environment and its Importance in the Ecology of Mammals and Birds," *Occas. Publ., Boreal Inst. Univ. of Alberta* (1946), pp. 1-143.

Freuchen, P., and F. Salomensen. *The Arctic Year*. NY: G. P. Putnam's Sons, 1958.

Gordon, M.S. *Animal Physiology: Principals and Adaptations*. 4th Ed. NY: MacMillan, 1982.

Guilday, J.E. "Differential Extinction during Late Pleistocene and Recent Times," In *Pleistocene Extinctions: The Search for a Cause*. Ed. P.S. Martin and H.E. Wright. New Haven: Yale Univ. Press, 1968, pp. 121-240.

Gunderson, H.L. *Mammalogy*. NY: McGraw-Hill, 1976.

Guthrie, R.D. "Paleoecology of the Large Mammal Community in Interior Alaska during the Late Pleistocene," *Am. Midl. Nat.*, 79 (1968), 346-363.

Harper, F. "The Mammals of Keewatin," *Miscellanous Publications, Univ. of Kansas Museum of Natural History*, 12 (1956), 1-94.

Hopkins, D.M., ed. *The Bering Land Bridge*. Stanford: Stanford Univ. Press, 1967.

Huxley, J. ed. *The Rand McNally Atlas of World Wildlife*. Chicago: Rand McNally, 1973.

Irving, L. *Arctic Life of Birds and Mammals*. NY: Springer-Verlag, 1972.

Kurtén, B. *The Age of Mammals*. NY: Columbia Univ. Press, 1971.

Kurtén, B., and E. Anderson. *Pleistocene Mammals of North America*. NY: Columbia Univ. Press, 1980.

Lincoln, F. *Migration of Birds*. Fish and Wildlife Service Circular, No. 16. Washington, D.C.: U.S. Department of Interior, 1950.

MacArthur, R.H., and E.O. Wilson. *The Theory of Island Biogeography*. Princeton, N.J.: Princeton Univ. Press, 1967.

MacLulich, D.A. *Fluctuations in the Numbers of the Varying Hare* (Lepus americanus). Biological Service Studies, No. 43. Toronto: Univ. of Toronto, 1937.

MacPherson, A.H. "The Origin of Diversity in Mammals of the Canadian Arctic Tundra," *Syst. Zool.*, 14 (1965), 153-173.

Martin, L.D., and A.M. Neuner. "The End of the Pleistocene in North America," *Trans. Nebraska Acad. Sci.*, VI (1978), 117-126.

Martin, P.S. "Pleistocene Ecology and Biogeography of North America," *Zoogeography*, 51 (1958), 1-509.

Martin, P. S. "Pleistocene Niches for Alien Animals," *Bioscience*, 20 (1970), 218-222.

Orr, R.T. *Animals in Migration*. NY: MacMillan, 1970.

Perry, R. *The World of the Walrus*. NY: Taplinger, 1967.

Pianka, E.R. *Evolutionary Ecology*. 2nd Ed. NY: Harper and Row, 1978.

Pruitt, W.O., Jr. "Animals in the Snow," *Scientific Amer.*, 202 (1960), 60-68.

Pruitt, W.O., Jr. *Boreal Ecology*. Inst. Biol. Studies in Biology, No. 91. London: Edward Arnold, 1978.

Remmert, H. *Arctic Animal Ecology*. Berlin: Springer-Verlag, 1980.

Simpson, G.G. "Species Density of North American Recent Mammals," *Syst. Zool.*, 13 (1964), 57-73.

Artist's Depiction of a Dorset Summer Dwelling, 1000 B.C.-A.D. 1000.

Eskimo Prehistory

Robert McGhee, Archaeological Survey of Canada,
National Museum of Man, National Museums of Canada, Ottawa, Ontario

Introduction: The Bering Land Bridge

Over the millions of years during which mankind was evolving from our primate ancestors in the tropical and subtropical areas of the Old World, the higher latitudes were subjected to a series of climatic events which periodically changed the entire nature of the Northern World. During a series of ice ages, continental glaciers covered vast areas of Northern Eurasia and North America, locking up much of the world's water. As a consequence, sea levels dropped substantially, exposing continental shelves and creating land bridges between continents.

One such land bridge joining Alaska and Northeastern Siberia was periodically exposed for tens of thousands of years. Called the Bering Land Bridge, this 1,000-kilometer-wide (600 miles) level plain served as a route by which northern animals and plants spread from one continent to the other.

During glacial periods, this northern region had a harsh continental climate with insufficient moisture to allow the formation of glaciers. Both the land bridge and the adjacent areas of Northeastern Siberia and Northwestern North America appear to have supported a relatively rich tundra vegetation grazed on by large herbivores including caribou, musk-ox, horse, bison, and mammoth.

By the time of the last ice age, humans had become efficient hunters of such animals. The discovery of fire and the use of protective clothing allowed them to live in northern climates. Groups of hunters were attracted by the previously unhunted animal herds to the Bering Land Bridge and adjacent areas of North America. The Arctic, thus, became the first part of the New World to see human occupation.

Remains of such occupations have been dated to approximately 15,000 years ago at Bluefish Cave in the Northern Yukon Territory, and finds in the nearby Old Crow Basin hint at even earlier inhabitants of the area. Some of these groups moved south, either during or at the end of the last ice age, to become the ancestors of the American Indians. By approximately 12,000 year ago, they had spread over most of North and South America.

While this was occurring, other hunting groups continued to move across the Land Bridge. With them they brought the more advanced technologies which had evolved in Eurasia during the closing phases of the glacial period. The last groups crossed the Land Bridge just before it was submerged beneath the rising waters of the Bering Sea approximately 10,000 years ago. Instead of moving south into the already populated regions of North America, they appear to have remained in Alaska and the adjacent parts of Arctic Canada.

Some of these peoples settled on the Pacific coast of Alaska and on the Aleutian Islands, developing a maritime-oriented economy and a way of life adapted to this new environment. It seems likely that these were the direct ancestors of the Aleuts, the peoples who occupied the Aleutian Islands in historic times and who are racially and linguistically the closest relatives of the Eskimos.

Other groups which crossed from Siberia moved into the interior of Alaska and continued their big-game hunting way of life in the tundra plains and valleys. Some speculate that these interior people were ancestral Eskimos. This seems unlikely, however, because it has thus far been impossible to provide archaeological evidence of continuity between these early hunters and later ancestral Eskimo groups.

The early millennia of the postglacial period saw the rapid melting of the glaciers, consequent rises in sea levels, and the northward advance of the forest into what had previously been tundra regions. By about 8,000 years ago, Northern North America was probably not very different from present-day conditions, and during the subsequent millennia it was probably somewhat warmer than today. During this period, Indian groups adapted to the northern forests and inhabited the interior of Alaska and the Yukon. Other Indians moved north into the Barren Grounds region to the west of Hudson Bay, probably following the caribou on their annual migrations from the forest to the summer tundra. In Labrador, maritime-oriented Indians spread northward along the coast, at least seasonally reaching areas that today are well north of the tree line.

Artist's Depiction of Early Humans Crossing the Bering Land Bridge to Alaska during the Last Ice Age.

N.J. PERKINS

None of these groups seems to have adapted to year-round life on the tundras and frozen seas of the Arctic. These areas, although certainly capable of supporting human hunters, remained unoccupied until they were discovered by people from an entirely different cultural tradition. These were the first people capable of freeing themselves from the shelter of the forests and of creating a new way of life which allowed them to spread rapidly across most of Arctic North America.

The Arctic Small Tool Tradition
Archaeological sites representing the remains of this new way of life appear simultaneously (within the two- or three-century range of precision of the radiocarbon-dating method) from Alaska to Greenland. This suggests an extremely rapid adaptation to life on the tundra and a swift expansion throughout the environmental zone approximately 4,000 years ago. The origins of this Palaeoeskimo way of life are unclear. It seems unlikely that it developed in Alaska, most of which appears to have been occupied during the previous millennia by distinctively Indian forest-dwelling hunting cultures. A more likely source area is Northeastern Siberia from whence the first Palaeoeskimos may have crossed the Bering Strait either by boat (although we have no evidence that they possessed such craft) or over the dangerously shifting winter ice.

The main reason for suspecting a Siberian origin for these people is seen in similarities between the stone tools of the Palaeoeskimos and those of the Neolithic peoples occupying Northeastern Siberia at about this time. These tools, very small and delicately made, have given the name Arctic Small Tool tradition to the archaeological remains of the Palaeoeskimos. They include points for harpoons, spears and arrows, blades for knives and scrapers, burins for carving bone, and tiny, sharp-edged microblades used for carving and cutting and perhaps mounted along the edges of weapons.

The Palaeoeskimos used the bow and arrow, previously unknown in the New World, giving them an advantage in tundra hunting of large game. Harpoons, derived from those used by North Pacific hunters or Siberian lake fishermen, allowed them to hunt seals and other sea mammals. They may have had more sophisticated tailored fur clothing than previous occupants of Arctic North America; historic Eskimo clothing conforms more closely to Asiatic than to American Indian patterns and may have been derived from the clothing of Palaeoeskimo times.

At a few Alaskan sites, there is evidence that the Palaeoeskimos lived in small, rectangular or square houses about 4 meters (13 feet) across. These houses probably had a light, pole framework covered with skins and perhaps turf for winter insulation. The floors of the houses were excavated 20 to 50 centimeters (8 to 20 inches) into the earth and had a central hearth built of slabs or cobbles. A somewhat different type of structure has been found at the early sites in Arctic Canada and Greenland. Oval to rectangular depressions a few centimeters (inches) deep, 3 to 4 meters (10 to 13 feet) across, were surrounded by a rim of gravel which must have secured the skirts of a tent. A square hearth of stone slabs was located in the center of the tent with each lateral edge extended from front to back to form a midpassage set off from the sleeping areas on either side. Such tents were probably occupied throughout the year and heated with small fires, burning rare sticks of driftwood, twigs of dwarf Arctic willow, animal bones, and probably the blubber of sea mammals.

The Alaskan Palaeoeskimos seem to have shown a preference for interior resources, primarily caribou and fish, although some groups must have depended on marine animals. The presence of animals which had never been hunted, and were therefore unafraid of human hunters, probably encouraged some groups to move eastward across Arctic Canada, where their remains are known to archaeologists as the Pre-Dorset culture. On the coasts and islands of the Canadian Arctic, marine resources must have been the basis of the Pre-Dorset economy, as they were for all later hunting groups inhabiting the region. Bones found in archaeological sites, however, suggest that several Pre-Dorset groups depended heavily on waterfowl, fox, and other small game as well as seals. In Ellesmere Island and the Pearyland region of Northern Greenland, they hunted primarily musk-oxen, a resource which is present in the area year-round but which is very vulnerable to human predation.

With the passage of time, climatic and environmental changes made necessary further adaptations to the regions inhabited by Palaeoeskimo populations. Approximately 3,500 years ago the Arctic climate, which up to that time had been slightly warmer than it is today, began to become noticeably cooler. The position of the tree line in Central Canada shifted to the south, and there was probably more sea ice which lasted longer each year in the gulfs and channels between the Arctic islands. The more severe climate may have also reduced the populations of terrestrial as well as marine animals.

Harpoon Technology. *In hunting sea mammals, two types of harpoons have been used by arctic hunters. The earliest evidence for harpoons of these types is from the Arctic Small Tool tradition (2000-1000 B.C.).*

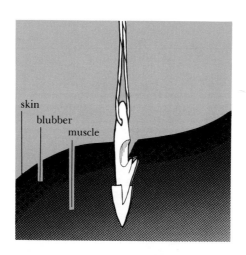

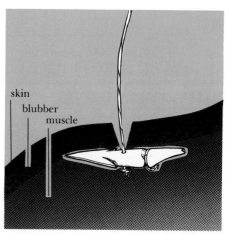

(A) ***Non-Toggling Harpoon.*** *The non-toggling harpoon is probably of older origin than the toggling harpoon. Because short barbs, alone, hold the harpoon in place, large animals can easily tear it loose or break it off. The non-toggling harpoon is, therefore, best suited for the hunting of smaller sea mammals.*

(B) ***Toggling Harpoon.*** *The harpoon head is attached by a line to the end of a foreshaft. When the head penetrates an animal's body, it detaches from the foreshaft. As the harpoon line tightens, an angled spur at the base turns the harpoon head sideways, anchoring it beneath the blubber. The animal, thus, cannot dislodge the harpoon by rubbing against a block of ice or a rock.*

(C) ***Prehistoric Toggling Harpoon Head.***

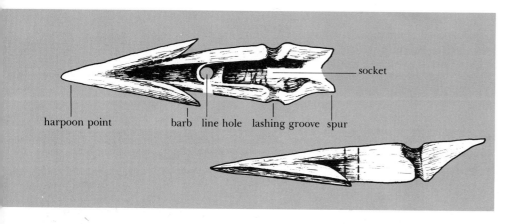

(D) ***Prehistoric Toggling Harpoon Components****.*

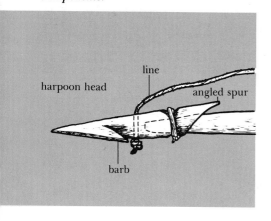

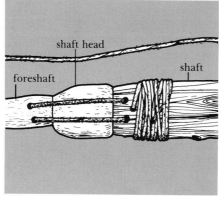

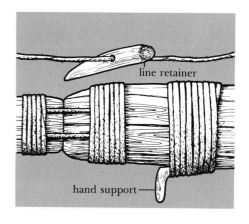

Small Tools of the Palaeoeskimos, 2000-1000 B.C.

Left to right:

A. Harpoon end blade *(Port Refuge, Devon Island, Canada). Chert, Arctic Small Tool tradition, 3.6 cm long. Cast courtesy of Archaeological Survey of Canada, National Museum of Man, National Museums of Canada, Ottawa #RbJu-1:666c.*

B. Non-toggling harpoon head *(Port Refuge, Devon Island, Canada). Ivory, Arctic Small Tool tradition, 6 cm long. Cast courtesy of Archaeological Survey of Canada, National Museum of Man, National Museums of Canada, Ottawa #RbJu-1:1080c.*

C. Toggling harpoon head *(Pond Inlet, Baffin Island, Canada). Antler, Arctic Small Tool tradition, 7.6 cm long. Cast courtesy of Archaeological Survey of Canada, National Museum of Man, National Museums of Canada, Ottawa #PeFr-1:7c.*

D. Arrow point *(Port Refuge, Devon Island, Canada). Chert, Arctic Small Tool tradition, 3 cm long. Cast courtesy of Archaeological Survey of Canada, National Museum of Man, National Museums of Canada, Ottawa #RbJu-1:767c.*

E. Side Scraper *(Port Refuge, Devon Island, Canada). Chert, Arctic Small Tool tradition, 3.6 cm long. Cast courtesy of Archaeological Survey of Canada, National Museum of Man, National Museums of Canada, Ottawa #RbJu-1:2018c.*

F. Biface point *(Port Refuge, Devon Island, Canada). Chert, Arctic Small Tool tradition, 3.7 cm long. Cast courtesy of Archaeological Survey of Canada, National Museum of Man, National Museums of Canada, Ottawa #RbJu-1:733c.*

Artist's Depiction of a Palaeoeskimo Dwelling, 2000-1000 B.C.

Summary of Eskimo Prehistory.

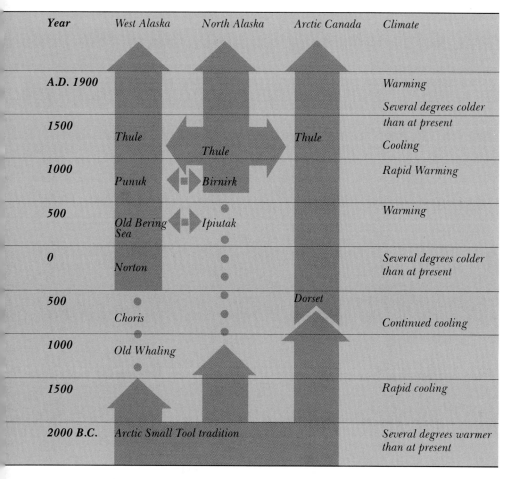

Year	West Alaska	North Alaska	Arctic Canada	Climate
A.D. 1900				Warming
				Several degrees colder than at present
1500	Thule	Thule	Thule	Cooling
1000	Punuk	Birnirk		Rapid Warming
500	Old Bering Sea	Ipiutak		Warming
0	Norton			Several degrees colder than at present
500	Choris		Dorset	Continued cooling
1000	Old Whaling			
1500				Rapid cooling
2000 B.C.	Arctic Small Tool tradition			Several degrees warmer than at present

Key

present=20th Century
temperature fluctuations=several degrees

◄■ *Cultural Relationship*

◄■► *Possible Cultural Relationship*

•••• *Possible Break in Cultural Continuity*

As a consequence, in Arctic Canada there were two notable shifts in Palaeoeskimo occupation. It seems that the people living in the High Arctic (in the islands to the north of Parry Channel and in Northern Greenland) either abandoned the area or became so scarce that they are not archaeologically visible. This very marginal zone of human occupation may simply have become untenable as the climate cooled and animal populations were reduced from their already meagre levels.

To the south, in the Barren Grounds to the west of Hudson Bay, a new zone of occupation was opened to the Palaeoeskimos. This zone, which extended as far south as the Great Bear and Great Slave Lakes, Lake Athabaska and Northern Manitoba, had been occupied for millennia by Indians. At about this time, archaeological remains of Indian occupation are replaced by those of Palaeoeskimos. This replacement, which lasted for a few centuries, may perhaps be explained by the southward shift of the tree line and consequent changes in the migratory patterns of the caribou which form the major resource for human hunters in the region.

By approximately 3,000 years ago, evidence of Palaeoeskimo occupation of Alaska disappears, although this may be due to lack of archaeological research rather than to a lack of people inhabiting the area. In Arctic Canada, however, and especially in the Eastern Arctic, we can trace continued occupation and the gradual development of an altered and, apparently, more economically successful way of life.

Early Eskimos Spread from Alaska across the Arctic, Reaching as far East as Greenland.

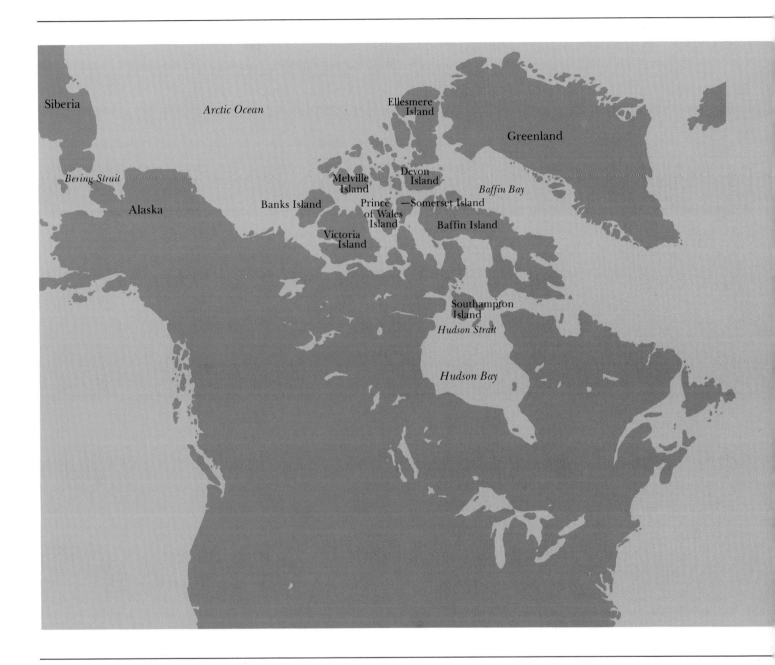

Siberia

Arctic Ocean

Ellesmere Island

Greenland

Bering Strait

Melville Island

Devon Island

Baffin Bay

Alaska

Banks Island

Prince of Wales Island

—Somerset Island

Baffin Island

Victoria Island

Southampton Island

Hudson Strait

Hudson Bay

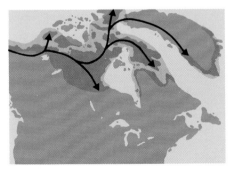

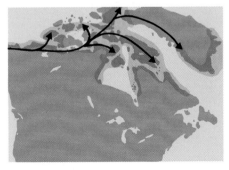

Migration Routes and Probable Area of Occupation for Palaeoeskimos of the Arctic Small Tool Tradition.

Probable Area Occupied by the Dorset Culture.

Thule Migration Routes and Probable Area of Occupation.

Artist's Depiction of a Dorset Winter Dwelling,
1000 B.C.-A.D. 1000.

The Dorset Culture

Major changes in Palaeoeskimo culture appear to have occurred between approximately 3,000 and 2,500 years ago and resulted in what is known as the Dorset culture. Technological changes are the ones most easily traced archaeologically, and several of these appear at approximately the same time. Small pots or lamps carved from soapstone occur for the first time; earlier containers, in which meat may have been boiled with stones heated in the hearths of Palaeoeskimo tents, must have been made from perishable wood or skin. The use of lamps fueled with sea-mammal oil now allowed the occupation of snow houses and, although it cannot be expected to leave many archaeological traces, the domed snow house may have been invented and used by the Dorset people. In the core area of Dorset occupation, on the southern islands and mainland coasts of the Eastern Arctic, some Dorset groups began to occupy substantial semi-subterranean winter houses, again probably heated with oil lamps.

Other elements of technology changed in style, if not in function. Ground stone, in the form of ground burin-like tools for working bone and small ground slate flensing knives, began to replace chipped stone tools. Bone sewing needles became larger and appeared in a new, flattened form. Harpoon heads, perhaps the most essential element of an arctic hunter's technology, gradually changed in style but cannot have been much more efficient than those of their predecessors. More striking is the apparent absence of bow and arrow equipment; although it is difficult to believe that such a useful weapon could have been dropped from use, it is equally difficult to make any other interpretation from the archaeological evidence. The same occurrence is well-documented archaeologically at a much later period, when the Polar Eskimos of Northwestern Greenland stopped hunting caribou in late prehistoric times, perhaps for religious reasons.

A few large canine skulls have been recovered from Dorset sites and tentatively identified as those of domestic dogs rather than wolves. Sled shoes, elongate pieces of bone lashed to the bottom of sled runners in order to prevent wear and easily identified by the grooves caused by the sled having been hauled over rocks, are also found. It is possible that the dog-sled may have been invented by the Dorsets, but the scarcity of dog remains and the absence of specialized harnessing equipment indicates that the technique was of little importance compared to that which it attained in later periods. A few wooden objects have been tentatively identified as kayak ribs; it is possible that at some period Dorset people may have invented this small hunting craft or learned of its use from their Alaskan relatives.

The major developments of Dorset culture occurred around 2,500 years ago in the context of a climate which was cooling, perhaps to conditions colder than at present. In most areas, sites dating to after 2,500 years ago are larger and appear to represent greater duration of occupation than those of earlier times. There is little evidence that this change was the result of technological developments producing a more efficient economy, and may have come about as a consequence of the climatic change itself.

Blubber-fueled lamps burn with a small flame and do not produce as much smoke or heat as an open fire. They are thus well-suited for heating and lighting snowhouses.

Lamp *(Provenience unknown). Soapstone, 29 cm long. CMNH #25413.*

A cooling climate in Arctic Canada would probably have resulted in more extensive sea ice, and sea ice which lasted later into the summer months. Despite the slight evidence that some Dorset people may have had kayaks, theirs was a technology adapted primarily to hunting sea animals either from the shore or from the ice. Seals, walrus, and small whales seem to have been hunted with harpoons which were either stabbed or thrown at the animals. The detachable harpoon head was tied to a line which was held in the hunter's hand or, for larger animals, must have been looped about something more stable—a rock, lump of ice, or perhaps an icepick jammed into the ice. With such a technology, a reduction in summerlike, open-water conditions may have resulted in more productive hunting and improved economic circumstances. If this is correct, it serves as a warning to historians and ecologists who generally associate a cooling climate with a deteriorating environment, especially in Arctic regions.

The Dorset Palaeoeskimos, at least during some periods, occupied most areas of Arctic Canada and Greenland later occupied by the Inuit.* An exception is the Barren Grounds region, which by Dorset times had been reclaimed by Indian caribou hunters. A northwestern extension of this region, the Arctic coast to the west of Coronation Gulf, was also unoccupied, as it was in historic times, probably because it provided few resources for an ice-hunting people. The 800-kilometer (500-mile) stretch of coast between Coronation Gulf and Mackenzie River seems to have served to insulate Dorset culture almost completely from Eskimo developments in Alaska.

Early in the Dorset period, and again in the centuries around A.D. 1000, the Dorset people occupied the islands of the eastern High Arctic, an area which was unoccupied during the historic period. During the first millennium B.C. they began to move south into subarctic regions, both on the west coast of Greenland and more importantly along the coast of Labrador. Reaching Southern Labrador, they crossed the Strait of

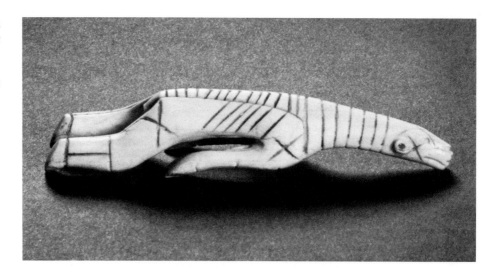

Belle Isle to Newfoundland where, although they may have shared some parts of the Island with Indians, they were the principal occupants between approximately 2,500 and 1,500 years ago. Here they demonstrated their ability to live in a forested as well as maritime environment. Despite the Dorsets' adaptation to a forest environment, their main resource remained the sea. The largest Dorset sites have been found in areas with access to the herds of harp seals, which give birth to their pups each spring on the drifting ice off the northern Newfoundland coast.

One aspect of Dorset culture which is rather surprising is the nature and quality of their three-dimensional art. Many carvings in wood and ivory have been recovered from their occupation sites. Most of the carvings are small, perhaps reflecting the tradition of miniaturization which they inherited from their Arctic Small Tool tradition ancestors. Many are realistic portrayals of arctic animals —caribou, seals, walrus, fish, birds, and, most frequently, polar bears. Sometimes only part of the animal is portrayed: a caribou hoof, a bear head, or even a bear skull. Some carvings, especially those of bears, are stylized representations with the animal's skeleton and major joints marked with incised lines. In fact, many bear carvings are so stylized that they can be recognized only by the characteristic skeletal designs.

A relatively large number of stylized polar bear carvings have been recovered from Dorset archaeological sites. Their presence suggests that these animals occupied an important position in Dorset ceremonial practices and beliefs.

Polar Bear Carving *(Alarnerk, Melville Peninsula, Canada). Ivory, Dorset (1000 B.C.-A.D. 1000), 15.5 cm length. Courtesy of Archaeological Survey of Canada, National Museum of Man, National Museums of Canada, Ottawa, #NhHd-1:2655c.*

This mask is representative of the highly developed art of the Dorset Period. Such masks were probably part of the shamans' paraphernalia.

Carved Mask (*Button Point, Bylot Island, Canada*). *Wood, Dorset (1000 B.C.-A.D. 1000), 18.5 cm long. Courtesy of Archaeological Survey of Canada, National Museum of Man, National Museums of Canada, Ottawa #PfFm-1:1728c.*

It has been suggested that many or all of these representations of bears, the most powerful animal in the arctic environment, portray not real bears but spirits. Such an interpretation is supported by other Dorset artifacts which also suggest the importance of shamanistic activities: life-sized masks, drums, sets of carved ivory animal teeth designed to be slipped into the mouth in order to portray an animal (perhaps a bear), miniature replicas of harpoon heads which may have been used as magical weapons, and wooden carvings of humans with a hole in the chest containing a sliver of wood. Thus, there seems little doubt that Dorset art was intimately connected with magical practices, and that it gives us a unique insight into the social and religious practices of a prehistoric people.

Both in the quality of carvings and in the very large number produced, Dorset art seems to have reached a crescendo during the latter part of the first millennium A.D. This same period saw the decline and eventual extinction of the Dorset culture. Newfoundland and Southern Labrador were the first areas abandoned, at some time after A.D. 500, perhaps because of the expansion of local Indian groups. When the Norse arrived in Southwestern Greenland during the late 10th century, they found traces of Dorset occupation but no people.

In the islands of the Canadian Arctic there was a widespread Dorset expansion just prior to A.D. 1000 and then sudden disappearance. Only in the Ungava region of Northern Quebec and on the adjacent Northern Labrador coast did the Dorset people continue to live their unique way of life for approximately another 500 years. In the centuries around A.D. 1000 the northern hemisphere began to experience a warming climate. In the Arctic, a reduction in sea ice and increase in open water resulted. These changing conditions may have contributed to the decline and eventual disappearance of the Dorset population.

Throughout most of Arctic Canada, however, a related but more important cause was the appearance of new people in the area, the ancestors of the Inuit who occupy the area today. Inuit legends state that when their ancestors arrived in Arctic Canada they found the area occupied by another race, the Tuniit, whom with fair confidence we can identify with the Dorset people known through archaeology. Although the legends often tell of good relations between Inuit and Tuniit, usually described as a large and gentle race of people who lacked bows and other items of technology, they inevitably end with the Tuniit being killed or driven from their native land.

In order to investigate the background of this event, we must look at developments in Alaska during the two millennia before the first contact between the Inuit and the Tuniit.

The Alaskan Maritime Tradition

While the Dorset people were developing their unique adaptation to Arctic Canada, in virtual isolation from the rest of the world, new developments were taking place along the coast of the Bering Sea. Ideas, and perhaps people, were entering the area from two directions. From the Pacific coast of Alaska came elements of technology which had been developed over the millennia during which people had lived in this rich maritime environmental zone. Such elements are probably first represented on the Bering Sea coast with the appearance of an, as yet, very poorly known archaeological complex known as the Old Whaling culture; this culture probably originated around 3,000 years ago. The next group to occupy the west coast of Alaska, at some time between 3,000 and 2,500 years ago, were the Choris people who lived in large oval houses and used pottery with linear-stamped designs. Neolithic peoples of adjacent Siberia used very similar pottery, and, thus, its appearance in Alaska bespeaks some form of contact between the two continents.

The third group appeared in the area about 2,500 years ago. They are much better known archaeologically and are the first people whom we can with certainty describe as ancestral Eskimos. Known as the

Norton culture, their archaeological remains contain a strange mixture of elements apparently derived from different sources. Norton chipped-stone artifacts resemble those of the earlier Palaeoeskimos of the area. Ground-slate knives, stone lamps, labrets to be worn in the lips or cheeks, and other elements seem to have developed from patterns long in use along the Pacific coast of South Alaska. Pottery decorated with check-stamped designs, somewhat different from that of the Choris culture, again suggests contact with Siberians.

Most archaeologists look at the Norton people as *in situ* descendants of Alaskan Palaeoeskimo populations who had picked up ideas and elements of technology from adjacent groups and combined them to form the first successful maritime adaptation to the coasts of the Bering and Chukchi seas. This would seem to be the simplest explanation, but there is an embarrassing 500-year gap between the latest-known Palaeo-eskimo site and the first appearance of Norton sites. An alternate theory sees the Norton people as South Alaskans, eastern neighbors of the Aleuts, who around 2,500 years ago learned to adapt their hunting to the seasonally frozen coasts of the Bering Sea and began to move northward. The evidence is simply too vague to allow us to say with certainty where the Norton people came from. Nevertheless, we know that between approximately 2,500 and 2,000 years ago they had spread their maritime-oriented "Neoeskimo" way of life along most of the western coast of Alaska.

Norton or Norton-like cultures served as the basis for the major cultural developments of the first millennium A.D. One of these developments, the Ipiutak culture of North Alaska, is best known from a large coastal site at Point Hope consisting of several hundred small, square, semisubterranean houses and numerous burials. Although most of Ipiutak technology is based on Norton models, there are surprising differences such as the absence of pottery, ground-slate tools, and oil lamps. Perhaps this site was used as a summer camp by small groups for brief periods, and, thus, these useful artifacts were simply not brought to this site. An alternative interpretation might be that the Ipiutak people actually never learned to use these materials.

The most impressive aspect of Ipiutak culture is its burials and the objects found in them, providing our earliest information on Eskimo burial practices. Because no graves have been found, we know nothing of the burial practices of the earlier Palaeo-eskimos of Alaska or Arctic Canada; we assume that Palaeoeskimos placed the bodies of their dead on the surface or on the sea ice. Only in Newfoundland have a few burials been found in limestone caves associated with Dorset artifacts; these serve only to show that the Dorset Palaeoeskimos were racially similar to modern Eskimos.

The Ipiutak skeletons are also of the Eskimo racial type but differ in a few skeletal characteristics from the recent occupants of the area. Many of the graves, excavated into gravel beaches, were accompanied by artifacts and carvings in ivory and other materials. Many of these carvings represent animals, others seem to portray fantastic creatures, and there are numerous ivory chains, swivels, and nonfunctional objects. Most impressive are the ivory death-masks found with a few individuals, perhaps the shamans of the tribe. The Ipiutak artistic style, with its hints of Siberian influences, is unlike any style known from other regions, and it is difficult to understand this prolific production of artistic works by what appears to have been a small, seminomadic population of Northwestern Alaska.

While Ipiutak culture remains an enigma, a great deal more is known of the roughly contemporaneous Okvik and Old Bering Sea cultures of the Bering Sea Islands and the adjacent coast of Siberia. Although these closely related cultures must have developed from a Norton or Norton-like base, no Norton culture sites are known from the area. The Okvik and Old Bering Sea cultures probably represent a recent movement of Alaskan peoples across the Bering Strait to Siberia where there was the rapid development of an economically rich and relatively sophisticated way of life. These people were specialized hunters of seals, walrus, and the smaller whales, with maritime hunting equipment considerably advanced over that used by earlier groups. The basic equipment for this way of life was the skin-covered boat, both the one-man hunting kayak and the larger umiak which could transport an entire camp. With the boats also came the float harpoon in which the harpoon line was attached to an inflated seal skin and which made possible the efficient hunting of larger sea mammals.

Hunting with such equipment in the animal-rich waters of the Bering Sea, these people could store enough meat to allow the occupation of permanent villages, probably the first such villages in the Eskimo world. The houses were semisubterranean and built of driftwood, covered with turf for insulation, and heated with pottery lamps burning sea-mammal oil.

Although it is impossible to estimate their population size, the Old Bering Sea populations were probably more concentrated than those of any earlier groups in Arctic North America. Such concentrations of people must have involved the development of new types of social organization, and much of the social and, perhaps, the religious culture of the traditional Eskimo way of life may be traced to the Old Bering Sea period.

The little that we know of the religion of these people comes from the interpretation of ivory carvings recovered from their houses and burials. Okvik and Old Bering Sea art is justly famous as one of the high points of Eskimo creativity. Elegant ivory carvings represent humans and animals, whereas utilitarian objects are often elaborately decorated with swirling designs of incised lines. The most highly decorated objects are generally harpoon heads and other equipment associated with the hunting of sea mammals, suggesting that the decoration may have been associated with hunting magic.

Objects of this type are commonly found at sites occupied by Old Bering Sea peoples. Although the exact use of such objects has not been established, they may have been used as counter-balances on throwing boards.

Winged Object (*Provenience unknown*). *Ivory, Old Bering Sea (A.D. 0-500), 20.3 cm long. CMNH #23102-15767.*

The function of this object is unknown. Incised, curvilinear lines are typical of the designs used by the Old Bering Sea people to decorate both utilitarian and nonutilitarian objects.

Carving (*Provenience unknown*). *Ivory, Old Bering Sea (A.D. 0-500), 12.8 cm long. CMNH #23102-15787.*

During the first millennium A.D., the Old Bering Sea culture gradually changed to a form known as Punuk. The Punuk period villages were larger, decorations became less elaborate, and we have the impression of a more efficient and functionally oriented way of life. New elements appeared, such as the Asiatic bow and slat armor, hinting that the patterns of Asiatic warfare which were at the same period expanding into Eastern Europe, were also reaching this most northeasterly part of Eurasia. Punuk influence extended eastward into North America in the centuries preceding A.D. 1000. In North Alaska, the Birnirk culture represented a curious amalgam of the Punuk way of life with elements of local technology. Some of these elements of local technology may have been derived from the earlier Ipiutak culture of the area. With the development of Birnirk culture, the stage was set for the next major event in Eskimo cultural development.

The Thule Migration

Towards the close of the first millennium A.D., the climate of the northern hemisphere began to become warmer, bringing to an end the cooling trend which had begun about 3,500 years ago. Such a change is well documented in Europe, where during the "Medieval Warm Period" grapes and other warmth-loving crops began to be grown farther north than was previously possible, and where more productive Scandinavian farming served as a basis for the Viking expansion.

Similar conditions in Northern North America are indicated from the study of glaciers, ice-cores, and botanical remains. For human hunters in Arctic North America, the most important change produced by such a warming trend would have been a reduction in the quantity and seasonal duration of sea ice. Summer breakup would have occurred earlier, open water areas would have been more extensive than they are today, and the ranges and populations of animals such as walrus and whales would have become larger. Conditions rather similar to those of the

Bering Sea may now have occurred along the North Alaskan coast and eastward into Arctic Canada.

At about the same time as the climatic change, the Birnirk culture of North Alaska began to change to what is known as Thule culture. The development from Birnirk to Thule culture is marked by generally minor technological changes, involving stylistic changes in the forms of harpoon heads, arrowheads, and other artifacts. The people continued to live in villages of semisubterranean wooden houses, and to subsist primarily on open-water hunting of sea mammals supplemented by caribou hunting and winter sealing from the ice.

The one major change was in the development of whaling techniques, which utilized umiaks and large bone whaling harpoon heads attached to drags and floats. Earlier populations had at least occasionally taken the bowhead whale, the slow-swimming, 10-to-20-meters-long (30-to-66 feet) whales which are the largest animals of the Arctic seas. But the Thule people seem to have become especially proficient in such hunting and came to depend on the whales as a major food source, as each animal would have provided several tonnes (tons) of meat and oil.

Toggling harpoon heads were made in a range of sizes for hunting various sea mammals. This medium-sized harpoon head was most likely used to capture walrus, beluga whale, and narwhal.

Toggling Harpoon Head (*Cape Prince of Wales or St. Lawrence Island, Alaska*). *Bone, Thule (A.D. 1000-1700), 12.8 cm long. CMNH #23784-30.*

*Artist's Depiction of a Thule Winter Dwelling,
A.D. 1000-1700.*

*Remains of a Thule Winter Village at
Brooman Point, Bathurst Island, Canada.*

The Thule people of the North
Alaskan coast probably hunted
bowheads in the same manner as
their present day descendants in the
area, concentrating on spring hunting
when the whales were confined by
narrow ice-leads during their eastward migration to their summering
grounds in Canadian Arctic waters.
We do not know what motivated the
first groups of Thule people to
follow the whales eastward—
perhaps the possibility of hunting
the animals throughout the summer
in Amundsen Gulf, or perhaps
simply because of social problems in
their home villages. However, once
such a movement was made, the
Thule people expanded rapidly
across Arctic Canada. Travelling by
umiak in the extended open-water
seasons of the period, small groups
of a few families would have been
capable of covering 100 kilometers
(62 miles) or more in a season,
setting up winter camp wherever a
whale was killed or where there was
evidence that winter food could be
obtained by other means. All of
the earlier Thule sites are located
along the migration and summering
grounds of the bowhead whale or
the Greenland whale, the Eastern
Arctic variant of the same species,
whose ranges may have overlapped
in Parry Channel during the Thule
period. Although no Canadian Thule
sites seem to date earlier than A.D.
1000, by A.D. 1200 the Thule people
had reached Northwestern Greenland, Baffin Island, and Northwestern Hudson Bay.

Within a very few centuries, these
maritime hunters had expanded their
territory from Alaska to Greenland.
From Alaska they brought most of
the cultural and technological elements developed by their ancestors
over the preceding millennia, but
several of these elements had to be
adapted to the conditions which they
found in their new environment.
Most of Arctic Canada, for example,
lacked the driftwood supplies of
Alaska, forcing the Thule people to
build a different style of winter
house. Houses were based on the
Alaskan pattern with a raised sleeping
platform at the rear, a semisubterranean floor area, and a sunken

cold-trap entrance tunnel. In the Canadian Arctic, however, building material included rock walls, flagstone floor and platform areas, and whalebone rafters which supported a roof of skins and turf. Another form of winter dwelling, the domed snow house, also was built. Specialized snow-knives and probes for testing the consistency of the snow, found at Thule sites, provide archaeological evidence of snowhouse construction. Such dwellings may have been necessary, because in many regions of Arctic Canada the Thule immigrants probably found it impossible to store enough food to allow them to live at one locality throughout the entire winter. Probable snow knives have been found in Dorset sites in Arctic Canada, and, thus, the Thule people may have learned to build domed snow houses from their Dorset predecessors.

Another element of Dorset technology which may have been borrowed by the Thule was the use of soapstone for the carving of lamps and cooking pots. With soapstone deposits widely distributed across the Arctic, this material rapidly replaced pottery in Thule technology throughout the Central and Eastern Arctic.

Dogsleds may have also been adopted from the Dorsets. Archaeological evidence indicates that specialized harness equipment for use with dogsleds first appears in early Canadian Thule sites, only later spreading westward to Alaska.

The ulu is a knife traditionally used by women. The blade would normally have been fitted into a handle of bone, ivory, or wood.

Ulu Blade *(Belcher Islands, Canada). Slate, Thule (A.D. 1000-1700), 9 cm long. CMNH #11958-56.*

Although some Thule winter villages consist of 20 or more houses, not all of which can have been occupied at the same time, most settlements must have been considerably smaller and less permanent than the North Alaskan communities from which the ancestral Thule people had come. It would seem likely that most such settlements would have considered themselves lucky to have captured a single whale during a summer, and food and fuel supplies must have been largely based on other resources. Thule people hunted seals, walrus, beluga, narwhal, caribou, musk-oxen, and fish—in fact, anything which was available in the area which they occupied. Such adaptability allowed them to penetrate regions which lacked whales and other large sea mammals. By at least A.D. 1400, most of Arctic Canada north of the tree line was occupied by a sparse Thule population.

With spring travel by sled and summer travel by boat, the Thule population was linked by at least a tenuous communication system. This can be traced archaeologically by the apparently rapid spread of new artifact styles and by the widespread distribution of trade goods. For this period, soapstone from the Central Arctic has been found in Northern Alaska, native copper from the Central Arctic spread as far north as Greenland, and meteoric iron from Northwestern Greenland has been found as far south as the west coast of Hudson Bay.

During their original expansion and subsequent travels, the Thule encountered other occupants of the region. In addition to snowhouses, soapstone, and dogsled equipment which may have been adopted through such contact, other archaeological evidence also suggests contact between the Thule and Dorset. These include harpoon head styles used by the Eastern Arctic Thule, styles which seem to have been based on Dorset patterns and elements of terminal Dorset technology which may reflect Thule influence. As noted earlier, contact between the two groups is suggested by Tuniit legends describing meeting with a race of people who were the original occupants of

the country. Such evidence can do no more than hint at the relationships between the two groups. Although the Dorset way of life disappeared from Arctic Canada and Greenland, it is possible that some local Dorset populations may have survived and been incorporated into the Thule population.

Another group with whom the Thule people came into contact were the Norse who had established colonies in Southwestern Greenland about A.D. 1000 and who continued to occupy the area for the next 500 years. Historical records of contacts between Eskimos and Norse are extremely few and vague, and most deal with hostility between the two groups. Archaeological materials of European origin—bronze artifacts, pieces of chain mail armor, scraps of smelted metal, oak wood, and pieces of woolen cloth—have been found in Thule sites dating to as early as the 12th century. Since the materials predate Norse mention of meetings with Eskimos by about a century, it seems possible that occasional encounters between the two populations may have occurred over a period of several centuries. Thus, sporadic trading relationships may have been established between the two groups.

The Norse settlements disappeared during the 14th and 15th centuries, and the areas previously occupied by the Norse were taken over by the Thule people. Yet there is little historical evidence and less archaeological evidence suggesting that the Eskimos had a hand in the extinction of the Greenland colonies.

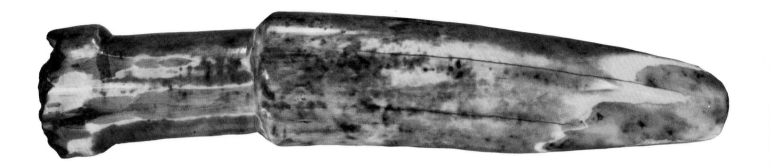

This tool was probably used for excavating the below-ground portion of Thule winter dwellings and for breaking up sod for the walls.

Mattock *(Provenience unknown). Ivory, Thule (A.D. 1000-1700), 33.5 cm long. CMNH #29691-255.*

Within four or five centuries of their ancestors having left Alaska, the Thule people had brought an essentially Alaskan way of life to most of Arctic Canada and Greenland. Although local Thule groups differed from one another to some extent in the local resources which they hunted and consequently in their weapons, tools, and seasonal rounds of activities, there remains an impression of a relatively uniform pattern of culture over an area of more than two-million-square kilometers (800,000-square miles). This prehistoric uniformity is reflected in the linguistic uniformity of the descendants of the Thule people: The Inuit from Greenland to Northwestern Alaska speak a single language, indicating a common linguistic ancestry in the very recent past. However, this same uniformity has not been maintained in Inuit culture. When 18th- and 19th-century European explorers and anthropologists began to penetrate the region, they found no widespread and uniform culture like that of the Thule people. Rather, they encountered small and more-or-less isolated groups of Inuit with a great variety of adaptations to local environments. The development of these divergent adaptations is best explained in terms of both environmental and historical events which influenced the Inuit way of life during the past few centuries.

The Little Ice Age

The relatively warm climates which had allowed the Thule people to expand their maritime hunting culture across Arctic Canada was to last for a very few centuries. Both historical and palaeoclimatological evidence indicates that the northern climate began to cool gradually after approximately A.D. 1200, and then more drastically between approximately A.D. 1600 and 1850, to produce conditions considerably harsher than those of the present century.

The period between A.D. 1600 and 1850 is known in Europe as the "Little Ice Age." During this period alpine glaciers advanced, increased sea ice in the North Atlantic hindered navigation between Europe and Iceland, and crop failures and famine occurred more frequently in northern countries.

In Arctic North America the colder climate and increased severity of sea ice seems to have had a significant influence on the Thule people and their way of life. In the Western and Eastern Arctic regions this influence was moderated by proximity to open water and by the relative richness of the sea-mammal resources in local waters, and an essentially Thule way of life could be maintained. In Alaska, the Thule culture continued to spread its influence southward to the Pacific coast, westward to Northeastern Siberia, and eastward as far as the Mackenzie River Delta where people continued to live in permanent villages of wooden houses and to develop a specialized way of life based on the hunting of beluga whale, seal, caribou, and fish.

In both Labrador and Greenland this period saw a southward movement by Thule people, perhaps in response to the climatic change which probably caused a southward extension in the ranges of the sea mammals which they hunted. During this period the Thule people supplanted the Dorset inhabitants of Northern Labrador and the Norse occupants of Southwestern Greenland. The southward expansion in Labrador continued during the 16th century, but this time, apparently in response to European presence in the area. Expeditions as far south as the Strait of Belle Isle were made in order to trade with or prey upon the early European fishing and whaling stations in the area.

In the areas of Baffin Island and Hudson Bay, although whaling seems to have ceased, the relatively rich sea-mammal resources of the region allowed the Inuit to maintain some aspects of their previous hunting and living patterns. Early winter continued to be spent in rock and turf-walled houses, with a move to snowhouses later in the season when supplies of stored food were exhausted. Summers were spent largely in hunting from kayaks, and umiaks continued to be used to some extent for transportation, if not for whaling.

In the Central and High Arctic, environmental conditions seem to have changed more drastically.

Whereas Thule people had previously occupied the eastern islands of the High Arctic as well as much of Northern Greenland, this area seems to have been abandoned during the Little Ice Age as local populations either starved during unexpectedly severe years or moved out of the area to join other groups. By the 19th century the only people remaining in this region were a small band of Polar Eskimos occupying Northwestern Greenland and hunting over the adjacent regions of Ellesmere Island. This group had lost the use of the kayak, bow and fish spear. They subsisted by hunting from the ice on the fringes of the North Water, an area of Northern Baffin Bay which rarely, if ever, freezes, and by exploiting the nesting cliffs of sea birds. Although they continued to occupy winter houses similar to those of their Thule ancestors, the entire Thule maritime-hunting culture had been dropped, as had contact with other groups. By the late 19th century they claimed to think of themselves as the only people in the world. These Polar Eskimos appear to have been on the road to extinction had it not been for the arrival in the area of a band of Canadian Inuit who reintroduced the kayak, and of the polar explorers who for several decades provided a major and probably necessary support for their way of life.

To the south, on the islands and adjacent mainland coast of the Central Arctic, Inuit continued to occupy most regions but found it necessary to make major changes in their ways of life. Most of these changes involved accentuating certain aspects of Thule life in the region while neglecting or even dropping other aspects. In the area between Melville Peninsula and MacKenzie River, the Thule people had always depended primarily on seals and caribou because the larger sea mammals were never available in quantities sufficient to support extensive hunting. Still, most Thule groups had managed to spend the winter in permanent winter villages, probably subsisting largely on seals hunted from kayaks during the summer and stored for winter use.

Although such hunting continued to be practiced during the Little Ice Age, by the 19th century it was no longer sufficiently productive to provide winter subsistence. Hunting of large sea mammals had been practically abandoned by the Copper Inuit and some Netsilik Inuit groups of the Central Arctic. These groups were now spending summers in the interior, hunting caribou and fishing in lakes and rivers, an activity which had probably been of relatively minor importance to their Thule ancestors. Such interior hunting allowed the accumulation of surplus food supplies only sufficient to tide the people over through autumn, between the time when most of the caribou had migrated to the south and the time when sea ice had formed. Winters were passed in temporary snowhouse villages on the sea ice, with food and fuel derived almost exclusively from the hunting of seals at breathing holes in the ice.

In at least parts of this region, other changes seem to have come about as a result of brief contacts with Europeans, or at least with European technology. Small amounts of European material had probably reached the area as early as the 18th century, traded from the Hudson Bay Inuit. However, there was a major influx of such materials during the latter half of the 19th century as the result of the Franklin Search Expeditions mounted by the British navy. One of the search ships, the *Investigator*, was abandoned in Northern Banks Island in 1853 and, according to local reports, was soon discovered by the Copper Inuit. A band of Copper Inuit appears to have moved to Banks Island where the people spent several decades living on musk-oxen and salvaging the cache of European materials. Material from the *Investigator* was traded widely through the Central Arctic and, to some extent, it influenced the development of local technology and trading patterns. In other areas of the Central Arctic, similar changes in pre-contact Inuit culture may have occurred as a result of the presence of European caches and abandoned ships.

Perhaps the most impressive example of rapid cultural change as a result of contact with Europeans occurred among the Inuit along the west coast of Hudson Bay. These people had probably always made some use of the caribou resources of the Barren Grounds to the west, but the primary occupants of this territory were the ancestors of the Chipewyan Indians.

During the late 18th century these Indians, who had long been involved in the European fur trade, were decimated by smallpox. The survivors moved to better trapping areas to the south. By the early 19th century, armed with guns and other European trade goods, the Inuit were capable of living year-round on caribou, and several groups moved into the interior. So completely transformed was their way of life that the first anthropologist to study them, during the early 20th century, thought of them as a surviving example of an ancient and primitive inland culture from which all Eskimos had developed by moving to the sea coast at some time in the past.

As can be seen from the above discussion, the diversity of historic Inuit culture was largely the result of rapid changes which had occurred in the centuries immediately prior to intensive contact with Europeans. Such changes came about as a response both to rapidly deteriorating environmental conditions, and to the intrusion into Arctic North America of Europeans and European material culture.

The Inuit way of life cannot be adequately described, as often has been the case, as the result of millennia of adaptation to the arctic environment. Such a characterization ignores the complexity of Eskimo history and the importance of changes in the environments in which these people lived. The cultures and adaptations described by European explorers and anthropologists, especially those of the Central Arctic Inuit, were those of peoples who had recently undergone profound environmental and cultural shocks. Only through their adaptability and their knowledge of their environment had they been able to maintain some elements of what, a few centuries previously, had been a relatively rich and sophisticated way of life.

*The term, *Inuit* is used by contemporary Eskimos, living between North Alaska and Greenland, to refer to themselves and their Thule ancestors.

Reading List

Bandi, H.G. *Eskimo Prehistory*. Seattle: University of Washington Press, 1969.

Dekin, A.A. *Arctic Archaeology: A Bibliography and History*. NY: Garland, 1978.

Dumond, D.E. *The Eskimos and Aleuts*. London: Thames and Hudson, 1977.

Dumond, D.E. *Archaeology of the Alaska Peninsula*. University of Oregon Anthropological Papers, No. 21. Eugene, OR: University of Oregon, 1981.

Giddings, J.L. *The Archaeology of Cape Dembigh, Alaska*. Providence: Brown University Press, 1964.

Giddings, J.L. *Ancient Men of the Arctic*. NY: Knopf, 1967.

Larsen, H., and F.G. Rainey. *Ipiutak and the Arctic Whale Hunting Culture*. American Museum of Natural History Anthropological Papers, No. 42. NY: American Museum of Natural History, 1948.

Mathiassen, T. *Archaeology of the Central Eskimos*. Report of the Fifth Thule Expedition, 1921-1924, Vol. IV. Copenhagen: Gyldendalske Boghandel, 1927.

McCartney, A.P. *Thule Eskimo Culture: An Anthropological Retrospective*. Archaeological Survey of Canada, No. 88. Mercury Series. Ottawa: National Museums of Canada, 1979.

McGhee, R. *Copper Eskimo Prehistory*. Publications in Archaeology, No. 2. Ottawa: National Museum of Man, National Museums of Canada, 1972.

McGhee, R. *Canadian Arctic Prehistory*. Toronto: Van Nostrand Reinhold, 1978.

Tuck, J.A. *Newfoundland and Labrador Prehistory*. Toronto: Van Nostrand Reinhold, 1976.

Color Plates

" . . . [O]nly about half the Arctic pack ice thaws during summer before starting its yearly expansion again in the autumn."
-Mary R. Dawson

During the summer the ice in Eclipse Sound, between Baffin and Bylot islands in the Central Canadian Arctic, retreats from land.

" . . . [P]olar environments . . . even with their cold, darkness, ice and snow, support plants and animals that have adapted to these conditions."
-Mary R. Dawson

The awesome, weathered cliffs of Prince Leopold Island form good nesting ground for many sea birds. Prince Leopold Island lies off the north coast of Somerset Island in the Eastern Canadian Arctic.

"The plants' low, compact, cushiony growth form serves to reduce heat loss as well as to resist dessication and mechanical abrasion caused by arctic winds and drifting snow."
-Frederick H. Utech

*Arctic willow, **Salix** sp., Salicaceae, (Willow Family).*

". . . [A]rctic animals have evolved adaptations that are finely tuned to the forbidding cold and seasonality of food resources." -Joseph F. Merritt

"*Unfortunately . . . [the marine mammal fauna] has been greatly depleted through systematic slaughter by commercial whalers, sealers, and walrus hunters.*"

"*During winter, the ringed seal survives under pack ice by establishing breathing holes. . . .*"   *-Joseph F. Merritt*

The walrus (Odobenus rosmarus) *is a member of the mammalian order Pinnipedia ("fin-footed"). Huge tusks, elongated upper canine teeth, are found in both male and female walrus. In combination with the lips, the tusks are used to rake mollusks from the sea floor.*

The ringed seal (Phoca hispida), *one of the most common arctic species, is a primary prey of the polar bear* (Ursus maritimus).

The king eider (Somateria spectabilis), *shown here, and the common eider* (Somateria mollissima) *are large ducks that regularly winter in the ice-free waters of the Arctic. Their heavy layer of down provides excellent insulation. Inuit use eider skins for clothing and robes. Icelandic farmers harvest eiderdown from the lining of the birds' nests.*

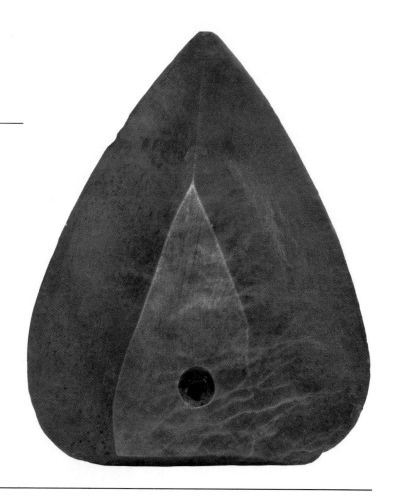

Lance blade or end blade for whaling harpoon (Belcher Islands, Canada). Greenstone, Thule (A.D. 1000-1700), 7.3 cm long. CMNH #28492-98.

"... [T]he Thule people ... came to depend on the whales as a major food source."

"Old Bering Sea art is justly famous as one of the high points of Eskimo creativity." -Robert McGhee

Mask fragment (Banks Island, Canada). Ivory, Old Bering Sea (A.D. 0-500), 12.8 cm long. CMNH #23102-15769.

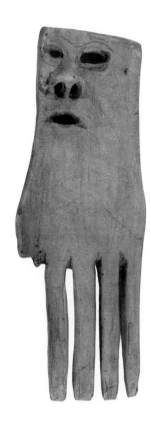

"One aspect of Dorset culture which is rather surprising is the nature and quality of their three-dimensional art." -Robert McGhee

Comb with face (Maxwell Bay, Devon Island, Canada). Ivory, Dorset (1000 B.C.-A.D. 1000), 6.2 cm long. Courtesy of Archaeological Survey of Canada, National Museum of Man, National Museums of Canada, Ottawa, #IX-C:2827c.

Carved mask (Button Point, Bylot Island, Canada). Wood, Dorset (1000 B.C.-A.D. 1000), 18.5 cm high. Courtesy of Archaeological Survey of Canada, National Museum of Man, National Museums of Canada, Ottawa, #PfFm-1:1728c.

"If the caribou were not frightened off by the approaching hunter, it was still necessary to get within close range for the bow and arrow to hit its target."
-David Damas

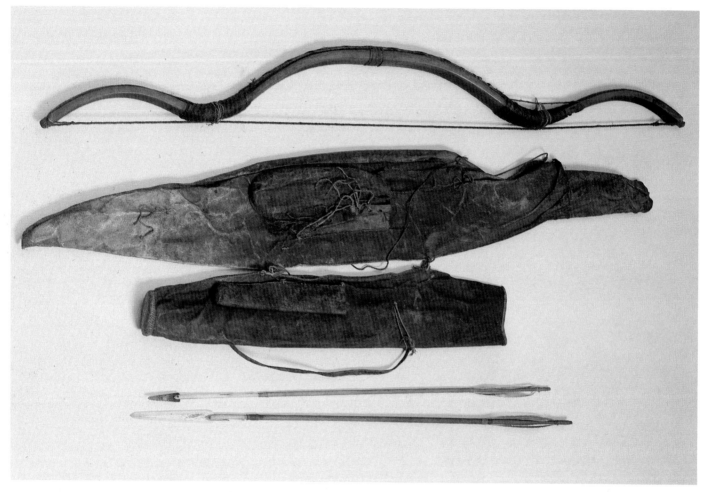

Top to bottom: Bow (Copper Eskimo, Victoria Island, Canada). Wood, sealskin, fiber; 137.5 cm long. Loaned by the University Museum, University of Pennsylvania, Philadelphia, #NA 4030B.

Bowcase and quiver (Copper Eskimo, Victoria Island, Canada). Sealskin, bone, cordage; 133 cm long. Loaned by the University Museum, University of Pennsylvania, Philadelphia, #NA 4030A.

Arrow (Copper Eskimo, Victoria Island, Canada). Wood, bone, steel, feather, sinew, copper; 85.7 cm long. Loaned by the University Museum, University of Pennsylvania, Philadelphia, #NA 4030L.

Arrow (Copper Eskimo, Victoria Island, Canada). Wood, ivory, bone, feather, sinew, copper; 92.3 cm long. Loaned by the University Museum, University of Pennsylvania, Philadelphia, #NA 4030R.

Back to front: Parka (Ungava/Labrador Eskimo, Belcher Islands, Canada). Sealskin, fur; 106 cm long. CMNH (Unaccessioned).

Parka (Baffinland Eskimo, Clyde River, Baffin Island, Canada). Caribou skin, fur; 113 cm long. CMNH #30947-1.

"The ingenuity of the Central Eskimo wardrobe provided another important element in the battle against wind and cold."

". . . [T]he skin-covered kayak was the chief watercraft: Light models for hunting in lakes and streams and heavier models for sea hunting were both used."
-David Damas

Kayak model (Ungava/Labrador Eskimo, Belcher Islands, Canada). Sealskin, wood, ivory, metal, sinew; 93 cm long. CMNH #32183-5.

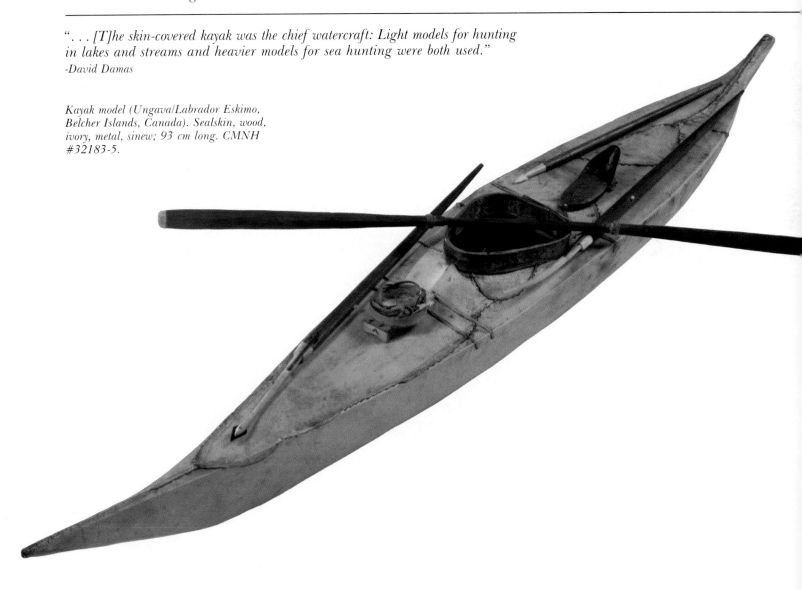

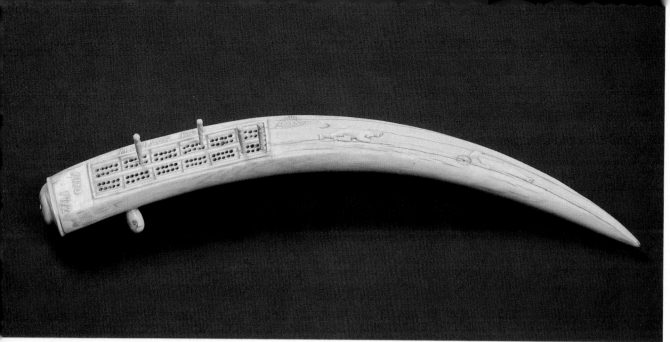

Cribbage board (Hudson Bay, Canada). Ivory,
50 cm long. CMNH #32078-1.

"... [I]nspired by the whalers, some Inuit perfected the art of scrimshaw, and,
consequently, an export trade in carved and engraved ivory developed ...."
-Nelson H. H. Graburn

"... [O]f no little importance to the native peoples of the Central Canadian
Arctic was the profusion of metal and wood available after the Franklin ships
were abandoned." *-James W. VanStone*

Top to bottom: Knife (Mackenzie Eskimo,
Mackenzie River Delta, Canada). Copper,
bone, hide, sinew; 43 cm long. CMNH
#23102-16530.

Knife (Provenience unknown). Bone, iron;
48.2 cm long. CMNH #23102-16527.

"Whaleboats were particularly significant trade items in that they increased family mobility, generally improved hunting capability, and created new forms of leadership."
-James W. VanStone

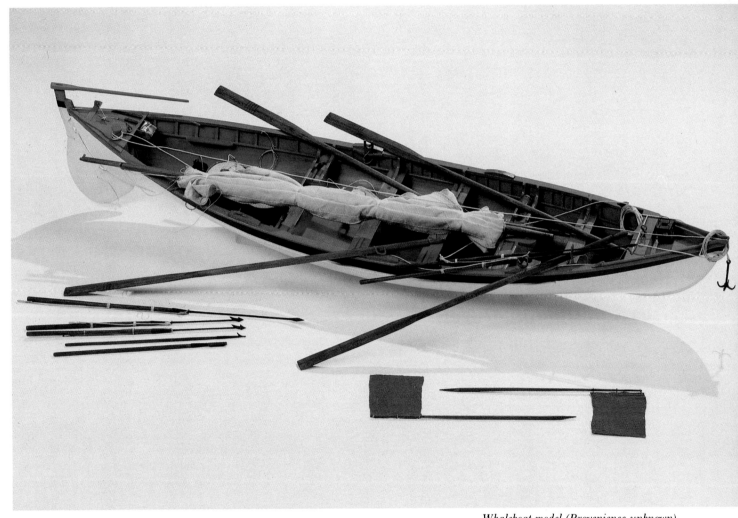

Whaleboat model (Provenience unknown). Wood, string, metal; 75 cm long. CMNH #24100-1.

Child's parka (Holman Island, Northwest
Territories, Canada). Wool, cotton, raccoon
fur, satin; 30.8 cm wide, 60 cm long.
CMNH #32142-2.

". . . Inuit women continue to sew beautiful parkas, mitts, and kamiks (boots)
out of traditional as well as introduced materials."
-Richard G. Condon

Woman's parka (Holman Island, Northwest
Territories, Canada). Wool, nylon, cotton,
timber wolf fur; 50.4 cm wide, 140 cm long.
CMNH #32142-1.

"... [M]odern Inuit material culture is still oriented toward the demands of ... coping with the extreme cold of the arctic climate."
-Richard G. Condon

Woman's boots (Holman Island, Northwest Territories, Canada). Sealskin, wool, leather; 20.4 cm long, 20.3 cm high. CMNH #32142-11.

Hunter dragging a seal by Tivi (Central Canada). Soapstone, 1960s-1970s, 17 cm high. CMNH #L-1980-4J.

" . . . [T]heir most intense interest focuses on the material and its possibilities rather than on the final form."

" . . . [A]spects of traditional culture such as igloos and tents, domestic activities . . . are also portrayed." -Nelson H. H. Graburn

Scene of summer camp by unknown artist (Pangnirtung, Northwest Territories, Canada). Paper, ink; 1972; 58 cm long. CMNH #31591-15.

"Some Inuit also view their arts as a chance to illustrate to their own children and to posterity 'what it was like to be Inuit,' because the younger generation has never known the . . . struggles for survival . . . ." -Nelson H. H. Graburn

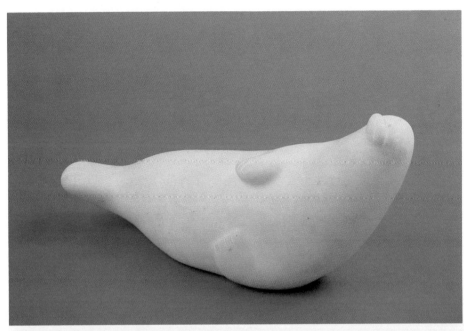

Seal by Ningeaseak (Cape Dorset, Northwest Territories, Canada) Quartzite, 1960s-1970s, 28.5 cm long. CMNH #31581-53.

Hunter and polar bear by unknown artist (Central Canada). Whalebone, 1970s, 36 cm high. CMNH #L-1980-4C.

"The term Arctic brings to mind cold, followed perhaps by thoughts of snow and ice, darkness and wind." -Mary R. Dawson

A View of Amundsen Gulf taken from Banks Island, Northwest Territories, Canada in October. The tracks in the snow (foreground) were made by a lone arctic fox (Alopex lagopus) searching for lemmings or other food. With the air temperature at minus 51 C (minus 60 F), the open water is freezing rapidly, in some cases forming "salt flowers" (center).

The Traditional Culture of the Central Eskimos

David Damas, Department of Anthropology,
McMaster University, Hamilton, Ontario

Hunting Birds from a Kayak. *As great flocks of waterfowl migrated north in the spring and summer, Eskimos hunted them from kayaks using the bird spear and throwing board. Use of the throwing board greatly increased the velocity and range of the bird spear.*

Introduction

Very few people have captured the public imagination as have the inhabitants of the Central Canadian Arctic who are known to anthropologists as the Central Eskimos. When the man on the street thinks of the Eskimo, his image is usually of someone who wears caribou fur clothing, lives in a snowhouse, drives a dogsled or navigates a kayak, lends his wife to other men as an expression of Northern hospitality, eats all of his meat raw, and prefers blubber above all other food. According to popular notions, Eskimos also abandon their old people and children in times of privation and live a short, precarious, but extremely active life. Most of these stereotypes are derived in some portion from fact. However, they can only be understood within the much larger context of environmental conditions and the unique history of the Central Eskimo.

The Life Cycle of the Central Eskimo

Each human in every society passes through a number of life events which provide a common base of human experience across cultural boundaries. In the case of the Eskimos, these important life events have had a special character, in part influenced by the conditions of life in the Arctic and in part reflecting customs which developed over centuries to become tenets of tradition.

When an Eskimo child was about to be born, the mother knelt inside the tent or snowhouse gripping a stick in her hands. She was assisted in childbirth by several of the village women. When birth was imminent, she uttered a series of names of deceased relatives. The name spoken when the infant emerged was the one the child carried through life unless some illness or accident brought him near death. After such events, the child would be called by the name of one of the other deceased relatives. Infants were usually nursed for long periods, even to the age of 5 or 6 if no other children were born to the mother before that time.

Very early in childhood the roles of males and females were ingrained;

These two Netsilik Eskimo girls, photographed in the early 1900s, were about 14 years old, the marriageable age.

children began early to imitate the activities of the appropriate parent. Children were shown great indulgence and only very gradually expected to master adult pursuits.

By the time a boy was eleven he began to accompany his father on hunting trips, to learn to handle the dogs, and to assist in building snowhouses. During his teens he made his first kills of caribou and seals. The first seal kill was often marked by special observances such as the practice of dragging the body of the seal over the boy as he lay in the snow. By the age of 17 or 18 the young man learned the adult male skills of traveling, hunting, and house building. If he were fortunate, by this age he also had acquired a wife.

Girls began to carry younger brothers or sisters on their backs as early as age 7 or 8 and by then had played at learning the various female household tasks. In most cases childhood was short for girls because they were betrothed at birth and married at puberty or even before; brides of twelve or thirteen were not uncommon in traditional times. The onset of marriage was marked by the very simple procedure of the bride moving her household implements into the dwelling of the groom. A number of these adolescent marriages failed to endure and were simply terminated by the girl leaving with her household possessions.

In spite of the apparent casualness of marriage arrangements among the Central Eskimos, an amazing number of marriages did persist throughout the lifetime of both partners. A few men in each Central Eskimo region had two or more wives, and, less frequently, women had two spouses. However, such joint unions were usually short lived.

Central Eskimo women were generally quite fertile and a fairly large number of children were born to most women. Nevertheless, infant mortality was always high. Infanticide was also practiced in some regions.

Adult life had its share of misfortunes and hardships as was decreed by the harsh climate and many uncertainties of life in the Arctic. At the same time the joys of parenthood, of companionship, and of success in life pursuits known to all people were not unfamiliar to the Central Eskimos. The stress of the climate and the rugged way of life undoubtedly played a role in bringing on rapid aging. Despite the fact that some of the diseases known to civilized people were absent from the Eskimos, few people lived beyond the age of 60.

When a person died, some of his important tools and possessions were left with the body. Burial as we know it was a rare phenomenon because even in midsummer the ground remains frozen a few centimeters (inches) below the surface. People who died during the warmer months were usually wrapped in skins and left on the surface of the land. A sled or kayak was sometimes left with a dead man. During winter, corpses were walled into snowhouses. Shortly after the death, the people of the village usually moved to another site.

The Central Eskimo Tribes and their Habitats

While the events in an individual's life cycle were probably similar throughout the Central Canadian Arctic, regional differences existed both in habitats and in many aspects of culture. The people of the Central Arctic referred to themselves as *Inuit* or "human beings" but used other, less flattering, terms of reference for Indians or people of European descent. The various regional groups of Eskimos were identified by their neighbors in terms which described characteristics of their hunting districts. Thus, for example, the term *Kiluhikturmiut* indicated "people of the head of the deep fjord," *Aivilingmiut* indicated "people of the place of the walrus" and *Utkuhiksalingmiut* indicated "people from the place of material for cooking pots."

Anthropologists have used larger divisions in referring to the various Central Eskimo subgroups. These divisions have been based on a shared culture and dialect; often the divisions also comprised the universe of people from which marriage partners were chosen.

The major anthropological divisions of the Central Eskimos include the Copper Eskimos of the regions

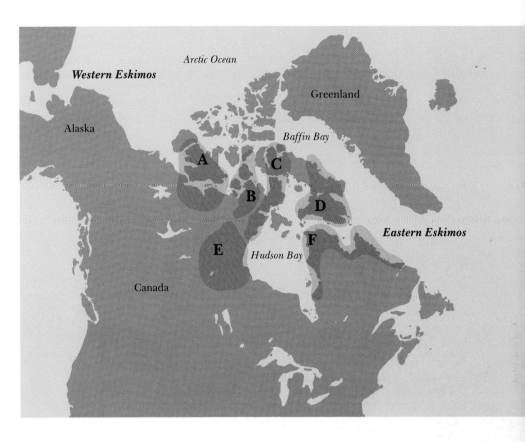

of Victoria Island and Coronation Gulf; the Netsilik Eskimos of King William Island, the Back River and Boothia Peninsula; the Iglulik Eskimos of Melville Peninsula and Northern Baffin Island; and the Baffinland Eskimos of the remainder of Baffin Island. In addition, the Caribou Eskimos represent a late movement into the Keewatin interior and the natives of Ungava-Labrador are considered transitional to the Eastern Eskimo groups.

There are distinct environmental zones which divide the Central Canadian Arctic. Each of these zones was inhabited by one or more Eskimo groups. The Copper and Netsilik Eskimos inhabited an area within which the islands and the mainland are connected during winter by a continuous expanse of stationary ice. The ice limited winter hunting largely to sealing at breathing holes. In this region of sparse resources, where famine was not unusual, the inhabitants resorted to such measures as infanticide and abandonment of the aged and infirm.

Distribution of the Central Eskimo Tribes

Key

Location of the Central Eskimo Tribes 1700-1900
A. *Copper Eskimos*
B. *Netsilik Eskimos*
C. *Iglulik Eskimos*
D. *Baffinland Eskimos*
E. *Caribou Eskimos*
F. *Ungava/Labrador Eskimos*

**Comparison of Typical Seasonal Activities
for the Copper, Netsilik, and Iglulik
Eskimos.**

	Jan.	Feb.	March	April	May	June	July	Aug.	Sept.	Oct.	Nov.	Dec.

Copper Eskimos

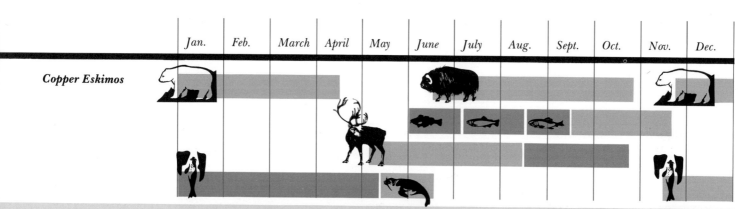

Eskimos lived on sea ice in large aggregations	Eskimos led nomadic life on land in small groups	Eskimos gathered at fish runs in large groups	Eskimos lived near the seashore in large aggregations

Netsilik

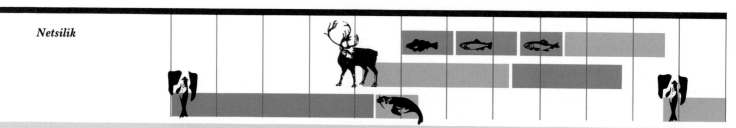

Eskimos lived on sea ice in large aggregations	Eskimos led nomadic life on land in small groups	Eskimos gathered at fish runs in large groups	Eskimos lived near the seashore in large aggregations

Iglulik

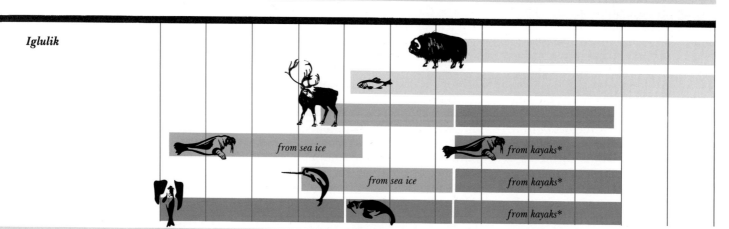

from sea ice

from kayaks*

from sea ice

from kayaks*

from kayaks*

Eskimos lived on sea ice in large aggregations as well as in smaller groups	Eskimos lived on sea ice in small groups	Eskimos lived near the seashore in small groups	Older men lived near the sea-shore; younger men lived inland	Eskimos lived near the seashore in large aggregations

Key

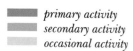 primary activity
 secondary activity
occasional activity

 polar bear   seal (at breathing-hole)

 musk-ox   seal (basking)

walrus   tomcod

narwhal   lake trout

caribou   char

Although all Eskimo groups used kayaks for hunting in rivers and lakes, the Iglulik also had large, ocean-going kayaks.

Adapted from David Damas, "Environment, History, and Central Eskimo Society," Contributions to Anthropology: Ecological Essays. National Museums of Canada Bulletin 230 (Ottawa, 1969).

The Iglulik Eskimos and the Eskimos of Baffinland occupied a second, more easterly, environmental zone. Fringed by open water areas in winter, this area allowed, in addition to breathing hole sealing, other occupations. These included the hunting of walrus through the thin ice which sometimes forms off the landfast ice floe edge. Conditions for survival were generally better than in the zone of the Copper and Netsilik Eskimos. Starvation was infrequent and the population control measures practiced by these latter people were usually absent. In this more eastern zone, sea-mammal hunting was also more highly developed and practiced throughout various seasons. In addition to winter hunting, the basking seals were commonly stalked in the spring and additional sea mammals were pursued from the kayak in the summer. Where driftwood was plentiful, as in Southern Baffinland, the umiak could be built and was used for travel and, sometimes, for whale hunting. Elsewhere, the skin-covered kayak was the chief watercraft: Light models for hunting in lakes and streams and heavier models for sea hunting were both used.

The Eskimos of the Ungava region south of Hudson Strait and those of the east coast of Hudson Bay shared an environmental zone similar in many respects to that of the Baffinland and Iglulik Eskimos. Along with the similar environment, the cultures shared many common features.

A third zone is found in the interior of the Keewatin area just west of Hudson Bay. Toward the end of the 18th century, this region became the home of the Caribou Eskimos who probably moved inland from the Hudson Bay coast when conditions for sea hunting worsened. Enormous herds of caribou which migrated through this region in the spring and in the fall were the chief

quarry of this Eskimo group. With the almost complete abandonment of sea-mammal hunting, the Caribou Eskimos represent an extreme adaptation. Often life was difficult for these people who spent winter in unheated snowhouses and frequently suffered privation. By the end of winter, stores of caribou meat often ran low and fish could not be reached through the thick lake ice.

The Eskimos living along the eastern coast of Labrador inhabited a relatively rich environment; their lifestyle closely resembled that of the Greenland Eskimos. Both groups had permanent winter dwellings and villages and practiced sea-mammal hunting and salmon fishing.

Yearly Cycle of the Central Eskimo
Just as the culture of the Eskimos continually changed throughout their long history, so too has each individual Eskimo's life been a response and adaptation to everchanging conditions. Each season brought its tone of life, its complex interaction of culture and habitat, and its particular pace. The very nature of the Arctic regions dictated that flux was ever-present. Nothing remained very much the same from week to week, from month to month and, especially, from season to season.

The extremes of the arctic zone had profound effects on most phases of Eskimo life. Not only did the fluctuations in temperature through the seasons involve changes in housing and in wardrobe, but they also affected methods of hunting and modes of travel. The freezing and thawing of the sea and of lakes and rivers along with the presence or disappearance of snow and the substantial variations in the amount of daylight which characterize arctic seasons—these together formed a background for the shifting patterns of economic and social life.

A number of barbed prongs attached to the center of the shaft provided a wider striking area. Several birds could be caught in one throw. The wings, neck, and feet of a struck waterfowl became wedged in the prongs.

Bird spear *(Provenience unknown). Wood, ivory, hide; 160 cm long. CMNH #13239-38.*

The fish spear was constructed with somewhat flexible prongs. After a fish was speared, the prongs were pulled apart and the fish easily removed.

Fish spear (Ungava/Labrador Eskimo, Povungnituk, Canada). Wood, ivory, metal; 168 cm long. CMNH #28492-19.

A group of Copper Eskimos is pictured spearing fish at a weir. The weir is composed of approximately four stone dams constructed along a shallow spot in a river. As the arctic char migrate upstream, they pass through narrow gaps in the lower dams that channel them into a completely enclosed upper dam. Here, the entrapped fish are easily caught.

The Copper Eskimo hunters are dressed in caribou-skin clothing. Both large and small land animals were hunted with the bow and arrow. The effective range of this weapon was from 68 to 80 meters (74 to 87 yards), although 27 meters (30 yards) was about the maximum range for an immediate kill.

Summer Life. The warmest months of the year marked the time of greatest dispersal for Central Eskimo groups. The land resources were most scattered at that time, because the caribou split into small groups after their spring migration northward from the tree line. Small game and migratory birds could be found almost anywhere, but their specific whereabouts was often unpredictable. Although fish could be caught in lakes and streams, they were never plentiful until the end of summer when the arctic char returned from the sea. The summer for the Copper, Netsilik, and Caribou Eskimo groups is best described by the anthropologist Jenness (1971) as follows:

. . . [T]he traveller will find scattered families roaming about from place to place, here today and gone tomorrow in their restless search for game. Days of feasting alternate with days of fasting according to their failure or success. No fowl of the air, no creature of the land, no fish of the waters is too great or too small to attract their notice at this time.

a time of greater specialization with simultaneous use of sea and land resources by different elements of the population. In those regions the younger, more mobile men and their immediate families moved inland and hunted and fished in much the same manner as the people farther west. These younger Iglulik and Baffinland Eskimos carried kayaks which they used to intercept caribou when they swam across lakes and streams. Small groups of older men, on the other hand, hunted in the sea. Heavier, less portable kayaks were used in pursuit of walrus, seals, narwhal, and the white whale.

In late summer, during August and September, the caribou were at their fattest and the new fur was suitable for clothing material. The caribou were, therefore, hunted most energetically at that season even though the herds were often still dispersed. Sometimes it was difficult for each hunter to secure enough skins to provide a complete new winter wardrobe for all his family members each year.

Any meat and fish not eaten immediately had to be dried. Strips of meat and fish were dried using the sun and wind because the Central Eskimos did not have wood or other fuel that could be used for smoking. With rain and fog being frequent occurrences during arctic summers, it took many days for the meat to dry properly.

Eskimos who hunted in the sea during the summer collected the blubber of sea mammals for winter fuel; the blubber was stored in skins of seals for later use. In spite of problems encountered in the summer, the people of the Canadian Arctic had an ideal natural method of food preservation for much of the year: For about nine months, freezing weather insured food preservation.

The great dispersal of people during the summer period resulted in less interaction. From time to time, however, bands of people met either by accident or according to plan and certain ceremonial events such as dancing, athletic contests, and games were held to lighten their lives.

It should be clear then that the coming of warmer weather with melting snow and ice did not herald days of unlimited plenty for these groups. This was a period of almost continual shifting of camps necessitated by the dispersed nature of the chief resources.

One of the effects of this omnivorous and free-ranging life was the fragmentation of groups according to the nature of their quarries. In the case of the Copper Eskimo, the exigencies of survival during the summer at times forced splitting of groups to the individual families of husband, wife, and small children. Larger groups tended to aggregate for those types of activities requiring a communal effort, such as caribou drives and fishing for char in weirs. Among the Netsilik Eskimos and Caribou Eskimos, summer groupings of about 10 to 20 people included a husband and wife, their married sons, their wives, and a number of small children.

In the country of the Iglulik and Baffinland Eskimos the summer was

119

Tools for sewing skin clothing, such as the two awls (center), thimble and holder (top), were often attached to the needle case (bottom). Bone, ivory, or metal needles were kept inside the hollow bone case.

Needle case with awls, thimbleholder, and thimble (Provenience unknown). Bone or ivory, hide, stone; 39 cm long. CMNH #23102-15573.

This style of scraper was used to soften caribou and other animal skins.

Skin scraper (Central Canada). Bone, 18 cm long. CMNH #L-1980-4 DD.

Autumn Life. As the days grew shorter and the nights longer, snow covered the ground and the lakes and streams froze. The inland roaming groups slowly made their way back to traditional gathering places, hunting and fishing through lake ice along the way. At times small numbers of musk-oxen and other game were encountered. After the musk-oxen were herded into a circular defensive formation with the aid of dogs, attempts were made to kill the entire herd.

In the Keewatin region west of Hudson Bay autumn was the time of the gathering and southward migration of the great caribou herds. Large groups of Caribou Eskimos came together for cooperative hunts. Positioned in kayaks, they intercepted the herds at crossing places; the caribou were also lanced or shot at from firing pits that were situated at the ends of converging rows of *inuksuit*, piles of stones constructed to appear like men and frighten the caribou.

Autumn was the most important time of the year for the Caribou Eskimo. Unlike other Eskimo groups, these people could not rely on seal hunting during the coldest and darkest months of the year. Therefore, it was extremely important to collect large stores of food when the great herds were present.

Sometime during October, when the snow drifts were hard enough to provide building material, snow-houses were constructed. At times, cold weather had to be endured in tents before conditions were right for snow-house building. Autumn gatherings at points of land near the sea were important occasions for reunification of kindred as well as for sewing the winter garments of caribou skin.

Tradition dictated that before the winter sealing could commence, garments had to be sewn in snow-houses built on the land. This practice related to an Eskimo belief in the importance of separating the products of the sea from those of land. The Sea Goddess who controlled the availability of sea mammals was believed to live in a cave at the bottom of the sea. If one of the numerous taboos that kept sea and land animals apart was broken, she could withhold the supplies of seals and walrus, narwhals and beluga whales.

Since the Caribou Eskimos had divorced themselves from the sea, they had a different set of traditions and deities. The Caribou Eskimos' chief deity was Pinga, the god of the air and winds.

Another important Iglulik and Baffinland Eskimo event emphasized the preoccupation with dividing the things of the land from things of the sea, as well as the change of seasons. This was the annual autumn tug of war. During the tug of war, those born during the time of year when people lived in tents, called squaw ducks, opposed those born in snow-houses, called the ptarmigans. The squaw ducks, true to the watery home of their namesakes, stood on the ice of the sea and the ptarmigans, representing as they did birds of the land, stood on the shore. Each side tugged on a sealskin rope until one side or the other was pulled from its base. If the ptarmigans won, it was believed that the winter would be longer and more severe than usual; if the squaw ducks won, the winter would be milder than usual. Farther west, among the Netsiliks, although the tug of war was not held, the squaw ducks' and ptarmigans' struggle over the length of seasons was preserved in myth.

After waiting motionless, sometimes for hours in the bitter cold, the Eskimo hunter thrust his harpoon into the breathing hole as the seal surfaced. Usually, the harpoon head penetrated the seal's body; the seal was pulled from the hole by the line attached to the harpoon head.

Winter Life. The period of time spent at the place for sewing garments depended in part on the amount of food accumulated during the summer and fall and in part on considerations of the rules for separating land and sea animals. While normally most Central Eskimo bands moved to the sea ice before the food stores had been exhausted, at times definite privation was suffered before the sewing of the caribou garments was completed. Among the Copper Eskimos, the sewing of winter garments had to be completed during two to four weeks in November because the products of the summer and autumn hunts were usually exhausted by the beginning of December. In more favorable locations, such as the Iglulik region around Repulse Bay, people could remain at the sewing place until some time in March. These people lived during that period on dried frozen fish and caribou meat and used the blubber accumulated in spring and summer sealing for fuel.

After this phase of the yearly cycle, the Central Eskimos (except for the inland dwelling Caribou Eskimos) moved to the frozen sea where they spent the remainder of the winter. Snowhouse villages were built on the smooth ice of gulfs, straits, or on the landfast floes that bordered areas of open water or drifting ice. Here, seals were hunted at their breathing holes.

Each autumn the newly forming ice traps the seals; each seal, thus, maintains several breathing holes. Although rapidly covered with snow, the holes can still provide air to the seals. Eskimos could locate the snow-covered holes only with the help of specially trained dogs.

Because every seal maintains a number of such holes, the chances of capture increased according to the number of holes covered by waiting hunters. For this very basic reason, groups of about 100 lived together during the winter sealing season. Generally, groups of 20 to 25 hunters had the best chance of reaping a reasonably rich return from a seal hunt.

If sealing were favorable in an area, the village might maintain one location throughout the winter. But, as was usually the case among the Netsilik and Copper Eskimos, an area of about an 8 kilometer radius (5 miles) would be hunted for about a month and the village then relocated at a distance of about 16 kilometers (10 miles). The move would open another previously unhunted area. Sixteen kilometers (10 miles) was also about the maximum day's travel possible, because only one or two dogs could be maintained by each hunter and men and women had to help pull the heavily loaded sleds.

These Copper Eskimo snowhouses were built on the sea ice. Sealing harpoons are planted in the walls; sleds are raised on snow blocks to keep them from being buried in the snow and to prevent dogs from eating their rawhide lashings.

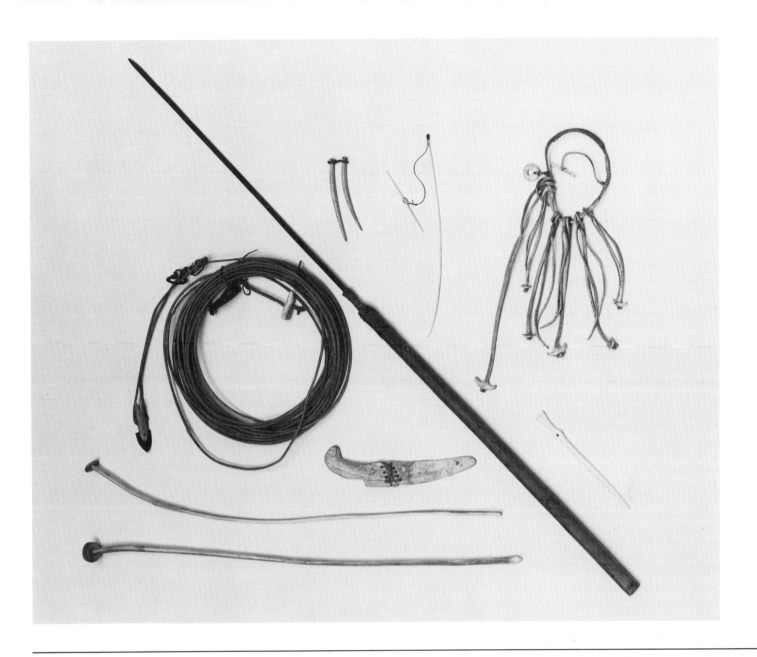

When Eskimos hunted seals at their breathing holes, these items were basic to their tool kit.

The harpoon shaft was fitted with the harpoon head and line. The length of the shaft was roughly equivalent to the height of its owner.
Harpoon shaft (Ungava/Labrador Eskimo; Great Whale River, Canada). Wood, steel, hide; 146.5 cm long. CMNH #11843-4.

(Clockwise:)

The seal indicator was inserted in the breathing hole until it almost touched the water. As the seal came to the breathing hole, it pushed against the indicator and provided a signal to the waiting hunter.
Seal indicator (Copper Eskimo; Victoria Island, Canada). Ivory, string; 58 cm long. Loaned by the University Museum, University of Pennsylvania, Philadelphia, #NA 4047.

An ivory toggle on the seal drag line was placed through a hole in the captured seal's lower jaw so that the hunter might transport the seal.
Seal drag line (Baffinland Eskimo; Cumberland Sound, Canada). Hide, ivory;

52 cm long. Courtesy of the Department of Anthropology, American Museum of Natural History, New York, #60/3127 B.

Two harpoon rests were pushed into the snow. While the hunter waited for the seal, the harpoon was supported on the rests.
Harpoon rest (Iglulik Eskimo; Repulse Bay, Canada). Bone, 25 cm long. Courtesy of the Department of Anthropology, American Museum of Natural History, New York, #60/6629 B.

The hunter enlarged the breathing hole with the snow knife and also used it to cut snow blocks for a seat and a protective barrier.
Snow knife (Iglulik Eskimo; Lyons Inlet, Canada). Bone, twine; 30.5 cm long. Courtesy of the Department of Anthropology, American Museum of Natural History, New York, #60/5315.

The seal breathing-hole tester was used to locate the center of the breathing hole, to determine its height, and to test ice and water conditions.
Seal breathing-hole tester (Copper Eskimo; Coronation Gulf, Canada). Bone, copper; 88 cm long. Courtesy of the Department of

Anthropology, American Museum of Natural History, New York, #60/6930.

The snow probe was used to determine the exact position of the breathing hole.
Snow probe (Copper Eskimo; Coronation Gulf, Canada). Bone, 89.5 cm long. Courtesy of the Department of Anthropology, American Museum of Natural History, New York #60/6941.

Once the harpoon head penetrated the seal's body, it slipped off the shaft and became lodged under the skin and blubber. The seal was retrieved with the line attached to the harpoon head.
Harpoon head and line (Provenience unknown). Hide, sealskin, bone, metal, ivory, sinew, baleen, tooth; 37 cm diameter. CMNH #9561-3.

The wound plug was placed in the wound made by the harpoon point to prevent an excessive loss of blood; seal blood formed an important part of the Eskimo diet.
Wound plugs (Copper Eskimo; Coronation Gulf, Canada). Bone, hide; 16 cm long. Courtesy of the Field Museum of Natural History, Chicago, #176057 A and B.

Eskimos, such as the Copper Eskimo family pictured here, frequently moved their villages during winter when seals became scarce around a village. All belongings were packed on sleds and pulled by men, women, and dogs to more favorable sealing grounds.

Dog Sled Assembly. The dog sled was the traditional method of travel over snow and ice. The flat, treeless terrain allowed the Central Eskimos to attach dogs to the sled in a fan-hitch arrangement. The basic sled had two wooden runners, 3 to 7 meters (10 to 24 feet) long, connected by cross bars. A thick thong (called a leader), looped across the front of the sled, held the dog traces (lines). One end of each dog trace was attached to the leader by a dog trace eye. The other end of the trace was attached to the dog's harness. The varying length of the dog traces resulted in the fan-hitch formation. One disadvantage of the fan hitch was that the dogs' traces continually became tangled during travel; frequent stops were, thus, necessary to separate them.

In the Iglulik area around Foxe Basin and in some parts of Baffinland Eskimo country, walrus hunting was another important winter occupation. Onshore winds bring cakes of floating ice to pack along the shore. While the ice floes are held in place by the winds, the adjoining edges begin to freeze. After feeding underwater on shell fish, a walrus rises to the surface and breaks through the newly formed ice in order to breathe. Walrus hunters traveled over ice cakes and the heaving surfaces of new ice to the points where walrus breathe. If a walrus were harpooned, traces were strung through its lip and the huge animal was dragged out onto the surface. The meat of even one walrus could feed a large number of people and dogs for a substantial period.

Walrus hunting was, however, highly dangerous. In addition to the possibility of frozen feet or drowning, winds could shift the newly formed ice and older ice cakes could break loose, leaving the hunters afloat at sea.

In contrast to Eskimos of the other areas, for the Caribou Eskimos, winter was a period of relatively slack activity. This group usually lived on the caribou killed during the big autumn drives and whatever fish they could obtain from the lakes. Although they tried to hunt whatever caribou remained in the country, the noise of a stalking hunter carried far in the cold air. If the caribou were not frightened off by the approaching hunter, it was still necessary to get within close range for the bow and arrow to hit its target.

For the Central Eskimos, social life climaxed during the winter months spent in the large villages. Even though men left and returned to camp in the dark, during December and January the hours for hunting were short. Many hunting days were lost because of storms. The drifting winds were often too cold and visibility too poor for successful hunting. A number of activities helped to pass the time during the long nights and storms. A large snowhouse called the *qagli* was specially built for these social activities.

Among the popular pastimes of the Central Eskimos were wrestling and certain trapeze tricks performed on a rawhide rope strung across the inside of the large ceremonial house. Disputes were sometimes settled by a form of fisticuffs witnessed by the village members who crowded into the *qagli*.

At other times the drum dance dominated the evening's activities. One large drum, sometimes as much as 1.23 meters (4 feet) in diameter, was used by the chief dancer and singer. The other members of the gathering usually formed a chorus. Sometimes the drum dancer sang songs of derision directed at other members of the group who had offended him in some way. These songs provided a surprisingly effective means of social control. However, the derided person might also reply with lampoons of his own as he banged the rim of the drum.

In the minds of the Central Eskimos, perhaps the most important gatherings were held to witness a shaman's performances. When the howling winds prevented the hunters from going to their breathing holes, inside the community house, seal oil lamps cast long, distorted shadows against the walls as the villagers attended the shaman's seances. These performances were not only prompted by bad weather but were held for other reasons such as sickness or the failure of game to appear.

Seances usually included tricks which served to prove the supernatural powers of the shaman. Skillful practitioners could effect ventriloquism so that it appeared that a voice of a spirit was coming from outside the house. Others could also bring on mass hypnosis to the extent that the audience could be convinced that the shaman was plunging a knife into his breast or reaching through the floor of the *qagli* to fetch objects from the bottom of the sea.

At times shamans would stage battles with evil spirits, showing the blood and bones of the defeated spirit. Such exhibitions convinced the people that whatever evil had

A Copper Eskimo man is shown beating a caribou-skin drum.

befallen them would be removed. Sometimes shamans also claimed to communicate with the Sea Goddess and, in doing so, learned which of her taboos had been broken and thus caused the bad weather, sickness, or lack of game.

The larger gatherings of winter also brought to the fore some of the important social ties which were unrealized during the summer period of dispersal. At such times, kinship ties, based either on blood relationships or those established through marriage, were extended and recognized beyond the immediate family. The obligations of kinship, whether those of food sharing, sharing of possessions, aid to aged or orphaned persons, were most evident during the winter period. In fact, those populating the winter village were usually interlinked by a continuous chain of such obligatory relationships.

Among most groups, snowhouses were built in compounds or clusters with the occupants consisting of father, mother, unmarried children, and married sons and their families. Only among the Copper Eskimos was the household confined to the nuclear family of husband and wife and unmarried children. Yet, even the Copper Eskimo sometimes expanded his family by the addition of an unmarried brother or sister of either spouse or by one of the widowed parents.

In addition to such ties of kinship which form the primary social cement in many societies, the Central Eskimos displayed great elaboration of partnerships which crosscut and expanded the kin network. Individuals often chose partners for whom special affection was felt. Some partners were based on sharing of the same name, or being born during the same month of the same year. Joking partners were those who would engage in witty and often ribald banter whenever they met. Other partners engaged in boxing or wrestling matches without malice. Special respect relationships with an individual involved avoiding the use of his or her name or avoiding direct communication with that person.

Anthropologists usually interpret such relationships as outlets for tensions built up under conditions of close personal contact where restrictions are placed on outbursts of temper or physical violence. This interpretation seems to apply to the Central Eskimo.

Another partnership system involved more practical considerations. The Eskimos had very definite and sometimes exceedingly precise rules for sharing food. The seal-sharing partnerships of the Copper and Netsilik tribes are a case in point.

As noted earlier, winter seal hunting, out of necessity, involved cooperative relationships. When a man brought home a seal, his wife would butcher it on the floor of the snowhouse. Specific portions were given to the children of the man's seal-sharing partners who came to the home representing their fathers. Thus, the liver would be given to the child of the "liver companion," or the hind flipper to the child of the "flipper companion." When any of the other hunters were successful, they would reciprocate with that same part of the animal.

This system provided a specific means of compensating for the unpredictability of the outcome of hunting. Other game was, likewise, shared according to membership in the hunt. Special food gifts were also given to the elderly to assure them of sustenance when they were without other means of support.

Thus, winter villages, rather than being amorphous, loosely knit and fortuitous aggregations, achieved a measure of internal unity through the extensive ties of kinship, supplemented and reinforced by an intricate series of partnerships.

Unlike other societies, this inner unity was not necessarily dependent upon a village chief. Leadership did exist, however, within the family unit. Among the Central Arctic Eskimos there was often a leader or *isumataaq* ("one who thinks for others") for each extended family, with the oldest male usually assuming this leadership role. However, for the Copper Eskimo, no real leader existed above the head of the individual biological family.

The ulu, or woman's knife, was the all-purpose tool of the Eskimo woman. Large ulus were used to butcher, skin, and remove blubber or flesh from skins. Small ulus were used to cut and trim skins and for eating.

Ulu *(Central Canada). Bone, steel; 11.5 cm long. CMNH #L-1980-4 II.*

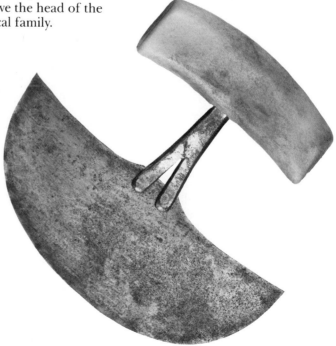

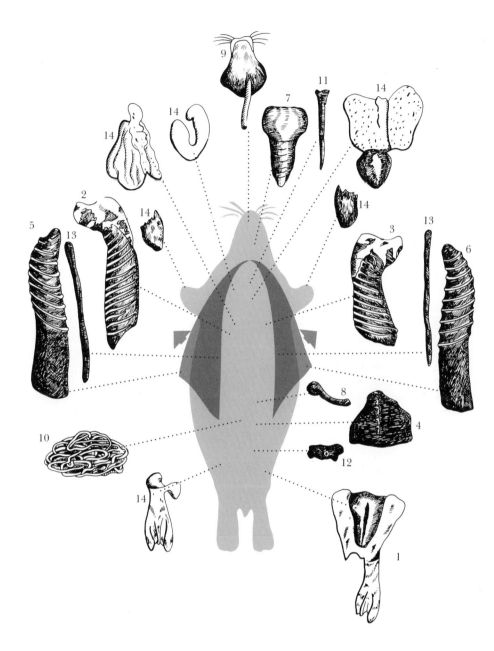

Seal Portions and their Pattern of Distribution to Seal-sharing Partners among the Netsilik Eskimos. *Both the Netsilik and Copper Eskimos had elaborate food-sharing partnerships with precise rules of distribution. When a man brought home a seal, his wife butchered the animal and distributed the portions to specific partners. This chart shows how the portions were distributed.*

1 = Rear portion that joins the spine and one rear flipper
2 = Ribs and front portion on the right side
3 = Upper ribs and front part on the left side
4 = Bottom four ribs on the left side and the end of the spine except for the last vertebra
5 = Right side of the belly
6 = Left side of the belly
7 = Neck and upper spinal column
8 = Two vertebrae and the fifth rib from the bottom on the left side
9 = Head
10 = Intestines
11 = Breastbone
12 = Last vertebra
13 = Slices from the flanks (given the village children)
14 = Viscera of the chest and abdominal remnants, stomach, dorsal membrane, front flippers, one rear flipper and the skin (given to the person who killed the seal)

Note:
The number of seal-sharing partners may vary; if there are fewer partners, the person who killed the seal would receive any remaining portions. The fat is distributed in a similar manner.

Adapted from Frans Van de Velde, O.M.I., "Rules Governing the Sharing of Seal after the 'Aglus' Hunt amongst the Arviligjuarmiut," Eskimo, Vol. 41 (1956).

Only among the Iglulik Eskimos was there a regular village-wide leader. Almost inevitably, the *isumataaq* of the entire winter village was the head of the largest close-knit kin group. His extended family and other relatives formed a nucleus to which other villagers attached through a variety of ties.

Inevitably, regardless of the mechanisms which worked toward unity and harmony, there were cases of conflict. While fisticuff contests and song duels served to defuse some conflicts, other means were necessary to settle more severe differences. In some cases, such as wife stealing or homicide, executions would be staged after agreement among the members of the community. However, the most common means of resolving disputes or responding to interpersonal frictions was withdrawal. With a network of kinship and other ties extending beyond the individual village to other tribal bands, it was usually not difficult to relocate if one did not find a particular group congenial. With the periodic reshuffling of people, resulting from various circumstances and conditions, shifts due to conflict did not receive major attention.

With the winter months came weather conditions considered to be among the worst known in the inhabited world. The Eskimos developed a number of techniques for adapting to the extreme weather conditions; these techniques have represented the supreme triumph of Eskimo culture over adverse environmental conditions.

One of the Eskimos' adaptations for fighting the cold was fortuitously provided by the all-meat diet. Even though the Central Eskimos' diet did not include carbohydrates as a source of quick energy, the slower burning fat and protein which made up the entirety of their diet kept the body warm for long periods. Raw meat also provided adequate amounts of vitamin C for their diet. Although probably an adaptation to the problem of fuel storage, the practice of eating raw meat undoubtedly kept the Eskimos from falling prey to scurvy, the bane of European sailors and polar explorers alike. When

sufficient seal oil was available, a meal of boiled meat and broth was served each day.

The ingenuity of the Central Eskimo wardrobe provided another important element in the battle against wind and cold. Caribou hide provided an ideal material for winter garments. While the heavier furs of autumn or winter-killed caribou were used largely for bedding, the lighter hides of animals killed in August and September were more flexible for clothing. When used in the customary double suit, these hides provided sufficient warmth for even the most severe weather conditions. The double suit was constructed with the fur toward the body in the inner suit and the fur facing outward in the over suit. Air heated by the body was trapped between the two layers of hide. In addition, each of the thousands of hollow hairs of the inner suit provided tiny reservoirs that stored the body heat. The suits of caribou fur were also skillfully cut so that easy movement was possible at all times. The large sleeve holes permitted the wearer to draw his arms inside and, thus, warm them against the body.

While the Central Eskimos did not have the earth and stone or whale-bone houses of their Thule forebears, the snowhouse provided adequate shelter from the cold winds. Snow was cut from a drift in blocks and used to build the dome which forms the walls and roof of the house. A snowhouse could be built by two people, with one doing the excavating and setting the blocks of snow in place from the inside and the second filling in the crevices between blocks with soft snow on the outside. The soft snow acted as cement to seal the blocks together and prevented wind from entering the house.

The snowhouse did not create an environment of tropical heat as did the permanent stone and sod houses of the Eskimos of Greenland and Alaska. Even when the stone lamps of seal oil were lighted, it was necessary to wear the inner suit of caribou furs. The snowhouse, however, did provide a windproof shelter that could not be matched by any tent. The seal oil lamps usually furnished

light and enough heat to melt snow and eventually to boil water for cooking. Clothes were usually dried by removing them and letting the body's moisture freeze in the garments as they lay on the floor. In the morning, the resulting frost was beaten loose from the garments with a stick.

The snowhouse rates as perhaps the greatest Eskimo invention. Building materials were usually at hand for about seven months of the year whether the builder was living on land or on the sea ice. In a land without plentiful supplies of wood and with the sod frozen for much of the year, it was a true godsend. The principle of the unsupported dome, achieved through blocks spiraling gradually inward as they formed the roof, was grasped by some early genius and provided the basis for a uniquely adaptive housing innovation.

While the Central Eskimos developed a number of clever hunting techniques which were practiced with great skill, the vagaries of the weather and game supply often brought on times of food shortages. These were most frequent during the winter months, given the weather conditions and the conditions of poor light which made hunting a difficult and uncertain business. Famine, together with the forced nomadic existence in many places, decreed that severe measures had to be taken.

At times of great cold and food shortages, when the fatigue of moving camp was most trying, elderly or disabled persons might ask to be left behind. Seldom were the aged or ill otherwise abandoned.

In times of famine, mothers also had difficulty providing milk for their babies. Caring for small infants was also a severe handicap while shifting camp. Under such circumstances, newborn infants were left exposed to the elements. Most often it was the female infants who suffered infanticide. Those Copper Eskimos and Netsiliks who practiced this measure extensively justified the selection of female infants on the basis that in such a hunting society the male's contribution was more valuable than that of the female.

Among the groups where female

infanticide was most widely praticed, the resultant shortage of women brought on some unfortunate social consequences. There was much rivalry over women, and wife stealing was a common social problem. At times homicide followed in its wake and might also expand into blood fueds.

Farther east, where economic conditions were superior, female infanticide was seldom practiced. More even sex ratios thus prevailed. However, with a greater emphasis on hunting at sea, men were sometimes lost to kayak drownings, thus causing a slight preponderance of females in the older age groups.

Spring Life. Toward the end of March, the days grew noticeably longer and warmer. Some Eskimos made excursions to regions where polar bears could be taken as their period of hibernation ended. Newborn seals could also be found in snow caves above the breathing holes of their mothers. For the most part, however, this period brought little change in the economic life and breathing-hole sealing continued as the chief activity until sometime in the latter part of May.

As the warm sun of May began to melt the roofs of snowhouses, most Central Eskimos covered them with skins or pitched tents within the walls of snow for shelter. For the Copper Eskimos and most Netsiliks, the season of sealing soon ended and the winter villages on the sea ice were abandoned.

As these Eskimos moved inland, trout and other fish caught through lake ice provided the most important source of food. Ducks and geese returning from the south were also useful sources of food.

Although caribou were now returning to the area in both small and large herds, they were generally not hunted because, during the spring, the animals are very lean and their hides burrowed by fly larvae. Caribou Eskimos, nonetheless, welcomed even this lean meat after the usual late winter and early spring food shortages.

As the spring sun began to melt their snow-houses built on the sea ice, the Copper Eskimos often erected dwellings with roofs made of skins and walls of snow. Snow blocks were used to form an entranceway and to insulate the sides of the structure.

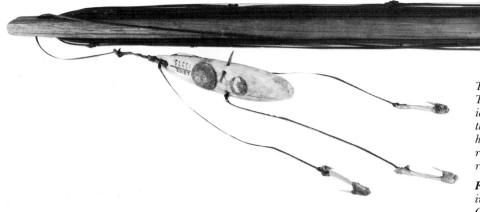

The fishing line was wound around the rod. The line was dangled through a hole in the ice. When the line was jigged up and down, the lure/sinker attracted fish to the hooks. A hooked fish was immediately hauled in and removed, and the hook and line rapidly returned to the water.

Fish jigger (Provenience unknown). Wood, ivory, baleen, stone, hide; 45 cm long. CMNH #23102.

An Eskimo woman is pictured jig fishing through lake ice. Both men and women fished for tomcod and lake trout through the ice. The chisel and scoop (left, middle) were used to make the hole in the ice. The snow knife (right) was used to construct the protective barrier of snow blocks as well as the seat.

Among the Iglulik and Baffinland Eskimos, the spring was the most productive period for sealing. The seals crawled from their holes which had been enlarged by melting and sunned themselves. Their naps were broken periodically by glances around the horizon for signs of approaching bears or men. Dressed in dark clothing, hunters stalked the seals by slowly crawling toward them while imitating their movements, thus, hoping to be mistaken for a fellow seal. Although it took great skill to approach close enough to harpoon a sunning seal, certain groups of Central Eskimos killed large numbers of the animal in this way.

Spring was also the great season of travel throughout the Central Eskimo region. The Iglulik Eskimos, thinly spread over a wide area and linked by a complex series of kinship ties, were the greatest travelers. They undertook trips of up to 960 kilometers (600 miles) during the course of a single spring, starting their journey when the sun reached substantial height and returning sometime in June before the ground was free of snow. These trips, thus, had various purposes including the arrangement of a marriage or a visit to relatives.

The long spring journeys of the Iglulik Eskimos were made possible by the availability of walrus as well as seal. Walrus provided food both for people and large teams of dogs. With sizeable dog teams it was possible to travel at intervals of 24 hours or more, stopping only briefly every few hours to rest the dogs and to untangle their traces.

The Copper Eskimos were also great travelers, but a shortage of dogs made it necessary for them to move in stages. The explorer and anthropologist Stefansson has told of such trips made by Copper Eskimos of Prince Albert Sound in Western Victoria Island. Nine-hundred-mile trips were made to the Thelon River in the Keewatin and back in order to trade with Caribou Eskimos who had direct access to trade goods. These trips, however, occupied periods of a year or more. Traveling began by dog sled and, as the snow melted, loads were carried overland by dogs

and humans. Copper Eskimos also made shorter trips to the tree line in order to get wood for tools and implements which were important to their material culture.

Regardless of the tribe or their motivation for travel, trips involved the danger of falling in with Indians or members of an alien Eskimo tribe. Small traveling groups were often raided; the men were killed and the women were captured along with any valuable goods.

In the ordinary rounds of travel, however, within a given tribal area, certain mechanisms could be employed to insure admittance into whatever group was encountered. One of these was the widely practiced Eskimo custom of spouse exchange. Through this system, which required approval by all involved, a quasi-kinship bond would be established between two Eskimo couples. Through spouse exchange, both couples and their children would be, henceforth, linked in a tight set of relationships.

Another mechanism for cementing relationships between the different bands of a tribe was partnerships established at dances. Trading partnerships also helped to alleviate hostilities or tensions when members of foreign tribes met. For example, when Iglulik and Netsilik Eskimos met at the base of Melville Peninsula, they channeled most of their trade through such formalized trading relationships.

Indeed, there was probably a great deal of intertribal trade even before the influence of white contact. Even the prehistoric cultures show evidence of such intertribal contact. Much of this trade resulted from uneven distribution of resources. For example, musk-oxen horns and hides, prized by the Iglulik Eskimos could be found in the Netsilik Eskimo region and were exchanged for walrus tusks and other products from large sea mammals.

Long before the hinterlands of the Northwest Passage were explored, trade goods from Churchill on Hudson Bay and from as far west as Siberia made their way into the Central Canadian Arctic. By the beginning of the 19th century, this

intertribal trade was well established and moved in a continuous link from Alaska to Hudson Bay. Later, intertribal trade was also stimulated by the discovery of abandoned exploring ships. Wood, metal, and other important products were discovered in Netsilik country aboard Ross's *Victory* and at the margins of the Copper Eskimo range aboard McClure's *Investigator*. In general, however, expeditions in search of the Northwest Passage or the missing Franklin parties had little effect on Eskimo economic and social life. The 19th century contacts of whalers at the eastern margins of the region did have greater impact, however. Through them, new goods were introduced into the regions, the yearly economic cycles were disrupted, and new diseases were introduced. Nevertheless, for most of these regions, it was not until trading posts were established in the second and third decades of the present century that the seasonal patterns of Inuit life were disturbed to any great degree. However, the stories of the fur trade, whaling, the establishment of missions, and government intervention and their impact upon the Central Canadian Eskimos are discussed by VanStone in the following chapter.

Reading List

Balikci, Asen. *The Netsilik Eskimos*. NY: Natural History Press, 1970.

Boas, Franz. *The Central Eskimo*. Lincoln, NE: University of Nebraska Press, 1964.

Freuchen, Peter. *Arctic Adventure*. 1935; rpt. NY: AMS Press, 1976.

Jenness, Diamond. *People of the Twilight*. Phoenix: Phoenix Books, 1971.

Rasmussen, Knud. *Across Arctic America*. 1927; rpt. Westport, CT: Greenwood, 1968.

Stefansson, Vilhjalmur. *My Life With the Eskimo*. NY: Collier Books, 1971.

Eskimos of Kotzebue Sound, Alaska, as depicted
by Ludwig Choris in 1816. From Choris, L.,
Voyage Pittoresque Autour du Monde.
(Paris: Fermin Didot, 1822).

Eskimo Culture Change: An Historical Perspective

James W. VanStone, Department of Anthropology,
Field Museum of Natural History, Chicago, Illinois

Introduction

Eskimos encountered in Southwest Greenland and along the coast of Labrador by Norse explorers in the 10th century A.D. were the first aboriginal New World inhabitants seen by Europeans. Although the Norse occupied Greenland until about 1500, their contacts with the Eskimos during this period were limited. Contacts between Eskimos and Europeans continued to be sporadic until the early 1700s and, in fact, isolated groups such as the Copper Eskimos may not have encountered outsiders until the early 20th century. Thus, in spite of limited early interaction with Europeans, Eskimos were among the last native peoples of North America to abandon their traditional way of life as a result of such interaction.

The most significant era of early contact began in the 18th century. In the Eastern Arctic, this era was marked by Denmark's re-establishment of the Greenland colony, and, in the west, by the coming of Russian fur hunters. The central Arctic regions remained isolated until the arrival of 19th century maritime expeditions searching for a Northwest Passage through North America. Whaling ships in Hudson Bay and the Mackenzie Delta were also significant agents of culture change. In the following pages these and other outside influences on Eskimo culture up to World War II (and more recently for Alaska) are examined.

In each of the three Arctic regions, the native people refer to themselves with different names. In Greenland native people refer to themselves as Greenlanders, in the Central Canadian Arctic they prefer to be called Inuit, whereas in Alaska they refer to themselves as Yupik or Inupiat Eskimos, depending on the language they speak. When referring to the native people of each region, the preferred designation is used in this chapter.

Europeans and Greenlanders

The natives of Greenland were the first inhabitants of the New World to have sustained interaction with Europeans. Norse settlers lived in Southwest Greenland from the 10th to the 15th century until their settlements eventually perished. Climate deterioration, loss of contact with Norway, and pressure from native neighbors are all possible explanations for the disappearance of the Norse from the area.

In the 16th and 17th centuries some of the first explorers searching for the Northwest Passage penetrated into Davis Strait and had brief encounters with Greenlanders. Dutch, Portuguese, and other European whaling ships also explored the area at about the same time. Of far greater significance, however, was the arrival of the Danish missionary Hans Egede in 1721. Egede came expecting to minister to the Norse settlements. Because they had long since disappeared, however, Egede concentrated his attention on converting the native population and establishing Danish influence.

Over the next 200 years there were a number of developments which had a profound effect on the culture of most Greenlanders. These developments, which resulted from both European contact and environmental factors unrelated to human activities, brought about significant habitat changes. Intensive whaling by Europeans throughout the 17th century, for example, virtually eliminated these large sea mammals which previously had played an important role in Greenlander subsistence. Since whales were also of considerable ceremonial importance, their decline had profound effects on the Greenlanders' ritual cycle.

A second significant development not related to the presence of man began during the 1920s. Oceanographic changes during this period resulted in the warming of the waters of the Labrador Sea. As a result, marine mammals no longer frequented the coast of Southwest Greenland in the same numbers characteristic of the past. As the seals and other marine mammals moved north, however, cod and other fish moved into coastal waters and formed the basis of commercial fishing that is of considerable importance to the Greenlanders of today.

A corresponding decline in the caribou population is also usually attributed to environmental changes rather than to the hunting activities of Greenlanders. Only in the Thule district of Northwest Greenland and the Angmagssalik district on the east coast have the natives been able to continue the basically traditional, seasonal round of subsistence activities. The persistence of these activities has been supported and encouraged by the Danish government.

The conversion of Greenlanders to Christianity took place through the establishment of a series of coastal mission and trading stations. As elsewhere in the Arctic, missionaries were gradually successful in undermining shamanisn through the introduction of church ritual and at least rudimentary health care. The missonaries' vigorous educational efforts were far more successful than those instituted among Eskimos elsewhere. By the 1860s a periodical

was being published in the Greenlandic language.

In 1774, the Danish government achieved a trade monopoly in Greenland which continued into the 1950s. Through this monopoly, an attempt was made to maintain reasonable prices and to control the types of goods offered to the Greenlanders. Efforts were also made to prohibit the export of subsistence materials, such as blubber and sealskins, which were deemed essential to the welfare of the Greenlanders. Even under such controlled, paternalistic conditions, however, trading posts introduced a variety of new, appealing items which greatly affected the basic Greenlander way of life.

In Greenland attempts to develop self-government and introduce social welfare programs began much earlier than in other Arctic regions. Representative councils were established in the 1860s on the local, regional, and provincial levels. These councils, consisting of Danish governmental, commercial, and medical representatives, as well as elected Greenlanders, were responsible for maintaining law and order, administering social programs, and exercising leadership in a variety of ways. Their activities were financed through a tax levied on items sold at the trading posts. This general pattern of representative government continued until the early 1950s, when a National Council was established for all of Greenland with 13 local municipal councils. At that time, Greenland also became a county of Denmark, with two elected members to the Danish Parliament.

The Western Impact on the Canadian Arctic

Although the first contact between Europeans and native North Americans took place when Norsemen from Greenland met the Skraelings, believed to have been Inuit, in Northern Newfoundland about A.D. 1000, further contact with Canadian Inuit did not take place until the 16th century.

In the 16th century, the seafaring nations of Europe were seeking a route through which merchants

could reach the Far East. Since the Spaniards were dominant in America and the Portuguese claimed a monopoly on trade by way of the Cape of Good Hope, the English were more or less forced to seek a Northwest Passage through northern waters. Thus, in 1576 the English navigator Martin Frobisher landed on the east shore of lower Baffin Island and sailed 150 miles up the Bay which today bears his name. Finding no end to it, Frobisher believed he had discovered the strait separating Asia and America. On two subsequent voyages, the navigator sought gold, and the Inuit he encountered, rejecting his friendly gestures, kidnapped five of his men.

Equally unfriendly relations were experienced in 1610 by Henry Hudson. Following the English navigator's discovery of Hudson Bay, native people were encountered at the west end of Hudson Strait. An apparently unprovoked attack resulted in the expedition's losing four of its number.

Other explorers followed the route pioneered by Hudson: the Welsh explorer Thomas Button (1612), the Danish explorer Jens Munk (1619-1620), and the English explorers Luke Foxe (1631) and Thomas James (1631-1632). Their explorations revealed excellent harbors at the mouths of the Nelson and Churchill rivers on the west coast of Hudson Bay. When the Hudson's Bay Company was established in 1670, posts were built at these points to open a fur trade with the Indians of the interior.

During the first half of the 18th century, occasional voyages were made up the western coast of the Bay to establish trade with the Inuit. Some explorations were carried out in connection with these trading voyages, and by the 1760s it was clear that no Northwest Passage led from Hudson Bay. This fact was further confirmed by the Englishman Samuel Hearne who, after two unsuccessful attempts, made a long and hazardous journey overland from Fort Churchill northwest to the shores of the Arctic Ocean in 1770-1772. Accompanying a party of Chipewyan Indians who had come to

In 1576, Sir Martin Frobisher became the first Englishman to search for a northwest passage to China. Although Frobisher never discovered a passage, he did make contact with the Thule Eskimos of Baffin Island. Encounters between the English and Eskimos were generally hostile, and a number of battles were fought.

the fort to trade, Hearne passed north of Great Slave Lake and descended the Coppermine River to its mouth, thus becoming the first white man to reach the Arctic coast of North America.

In the second half of the 18th century, historical circumstances forced the Hudson's Bay Company to adopt a more aggressive trade policy. Montreal traders opened up trade routes by rivers and lakes across the continent, northwest to Great Slave Lake, and eventually to the Arctic Ocean. Traders on Hudson Bay were forced to move inland or see their trade cut off at its sources. Although there was no trade with Inuit by these interior routes, easy access was provided to areas occupied by Inuit. Meanwhile, along the west coast of Hudson Bay, the Hudson's Bay Company continued to send ships annually to trade with the Inuit. Products from the environment were traded for metal tools, glass beads, twine for netting, and, beginning in the 1770s, firearms. These trading voyages were discontinued after 1790, and only the more southern groups of Inuit traveled to Fort Churchill to trade and to be hired for brief periods in summer as hunters.

Serious efforts to discover a Northwest Passage were renewed in the 19th century, but commercial aims no longer supplied the impetus for the search. The British wished to confirm their territorial claims in the Arctic regions as well as to promote geography and the other natural sciences. Although it was obvious that Hudson Bay did not provide access to a passage, it was hoped that a route could be discovered farther north. The explorations of Captain John Ross (1818), Lieutenant Edward Parry (1819-20, 1824-25), John Franklin (1819-22), Lieutenant Edward Parry and Commander George F. Lyon (1821-23), Commander George F. Lyon (1824), and Captain John Ross (1829-33) all had at least some contact with and were assisted by Inuit.

Of particular interest was the last voyage of Ross who, during his first winter, was permanently ice-bound in Lord Mayor's Bay at the bottom of

When he sailed from England in 1845, Franklin was already a veteran arctic explorer. Unpredictable arctic ice conditions, however, brought this expedition to a disastrous end. For 20 months, Franklin's ships were trapped in ice to the north of King William Island. Franklin died there on June 11, 1847. The surviving crew members perished sometime during 1848 as they attempted an overland journey to the south.

Regent's Inlet. After three years, the crew finally escaped with the aid of whalers, but all would have perished had it not been for the assistance of the Inuit living on Boothia Peninsula. They not only supplied members of the expedition with fresh meat but also instructed James Ross, the Captain's nephew, in the techniques of sled travel. Previously, the British had explored the Arctic almost exclusively with ships or boats. The skills that Ross learned from the Inuit of Boothia Peninsula made possible the long journeys and extensive discoveries of the subsequent Franklin search expeditions.

In 1845, Franklin sought a navigable channel through the northernmost areas of the Arctic. By 1847, no word was received from Franklin and search parties were sent out the following year, providing a new impetus for arctic explorations. Between 1848 and 1859, 42 search parties were organized to approach the Arctic regions from the east; a few sought Franklin along the Bering Sea coast. Although Franklin was never found, the frontiers of geographical knowledge in virtually all regions of the Arctic were greatly expanded by the Franklin search expeditions.

Most of these expeditions had at least some contact with the Inuit, and of no little importance to the native peoples of the Central Canadian Arctic was the profusion of metal and wood available after the Franklin ships were abandoned.

About 1840, sustained relations with the Canadian Inuit were established by New England and Scottish whaling ships on northern and eastern portions of Baffin Island. Somewhat later, relations were established along the northwest shore of Hudson Bay. Many whaling ships spent the winter in the Arctic in order to take advantage of spring and summer whaling seasons. During the long periods of winter isolation, the whalers were, to a large degree, dependent on their contacts with local Inuit for food and clothing. The goods received in exchange by the Inuit were of considerable significance: They represented the first large-scale replacement of traditional Inuit material culture.

Inuit were employed to assist the whalers in hunting, particularly in spring when the open sea was navigable but the ships were still locked in the ice of a sheltered anchorage. These native whalers were

paid in trade goods. Firearms, greatly desired by the Inuit, brought about significant changes in hunting techniques. Their use made open-water hunting more important than the traditional ice hunting. With the necessity of obtaining continuous supplies of ammunition, firearms also committed the Inuit to continued contacts with whalers and, later, with trading posts.

This drawing of the American whaling fleet in winter quarters at Marble Island, Hudson Bay, Canada (1878-1879) was done by Henry Klutschak, a member of the Schwatka expedition that searched for information about Sir John Franklin. Ships are shown frozen in ice and insulated with snow blocks.

Early missions, such as this one pictured on Southampton Island, Hudson Bay, Canada, in 1930, provided the Inuit with essential health care and educational services. At the time, such services were not being supplied by the government.

Thus diverted from full-time subsistence activities by the demands of the whale fishery, the Inuit also gave up to some degree their traditional settlement patterns since the acquisition of whale boats encouraged them to settle along the coast in summer. They were likely to cluster around a whaling base which might eventually become the site of a trading post. Whaleboats were particularly significant trade items in that they increased family mobility, generally improved hunting capability, and created new forms of leadership.

It is clear, therefore, that in a variety of ways, commercial whaling had an extremely disruptive influence on traditional Inuit life. As the first sustained agent of contact in the Canadian Arctic, whaling created many of the problems for arctic peoples with which government agencies had to cope at a later date. In addition to the introduction of manufactured goods, the whalers, as well as the early explorers, brought a variety of exotic diseases that took a fearful toll among a people who had no natural immunity to them. These diseases resulted in a severe depletion of the Inuit population in most areas of the Arctic.

By the beginning of the 20th century, commerical whaling was no longer profitable and intensive hunting had severely depleted the whale population. Baleen, the long flexible strips in the whale's mouth used for filtering food, had been valued for a variety of commercial purposes. In addition to taking large quantities of baleen with their own vessels, whalers traded with the Inuit for baleen. When the demand for baleen fell, the whaling ships departed and Inuit were left with a depleted resource base as well as a loss of access to trade goods.

Fortunately, for the welfare of many Inuit, another local resource attracted the interest of outsiders at about this time. The trapping of fur-bearing animals, particularly the Arctic fox, became important and the Inuit, like the Indians in the Canadian Subarctic, were swept into the uncertainties of a trapping trading economy.

During the period of baleen whaling, the Hudson's Bay Company did not extend its operations into the Far North but was content to operate from its traditional subarctic bases. Between 1900 and 1920, however, not only the Hudson's Bay Company but other trading companies and independent traders moved north to take advantage of the increased demand for furs on the world market. Even more than the whalers, the traders encouraged the Inuit to become dependent on imported products and to emphasize the trapping of white foxes at the expense of their traditional subsistence activities.

In 1903 the Canadian government for the first time began to exercise jurisdiction over the Northwest Territories. The Royal Canadian Mounted Police (RCMP) acted as government representatives; their posts were established in selected locations, often at places where trading posts already existed. In addition to their peace-keeping duties, the RCMP were responsible for the administration of most Inuit affairs until after World War II.

During the 1920s the fur trade prospered, with each Arctic fox skin bringing as much as $70. As a result, Inuit, particularly in the Hudson Bay and Mackenzie Delta regions, became affluent and purchased large gasoline-powered vessels and other equipment. In the latter area, muskrat, unknown elsewhere in the Arctic, were an added source of income. The collapse of fur prices in the 1930s, along with the depletion of fur-bearing animals and a decline in large game animals due to over-hunting, brought to an end this period of affluence. In some areas, large numbers of Inuit would have starved had it not been for aid furnished by the Canadian government and, in some cases, traders.

Before the turn-of-the-century, there had been relatively few missionaries in the Canadian Arctic, particularly in the east. In the early 1900s Anglican and Roman Catholic missions began to proliferate. In some areas missions of the two denominations were located side by side and competed vigorously with one another for converts.

Missionaries also frequently found themselves at odds with the trading companies. The latter emphasized the importance of trapping which, of necessity, required the Inuit to be dispersed over a wide area for long periods of time. Missionaries, on the other hand, liked to have their parishioners settled permanently in one place so that they might exert maximum pressures for conversion and social change. The presence of missions and trading stations in the same locations, often along with RCMP detachments, served as a focus for Inuit settlement. When, after World War II, representatives of government agencies joined these settlements, the impetus for permanent communities clearly existed.

Many of the earliest missionaries, particularly those of the Roman Catholic faith, were skilled linguists and translated prayer books, the Bible, and hymnals into local dialects. In 1894 an Anglican missionary developed a syllabic script for use by the Inuit of Baffin Island. This writing system has come to be widely used in the Eastern Arctic. In addition to religion, missions also provided health care and education until these services were taken over by the Canadian government in the mid-1940s.

World War II marked the beginning of intensive government, military, and industrial interests in the Canadian North. Following the war, the Canadian government accepted responsibility for providing isolated Inuit settlements with the same services available to Canadians in Southern urban centers. A settled life was encouraged simply because settled people are much easier to administer than those who are dispersed. The tendency for Inuit to settle permanently in communities administered by the federal government and serviced by missionaries and traders brought with it new problems relevant to social organization and a new relationship with the resource base, both significant aspects of the modern period.

The Russian Era in Alaska

Before the end of the 16th century, Russian fur traders had crossed the Ural Mountains, expanded eastward across Northern Asia, and established themselves on the eastern coast of Siberia. By the early 18th century, rumors began to circulate among these intrepid travelers and traders concerning a continent to the east. These rumors eventually reached St. Petersburg where Czar Peter the Great was quick to realize their importance. He dispatched an expedition under the command of Vitus Bering, a Dane serving in the Russian navy, to verify the separation of Asia and North America. In 1728 Bering sailed northward along the Asian coast as far as Cape Dezhnev, and, after passing through the strait that today bears his name, he believed he had definitely established the

separation of the two continents.

The interest aroused by Bering's first voyage led to the organization of a second expedition which sailed in 1741 from Kamchatka on Russia's eastern coast. The expedition's vessels were commanded by Bering and Aleksey Chirikov. The North American continent was sighted by Chirikov near Cross Sound, but an attempt to land resulted in the loss of two row boats and the death of nearly a third of the crew at the hands of Tlingit Indians. Chirikov hastily returned to Kamchatka, sighting a few of the Aleutian Islands on his way.

Bering sighted the American coast in the vicinity of Mt. St. Elias and landed on Kayak Island where Georg W. Steller, the naturalist accompanying the expedition, located an abandoned camp. Although the identity of the campers cannot be established with certainty, they may have been Eskimos. Bering then sailed west along the Aleutian Islands and on to Bering Island where his ship was wrecked. Bering and many of his crew died during the winter. The next summer, the survivors built a small vessel from the wreckage and returned to Kamchatka. Despite the hardships of the voyage, they brought back a rich harvest of furs which set the stage for further developments.

Soon after Bering's second voyage, Russian fur hunters ventured to the Aleutian Islands where they reaped fabulously rich harvests of foxes and sea otters. By 1762 they had reached Kodiak Island and made their first extensive contacts with Eskimos. Both the Aleuts and Koniag Eskimos were ruthlessly exploited by the Russians and forced to trap furs. Neither population ever recovered from the negative impact of their experiences.

Conditions became somewhat better for these people after Gregori Shelikov, a Siberian merchant, formed a company to exploit the American fur trade. In 1783, Shelikov established a small colony at Three Saints Bay on Kodiak Island. Aleksandr Baranov assumed control of the company's American interests in 1792 and directed its operation for 25 years. Virtually alone, he developed the trade to the point that

this company was able to overcome all rivals. By imperial decree, it became the Russian-American Company as a state monopoly in 1799. Baranov moved his headquarters to Sitka in 1800, and this small settlement then became the capital of Russian America.

In 1778 on his third voyage, the English explorer, Captain James Cook, mapped much of Alaska's coastline as far north as Icy Cape. Cook was the first person to recognize fully the widespread uniformity of Eskimo culture. While in Prince William Sound, he noted how much the local people fit descriptions of Greenlanders made by David Crantz, a Moravian missionary. Cook's observations provide considerable cultural detail about Pacific Eskimos, and John Weber, the artist accompanying the expedition, accurately depicted Western Eskimo habitat, clothing, and dwellings.

Other British naval officers, notably John Franklin and Frederick W. Beechey, also explored Northwestern Alaska, but their impact on the Eskimos was minimal. Otto von Kotzebue and Aleksandr F. Kashevarov led the only Russian parties to penetrate the northern region examined by Cook. The exploring party led by Kotzebue in 1816 had few contacts with Eskimos, but the expedition artist, Ludwig Choris, produced some fine portraits of those in the northwestern region. During coastal explorations in 1838, Kashevarov met Eskimos between Kotzebue Sound and Point Barrow, and his notes contribute to our knowledge of their social life. Neither explorer attempted to extend the fur trade to this region.

Early in the 19th century the number of fur-bearing animals declined abruptly along the North Pacific Arc, and the Russian-American Company turned its attention to Southwestern Alaska. When the Company established trading posts in this region, it found that the local Eskimos already possessed Russian trade goods which they had obtained from posts along the Kolyma River in Siberia and received via the Chukchi people. The middlemen in this long-distance trade were the

Eskimos of Sledge and King islands in the Northern Bering Sea. This trading network, reaching deep into the interior of Alaska, was obviously detrimental to the effectiveness of the newly established Russian-American Company posts in Southwestern Alaska. Efforts to overcome this direct Siberian trade led to the most significant Russian explorations in Southwestern Alaska, those of Lieutenant Lavrentiy A. Zagoskin.

In 1842-1844 Zagoskin, who explored large sectors of the Yukon and Kuskokwim rivers, was under instructions to learn as much as possible about present conditions in the area relevant to the potential future of the Russian fur trade. His report contains valuable information about the life-style of the Eskimos and their involvement in the fur trade. Zagoskin recommended that the number of posts be expanded and the quality as well as the variety of trade goods be improved. His recommendations were not followed, and the Russian-American Company had not succeeded in diverting the Siberian-Alaskan trade to its own posts when Alaska was sold to the United States in 1867.

After the Russian-American Company received a renewal of its charter in 1821, several Russian Orthodox Church priests were sent from Irkutsk in Southern Siberia to Alaska at the request of the company's administration. Serving first at Sitka and on Kodiak Island, churchmen were later sent to trading posts along the Nushagak, Kuskokwim, and Yukon rivers in Southwestern Alaska. In the immediate vicinity of the trading posts, the priests had some success in converting Eskimos to Christianity. Their influence was far more ephemeral, however, in remote villages which were visited not more than once or twice a year. Nonetheless, throughout Southwestern Alaska large numbers of Eskimos were baptized, lay readers were trained, and some community chapels were constructed. Parish schools were established at the mission centers, but the pupils were mainly the children of company employees.

A major obstacle confronting Orthodox priests during their early years in the southwest was hostility resulting from the devastating small-pox epidemic of 1838-1839 which the Eskimos and Indians blamed on the Russians. Early European contacts in Alaska had led to the rapid spread of several exotic diseases that decimated the population. The smallpox epidemic was especially severe in some areas where as many as two-thirds of the people died. Such extensive population losses were no doubt accompanied by serious social, economic, and political disruptions.

In assessing the effects of Russian contact on the Eskimos of Western and Southwestern Alaska, the role of the fur trade and fur traders is of primary significance. There is little doubt that after 1840 the Eskimos devoted an ever-increasing amount of time and effort to trapping. To some extent, fur production was a by-product of modified traditional subsistence activities, but most of the fur-bearing animals sought by traders were actually of little intrinsic value to the Eskimos. The diversion of effort from subsistence hunting to trapping resulted in a substantial loss of food since commercially valuable fur bearers provide considerably less meat per animal than do caribou or seals. Thus, the Eskimos were forced to become increasingly dependent on traders to fulfill food needs that might otherwise have been satisfied by the local habitat.

The Russian impact on Alaska did not end with its sale in 1867 to the United States. The Russian Orthodox Church remained, although the priests faced vigorous competition from Roman Catholic and Protestant missionaries. Nonetheless, the Orthodox Church retained and has continued to acquire many converts among the Eskimos of Western and Southwestern Alaska. Russian place names occur along the Yukon and Kuskokwim rivers, and many Russian words have been incorporated into the Yupik Eskimo language. Much of the area of Russian influence in Alaska is occupied by Indians, but in the west and southwest, the Russian heritage is very much a part of contemporary Eskimo culture. In contrast, early Anglo-Americans were to make their presence felt most strongly in areas north of Norton Sound which, strictly speaking, were never really part of Russian America.

The American Era in Alaska to World War II

The advent of American control over Alaska brought no immediate changes, and if the transfer received only passing notice from the few whites in the newly acquired territory, it can easily be understood that most native Alaskans were unaware of the change. In fact, as late as 1908, when an official of the U.S. Bureau of Education made his annual tour of inspection in the territory and visited settlements along Bristol Bay in Southwestern Alaska, he was shocked to learn that many Eskimos had no knowledge of the United States government and still believed themselves under the rule of Russia.

At the time of the sale of Alaska, American members of the Western Union Telegraph Expedition, a private undertaking, were already exploring the newly acquired territory. Their purpose was to survey a route for a telegraph line that would cross the Bering Strait and connect America with Europe. In 1865, the telegraph expedition was headquartered on the west coast of Alaska at St. Michael. Although much of the work was in interior sectors occupied by Athapaskan Indians, surveys were also made farther north, along Norton Sound and on Seward Peninsula. Here, useful information about Eskimos was collected by William H. Dall, a natural historian who was to have a lifetime interest in all aspects of science in Alaska.

Following the Western Union Telegraph Expedition, all significant explorations in Alaska were sponsored by the federal government. The first systematic surveys of conditions among native Alaskans are included in the 10th U.S. Census report of 1880 and the 11th Census of 1890. To obtain data for these reports, Ivan Petroff and others traveled extensively throughout the territory, counting as many individuals and settlements as possible and collecting data about Eskimo and Indian lifestyles. The earlier accounts about Eskimos by Dall,

Eskimo houses at Nushagak, Alaska, 1880s.

Eskimos making souvenirs at Port Clarence, Alaska, c. 1900.

combined with those of Petroff, delineated Eskimo tribal boundaries and major ecological adaptations with reasonable clarity.

The earliest systematic accounts of Eskimo life, the very heart of ethnographic research, were made by young men in the service of the federal government. They were largely self-trained and interested in all aspects of natural history. The most outstanding of these investigators was Edward W. Nelson of the U. S. Army Signal Service. In 1877 Nelson was stationed at St. Michael and, although his primary duty was to make meteorological observations, he was also instructed to collect data about local geography, zoology, and Eskimos. During his term of duty, which ended in 1881, he traveled widely in Western Alaska and obtained more than 10,000 ethnographic specimens that are now in the Smithsonian Institution's National Museum of Natural History. The publication of Nelson's ethnographic information about Eskimos in the vicinity of Bering Strait was a notable landmark in the study of Eskimo culture.

The International Polar Expedition brought John Murdoch, as an observer and naturalist, to Point Barrow in Northern Alaska from 1881 to 1883. He compiled a wealth of valuable ethnographic data about the Eskimos of the Barrow region, and his published report stands second to that of Nelson as a major contribution to Alaskan Eskimo ethnography in the early American era. Of lesser importance, but still highly significant, are the reports about the Eskimos of the Kobuk River in Northwestern Alaska by John C. Cantwell of the Revenue Marine (Coast Guard) in 1884 and 1885. A competing Kobuk-area expedition led by George M. Stoney of the U.S. Navy in 1884-1886 obtained greater amounts of information, but a comprehensive report of its findings was never published. From this time until the eve of World War II much of the information about the changing nature of Eskimo life came from observations by U.S. Geological Survey geologists, who, of necessity, were less interested in the people of the area than earlier government employees.

As was true in the Central Canadian Arctic, by the mid-1800s commercial whalers had a significant impact on the Alaskan Eskimos. Each summer, whaling ships passed through the Bering Strait to hunt bowhead whales. In exchange for baleen from the whales, Eskimos along the Northwestern Alaska coast first received large quantities of trade goods from these whalers. In spring the villagers at coastal settlements between Port Clarence on the Bering Strait and Point Barrow on the northern coast eagerly awaited the arrival of the whaling ships. With the introduction of steam-powered vessels after 1880, many whalers wintered in the Arctic. Contacts with the native people, thus, were greatly increased.

By the early 20th century, when the demand for baleen had begun to fall off, some vessels found it profitable to intensify their trade with Eskimos. By the time commercial whaling came to an end in the second decade of the present century, resident traders were already established in some of the villages.

In the same year that Russia sold Alaska to the United States, the assets of the Russian-American Company were acquired by a San Francisco firm. Reorganized as the Alaska Commercial Company, the new organization dominated trade in Western and Southwestern Alaska well into the 20th century. The small-scale traders of the early American period were unable to compete, and, in 1883, the Alaska Commercial Company achieved a monopoly. During the period in which competition still existed, Eskimos were able to manipulate traders rather effectively. However, the combined factors of the trade monopoly, the Eskimos' greater dependence on trade goods, and a decline in fur-bearing animals, consolidated the power and authority of the merchant. As a consequence of the early American trade, Eskimos adopted many new items of material culture but with a minimum of disruption of their modified-traditional way of life. More disruptive was the continuing loss of subsistence autonomy that had begun much earlier during the Russian era.

Somewhat paralleling the effects of whaling upon the Eskimo population of Northern Alaska was the development of a commercial salmon fishing industry in the Bristol Bay area of Southwestern Alaska in the 1880s. Eskimos from the surrounding area were attracted to Bristol Bay during the summer where they encountered many different races and lifestyles.

During the industry's early years, most of the actual fishing was done by Euro-Americans while imported Chinese laborers performed the cannery work. Despite considerable prejudice, some Eskimos gradually obtained employment in the canneries. It was not until World War II, however, that Eskimos began to participate more fully in the industry.

Although the Russian Orthodox Church continued to maintain most of its missions after the United States' purchase of Alaska, competition increased early in the American era. By the late 1880s the Moravians had established missions at Bethel on the Kuskokwim River in Southwestern Alaska and near Nushagak, along Bristol Bay. Around the same time, the Roman Catholics began work at Holy Cross, located along the Yukon River in Southwestern Alaska. Protestant missions were established in Northwestern Alaska at Cape Prince of Wales, Point Hope, and Point Barrow in 1890. Sheldon Jackson, the first general agent for education in Alaska and a clergyman as well, was responsible for the establishment of the Protestant missions. Additional Protestant missions were begun on Seward Peninsula and in the Kotzebue Sound area.

The Roman Catholics and Protestants were successful, at least in part, because they began work at a time when the traditional Eskimo belief system was disintegrating. Shamans and other part-time religious specialists were no longer able to keep the supernatural world in harmony with the real one. A decline in the number of game animals, increased indebtedness to traders, the high incidence of illness and death from introduced diseases, and the failure of traditional religious leaders to cope successfully with these problems, created an emotional climate amenable to the concept of individual salvation.

All Christian missionaries firmly believed that the education of children was the key to their eventual success, and, thus, the early history of formal education for Alaskan Eskimos is intimately connected with the history of missions. The distinction between secular and religious teaching was not a strong one in the minds of those who conducted the schools. The educational setting was an integral part of their effort to introduce Christianity, and the fact that the schools were supported by government grants during these early years in no way altered the situation.

Secular education eventually developed from this mission school base, with public education beginning in most Eskimo communities around 1905. The steady increase in federal schools brought a decline in mobility and greater government control over the people. Families were strongly encouraged to keep their children in school from September through May, and Eskimos came to recognize the advantages of having their children learn English. Young people were, thus, frequently unable to participate in subsistence activities during this critical learning period of their lives.

Health care was another important service provided by teachers and missionaries. Despite the inadequacy of the treatment provided, Eskimos came to rely on this aid when they were ill, particularly during epidemics. Faith in shamans, the traditional healers, was declining because of their inability to combat introduced diseases. During the early 1900s, tuberculosis became epidemic and was killing or maiming large numbers of Eskimos. Government-sponsored medical services began in most communities at this time. However, this government aid was far from adequate. The debilitating nature of introduced diseases weakened the surviving Eskimos and left them unable to either pursue modified-traditional subsistence activities or cope with the many problems created by a rapidly changing cultural setting. It was not until after World War II that villages were provided with reasonably effective health care.

With the decline in sea mammals caused by unrestricted commercial hunting, the federal government, in 1892, instituted a reindeer-herding program in Western and Northwestern Alaska with the hope of providing the Eskimos with a new source of food. Although many Eskimos tried herding, the program eventually failed. Some young Eskimos were willing to become involved for a while, but few looked upon herding as a reasonable lifetime occupation. Accustomed to exploiting animal resources, they could not adjust to the different lifestyle required by herding. The people were also accustomed to a relatively stable village life and found the isolation of reindeer camps difficult to accept.

From the first influx of miners into the Klondike region of Canada's Yukon Valley at the beginning of the gold rush in 1897 until the marked decline of diggings in West-central Alaska about 1920, Alaskan natives were exposed to a new force in their lives and to an unprecedented but limited economic opportunity. Indians were far more involved in the gold rush than Eskimos, since most gold was found in areas they inhabited. With little gold found in Southwest Alaska, the Eskimos living there had relatively little contact with miners.

The stampede at Nome in 1900, however, led to the first interaction of the Eskimos of Northwest Alaska with Euro-Americans other than whalers, traders, and missionaries. Eskimos had no active role in gold mining except to the extent they could provide services useful to the miner. Employment opportunities were, however, frequently available, with Eskimos providing fish and game and performing menial chores. For most, it was their first experience with wage labor and with outsiders who came into the country to exploit resources different from those exploited by the indigenous inhabitants. The experience clearly established the Eskimos' subordinate role as second-class citizens in their own environment.

The years following the decline of Alaskan gold digging were relatively stable as far as relations between Eskimos and Euro-Americans were concerned. Although commercial fishing continued to grow in the Bristol Bay region, most miners left the territory and many areas once more became isolated backwaters.

It was not until the beginning of World War II that rapid population growth and intensive culture change ushered the Alaskan Eskimo into the modern era.

The American Era Since 1940

By the eve of World War II, the few outsiders still involved with Alaskan Eskimos were traders, missionaries, teachers, and a small number of administrators. The Japanese attack on Pearl Harbor and their occupation of Attu and Kiska islands in the Aleutians foretold major changes in Eskimo life. Military construction projects enabled many Eskimos to enter the job market for the first time, sometimes close to their home villages. The war made it impossible to recruit cannery workers from outside Alaska, and increasing numbers of Eskimos began working at Bristol Bay area canneries. Beginning in 1943, this became a dependable source of cash income during the summers. Of even greater immediate impact on the lives of isolated villagers was the formation of the Alaska Territorial Guard (ATG). Nearly every physically able adult Eskimo male from Egegik to Point Barrow joined the "Tundra Army," which was trained as a first-line of warning and defense in coastal Alaska. The ATG was disbanded in 1947, but after its reorganization as the Alaska National Guard, it continued to include many village units, especially during the Cold War. The impact of these military organizations on village life can hardly be underestimated. The hierarchy of command, rigid discipline, importance of youthful Eskimo leaders, and training to distrust outsiders undermined traditional ideas of leadership and harmony in many villages. The pay for soldiering, combined with participation in a wage-labor economy, made the subsistence base and work patterns of old become far less meaningful.

By the 1950s village life was permanently altered in many ways apart from leadership and subsistence activities. Despite the aptness of aboriginal Eskimo technology, it was nearly gone, and apart from some items of clothing and boats, the material inventory consisted of imported industrial manufactures. Most families lived in log or frame houses, and trips by airplane were becoming as commonplace as dog-sled travel. Educational opportunities for village children expanded as increasing numbers attended high schools away from home. In most communities traditional ceremonial life had been abandoned, and motion pictures became an important form of entertainment. In some communities cooperative stores flourished, as they had for some time, and village councils were organized under federal auspices. Direct control of village affairs by missionaries, traders, and teachers declined as the Eskimos themselves became increasingly Americanized.

In human terms the most dramatic change in Eskimo life began during the 1950s with vast improvement in their health care. In 1955 the U.S. Public Health Service (USPHS) became responsible for providing medical facilities and personnel. Tuberculosis was the major health problem, and the death rate from this disease among native Alaskans in 1950 was 37 times greater than among Caucasians in the United States. The USPHS launched an ambulatory chemotherapy program so that most patients could take drugs at home rather than be hospitalized, and this was followed by an intense program of preventive treatment. These efforts were so successful that in 1970 no native Alaskan died from tuberculosis during the entire year, a remarkable point to reach in less than 15 years. As the health care delivery system improved, along with better living conditions, the overall death rate declined abruptly, and village populations began a rapid increase.

Before World War II teachers, missionaries, and traders alike had a limited capacity to provide social services to Eskimos, yet they all clearly recognized that in many villages abject poverty and dismal living conditions were common. At the end of the war Social Security benefits became available, the federal government distributed special relief funds to the needy, and eligible persons began receiving Old-Age Assistance,

Aid to Dependent Children, and Aid to the Blind. Shortly before and especially after the War on Poverty bill was passed in 1964, a systematic effort was made to improve living conditions in the villages. Substandard homes in most communities were replaced by frame houses meant to be an improvement, although they were often of poor design and construction. Wells were drilled to provide safe and abundant water, and indoor plumbing was installed in some homes. Generators were set up to provide electricity, and old school buildings were replaced by larger, more modern ones. These innovations of federal inspiration made the villages, within a comparatively few years, more pleasant and healthful places in which to live. Furthermore, the food stamp program insured that the poor would not continue to go hungry.

Surprising as it may seem, Eskimo rights to their land were ill-defined by the federal government until the 1960s. A few small reservations had been established. and after 1906 Eskimos could, in theory, obtain title to 64 hectares (160 acres) of unreserved federal land, but few persons participated in the program. Neither was there any effort to resolve aboriginal Eskimo land claims based on their use and occupancy when Alaska became a state in 1959.

Children in front of the school at the Moravian Mission of Carmel near Nushagak, Alaska, c. 1900.

This was largely because native Alaskans were not effectively organized and had no real voice in decisions about statehood. The situation began to change in 1962 when an Eskimo, Howard Rock, launched a Fairbanks newspaper, *Tundra Times*, as the voice of native Alaskans. The question of Aleut, Eskimo, and Indian land rights was a paramount concern, and before long Eskimos organized on a regional basis to seek some form of settlement with the federal government. The founding of the Alaska Federation of Natives in 1966 was a major step forward because this organization represented the interests of all native Alaskans. The year 1966 was critical in another respect: Native Alaskans, lacking a land settlement, protested the federal sale of gas and oil leases along the northern coast; the leases were consequently suspended by the Secretary of the Interior. This situation produced a strange alliance of native Alaskans, the State of Alaska, and major oil companies, all seeking to resolve the land issue, finally achieving their goal in 1971.

The Alaska Native Claims Settlement Act (ANCSA) of 1971 extinguished all aboriginal native Alaskan rights based on land use and occupancy, including hunting and fishing rights. Native Alaskans would receive fee simple title to 16,000,000 hectares (40,000,000 acres) of land, including mineral rights, and $962.5 million over a number of years. For this land they relinquished claim to 130,000,000 hectares (325,000,000 acres). Those eligible were Alaskans with one-quarter or more Aleut, Eskimo, or Indian blood, alive at the time the act became law. Twelve regional corporations were established within the state (a thirteenth was later added for persons not living in Alaska), and each corporation was to manage the assets of a particular region. The act also provided for the creation of village corporations within each Alaskan regional corporation. The goals of the ANCSA were forthright, but the charters under which the corporations were established proved immensely complicated. They are, in fact, a nightmare of complexity

because so many state and federal agencies, each with its own jurisdiction to protect, are involved in implementing the terms of the act.

The corporations established under the 1971 settlement act are business organizations in a strict sense, and as the act now stands, corporate stock can be sold publicly after 1991. This means that, if the corporations survive until then, their control may pass out of native Alaskan hands. Thus far, most Eskimos have derived neither significant nor steady income through the investments of their corporations, and it is possible that they may never do so. Instead corporate bureaucracies have absorbed much of the available money in their administration. Positions in the corporations have created a middle-management power elite of part-natives but few, if any, human problems have been resolved. It was clearly the intent of the federal government that title to the lands under the settlement promptly be conveyed to the corporations, but by 1981 one corporation, Chugach Incorporated, had not received title to a single piece of land and most other corporations had received title to only about 12 percent of their primary entitlement. Contrary to the opinion held by some, Alaska natives are not the "Arabs of the North," because individual shareholders have received only small amounts of money under the terms of the act; for example, members of the Calista Corporation in the lower Yukon and Kuskokwim area have received only about $500 each in 10 years. One major barrier to potential development of the land is that the corporations must have title before it can be developed.

An indirect and positive benefit of the settlement act has been the emergence of a far clearer sense of ethnic identity among Eskimos in Alaska. They are now working together in their own organizations for their own future for the first time. They have an expanding pride in being Eskimo and a far clearer feeling of purpose. Efforts are being made to preserve and revive select aspects of old traditions in a developing atmosphere of cultural awareness.

This thrust is reflected in bilingual education programs and the efforts by Alaskan high school and college students to collect ethnographic information and publish it in their own journals. The revival of Eskimo dances, exchange feasts, and a far greater sense of their own history than ever before are additional manifestations of a revitalization of Eskimo culture. Furthermore, the people of most communities have never lost their identity with the land and a deep emotional attachment to it. Their dependence on local resources continues to dominate the lives and livelihood of most villagers. Few of them would want to return to an aboriginal lifestyle, even if this were possible, but few have abandoned their cultural heritage, which is possible. Instead, most Eskimos seek a continuing accommodation with the ways of Euro-Americans while retaining and fostering their primary identity as "real people," either Yupik or Inupiat.

Conclusion

The preceding pages suggest significant regional differences in responses to European contact as well as some that appear to have been almost universal throughout the Eskimo areas. Perhaps the most obvious of the latter type of response was the pervasive importance of trade. Eskimos throughout the Arctic invariably viewed contacts with Europeans as opportunities for trade. Items of European manufacture were eagerly received in exchange for products from the natural environment, and as opportunities for trade increased, virtually all Eskimos rapidly abandoned most of their old material culture. Only in certain isolated areas of North-central Canada, Northwest Greenland and West Alaska are selected traditional artifacts still in use.

Traders were the outsiders with the greatest initial impact on Eskimo life because they controlled access to European goods. Eskimos in Alaska, Canada, and Greenland dealt with the agents of large trading companies which, for the most part, operated under monopolistic conditions. Only in Greenland, however, was the trading company under full control of the government and thus in a position to protect Greenlanders from certain excesses of the market place characteristic of other areas: high prices and shoddy, non-essential trade goods. Although the Greenland form of commercial paternalism was unique in the Arctic, the end result of interaction with traders was everywhere the same: People, in their desire for goods of Western manufacture, were increasingly alienated from their traditional subsistence pursuits.

Throughout the Arctic, missionaries had a profound influence on native intellectual life. Regardless of the denomination they represented, all wished to replace Eskimo religion and social behavior with Christian beliefs and behavior. Since shamans symbolized the native belief system, missionaries measured their success or failure in terms of the extent to which they were able to overcome shamanistic influence. The education of young people was also an important aspect of mission work since missionaries believed their best chance of success lay in reaching the younger generation with the Christian message. As noted previously, progress in education was achieved at a much earlier date in Greenland than elsewhere and some of this progress can be attributed to teaching in the native language. In Greenland and Canada, Eskimo education was not secularized until after World War II, whereas in Alaska this change took place at the end of the 19th century. Mission education in general was inadequate, being highly selective and failing to prepare native peoples to deal adequately with a rapidly changing world. Early secular education in Alaska, aimed at integrating Eskimos into the greater American society, was equally unsuccessful.

The impact of introduced diseases was great throughout the Arctic, population depletion resulting not just from the diseases themselves, but also from the inability of weakened survivors to obtain food. Tuberculosis was generally destructive, and although successful treatment was eventually achieved prior to the 1950s, many people died or were disabled by this widespread progressive illness.

From a broad perspective, historic contact up until World War II brought several economic changes to arctic peoples. Among these were the fur trade and regional economic pursuits such as commercial fishing and whaling. Fluctuating prices paid for products from the environment, combined with low wages, kept the standard of living low until the 1930s when Eskimos benefitted from generally higher fur prices. Declining populations of game animals and changing settlement patterns restricted access to traditionally hunted species. Only in Greenland where the Danish government maintained a protected environment were natives able to hunt and fish somewhat as they had in the past. With the increased availability of wage labor opportunities after World War II, Eskimos throughout the Arctic adapted, with regional variations, to a general economic pattern that included wage labor, welfare, and a limited amount of traditional hunting and fishing.

Reading List

Although more books and articles have been written about Eskimos than about any other aboriginal people, comprehensive studies about historic changes in their culture are relatively rare. The following sources, all with excellent bibliographies, are suggested for the reader who wishes to delve deeper into the subject of Eskimo culture change.

Birket-Smith, K. *The Eskimos*. London: Methuen, 1959. (Also 1936 and 1971 editions.)

Gad, F. *The History of Greenland*. Montreal: McGill-Queen's University Press, Vol. I, 1971; Vol. II, 1973.

Hughes, C.C. "Under Four Flags." *Current Anthropology*, 6 (1965), 3-69.

Jenness, D. *Eskimo Administration: Alaska*. Vol I. Arctic Institute of North America Technical Paper, No. 10. Calgary, Alberta: University of Calgary, 1962.

Jenness, D. *Eskimo Administration: Canada*. Vol. II. Arctic Insitute of North America Technical Paper, No. 14. Calgary, Alberta: University of Calgary, 1964.

Jenness, D. *Eskimo Administration: Labrador*. Vol. III. Arctic Institute of North America Technical Paper, No. 16. Calgary, Alberta: University of Calgary, 1965.

Jenness, D. *Eskimo Administration: Greenland*. Vol. IV. Arctic Insitute of North America Technical Paper, No. 19. Calgary, Alberta: University of Calgary, 1967.

Jenness, D. *Eskimo Administration: Analysis and Reflections*. Vol. V. Arctic Institute of North America Technical Paper, No. 21. Calgary, Alberta: University of Calgary, 1968.

Oswalt, W.H. *Eskimos and Explorers*. Novato, CA: Chandler & Sharp, 1979.

Modern Inuit Culture and Society

Richard G. Condon, Department of Anthropology,
Harvard University, Cambridge, Massachusetts

Introduction

For millenia, the Inuit[1] of the Canadian Arctic have been dominated by dramatic, and often severe, seasonal changes in temperature, photoperiod, wind conditions, ice conditions, and food availability. As a result of thousands of years of adaptation to such extreme climatic conditions, these remarkable people learned to adjust their social organization, population distribution, hunting strategies, and even material culture to cope with the annual fluctuation of resource availability in the arctic ecosystem. Such responsiveness to change, however, could not prepare the Inuit for the dramatic transformations which they began to experience in interacting with an intrusive southern culture.[2] The technical knowledge which once enabled the Inuit hunter to contend with a harsh and ever-changing environment could not aid him in coping with the new ways introduced by whalers, trappers, traders, missionaries, Royal Canadian Mounted Police (RCMP) officers, schools, government administrators, and oil companies.

While the Inuit of today are no longer culturally identical with the Inuit encountered by the earliest explorers and whalers, neither have they become completely imprinted with the Euro-Canadian culture which seeks to integrate them into its mainstream. The modern Inuit are members of a dynamic culture which strives to maintain its traditionally close ties to the land for the purposes of hunting and trapping, while at the same time remaining receptive to responsible development of the Inuit homeland.

The present chapter will provide a summary of modern Inuit culture through the examination of contemporary Inuit economics, material culture, family organization, education, health, and political activity. In the process, those popular, but unintentionally erroneous, stereotypes of Inuit culture and society will be identified and re-evaluated. The task of describing contemporary Inuit culture in such a short space is, admittedly, an ambitious undertaking in light of the complexities of Northern life and the fact that there is substantial regional variation among the Inuit groups of the Northwest Territories, Northern Quebec, and Labrador. Nevertheless, this summary description of the contemporary situation in the Canadian Arctic should give readers a general understanding of what it means to be Inuit in the context of modern Canadian society, as well as provide some insight into the continuity of social and economic adaptation from the late post-contact period of the 1940s into the latter part of the 20th century.

Woman stretching a sealskin on the ground outside of her home; the skin will be left to dry in the July sun. Holman Island, Northwest Territories, Canada.

Never to Return

By the end of World War II, dramatic and irreversible social change had occurred throughout the Canadian Arctic. In addition to the introduction of new material goods such as guns, steel traps, boats, and canned foods, the Inuit had been drawn slowly into increasing dependence upon the Southern economy via wage employment and the trading of renewable resources. The resulting over-utilization of many arctic regions effectively prevented any return to a more traditional and self-sufficient way of life.

For decades, the only outside agents actively involved in the Canadian North had been missionaries, Royal Canadian Mounted Police (RCMP) officers, and various independent traders and trading companies, most notably the Hudson's Bay Company. The 1940s and 1950s, however, marked a period of increasing government involvement in Northern affairs and Inuit welfare. Recognition of the strategic importance of Northern Canada during and immediately after World War II resulted in the construction of weather stations, military bases, air strips, and eventually the Distant Early Warning System (DEW-line) in the mid-1950s.

These large-scale construction projects not only provided employment for large numbers of Inuit, but also called attention to an Inuit population facing famine (due to low fur prices and poor hunting conditions) and in dire need of social and medical assistance.

Up until the 1950s, responsibility for the Canadian Inuit was passed from one government department to another. In 1939, a ruling of the Canadian Supreme Court accorded the Inuit the same health, education, and welfare benefits as Canadian Indians. It was not, however, until the establishment of the Department of Northern Affairs and National Resources in 1953 that the Inuit finally began receiving these benefits.[3] With the organization of this department, a new phase of government activity was initiated. The Department of Northern Affairs and National Resources provided social services for the impoverished and disease-plagued populations of Canada's Northlands. In addition, the Department of National Health and Welfare began yearly medical surveys in the North to administer health care and to screen for tuberculosis and other debilitating diseases.

Population Concentration

Before the arrival of Euro-Canadian culture, the Central Arctic Inuit lived a precariously nomadic existence, extracting a living from a biologically marginal environment. This was a world in which only the healthiest individuals could survive and where famine and hunting accidents were accepted facts of life. During this period, Inuit households divided their annual cycle of activities between large snowhouse settlements located on the winter sea ice and nomadic hunting and fishing camps on the summer tundra. With the introduction of trapping, the centers of social and economic life were relocated to the trading posts which started to dot the Arctic Coast in the opening decades of the 20th century. It was at these locations that the Inuit came at various times of the year to trade and socialize before returning to the relative isolation of camp life.

As the federal government of Canada started to expand its services to this widely dispersed population, the Inuit were encouraged to move into centralized settlements, thus allowing for more efficient administration of health care, social assistance, and schooling. Most of these settlements were established next to already existing trading posts. In fact, of the approximately 50 population centers spread throughout the Northwest Territories, over 75 percent had been established specifically for the fur trade.

Most of the early settlements consisted of only a trading post, a mission, and perhaps an RCMP detachment. While most Inuit families continued to live in isolated trapping camps for much of the year, a few families made these early settlements their homes. Employment was sought at missions and trading posts. Makeshift houses were often built from scrap wood, metal, cloth, and cardboard. When no such materials were available, families lived in double-walled tents, with brush used as insulation between the tent walls.

In order to make the settlements more attractive to those living out on the land, the federal government started to build medical facilities, schools, and government-subsidized housing. These prefabricated housing units represented a vast improvement over the crowded and poorly insulated housing built by the Inuit themselves. As it became more difficult for the Inuit to support themselves in the outlying trapping camps, families gradually moved into the settlements, first on a seasonal basis and then permanently. By the late 1960s, the vast majority of Canadian Inuit had become drawn to the greater social and economic security of these communities.

Distribution of Modern Inuit Settlements

Today, the Canadian Inuit inhabit approximately 50 settlements and towns in the northern reaches of the Northwest Territories, Quebec, and Labrador. Of the approximately 20,000 Inuit who reside in Northern Canada, 15,000 are located in the Northwest Territories, 5,000 in Northern Quebec, and 1,300 in Northwestern Labrador. Modern Inuit communities vary significantly in size, accessibility, economic adaptation, and the degree to which they hold to traditions. Populations range from a few hundred in places such as Sachs Harbour and Holman Island to several thousand in the regional centers of Inuvik and Frobisher Bay. Most of these Northern communities also have substantial white populations whose members fill various government and administrative positions as teachers, mechanics, nurses, managers and military personnel. Although these whites tend to be fairly transient, spending an average of one to three years in the North, an increasing number are taking up permanent residence in the Arctic. Larger settlements such as Frobisher Bay, Inuvik, and Cambridge Bay tend to have substantial numbers of Euro-Canadian residents, whereas more isolated communities

View of the Inuit community of Holman Island, Northwest Territories, Canada, in September.

A barge, loaded with a year's supply of materials, arrives at Holman Island, Northwest Territories, Canada, in late August.

such as Spence Bay, Pelly Bay, Holman Island, and Gjoa Haven have only a handful. Because local Inuit are now being trained to carry out many of the services at present supplied by Euro-Canadians, a decreasing number of these transients will come North to supply their skills.

Traditionally, Inuit populations were spread over an extremely vast area of Northern Canada. Surprisingly, from Northern Alaska to Greenland and Labrador, a marked uniformity of language and culture has existed. In fact, in the early 1920s when the famous arctic explorer and anthropologist Knud Rasmussen travelled across Arctic Canada from Greenland to North Alaska, he was able to communicate with all of the Inuit groups that he met using his native Greenlandic dialect. Although regional Inuit populations are now concentrated in settlements and towns, this extensive distribution persists to the present day. Difficulties in bringing modern communication and transportation systems to the North have been, in part, attributed to the Inuit's persistent geographic spread.

Prior to World War II and the construction of landing strips in many arctic communities, travel to and from the Arctic was a long and tedious affair. This was due not only to the extreme isolation of Inuit communities, but also to severe weather conditions which restricted travel to the warm summer months. In many cases, teachers, nurses, and missionaries who headed north would have to wait for yearly barges or medical survey planes to transport them to their destinations.

Today, transportation to, from, and between arctic communities has been vastly improved with the construction of airports and the implementation of scheduled air service. Even the most isolated communities (and some outpost camps) have air strips, while many have airports as large as municipal airports in Southern Canada. Most of these air strips were built by the United States government during and immediately after World War II.

More recent additions and improvements in this system of interconnecting arctic airports have been built by the Canadian Department of Transportation. Today, people who wish to travel to an arctic community no longer have to wait for months, but can fly in at any season of the year on scheduled flights.

Because of the maritime adaptation of the Inuit people, most settlements have been built on coastal areas, either along the arctic mainland or in the Canadian archipelago. Consequently, all but the most isolated settlements are serviced by barge at least once a year. Because of the extremely high cost of air transport, such things as building supplies, motor vehicles, snowmobiles, oil, gas, and nonperishable foodstuffs can be shipped northward by barge at a fraction of the air cost. Planes, however, can fly into these communities at any time of year, whereas barges can sail northward only during the brief summer period of open water.

Contemporary Material Culture

Changes in the material and economic spheres of Inuit life represent the most visible index of social change in the Canadian Arctic. The Inuit no longer live in snowhouses, travel by dog sled, hunt with harpoons, or wear caribou-skin clothing. Rather, they have successfully incorporated a large number of southern material goods and economic strategies, while retaining the integrity of the Inuit lifestyle.

When stepping off the plane in any modern Inuit settlement, one is confronted by a surprising number of southern-produced goods which have been transported to the community by plane or barge. The taxi cab or truck which takes new arrivals into any town may strike the unexpecting visitor as an anomalous mode of travel for the arctic tundra. And the surprises may not end here. When visiting local households, guests will see televisions, radios, stereos, sewing machines, coffeemakers, freezers, electric guitars, and Monopoly boards. In most communities, these visitors can shop at the Hudson's Bay Store (or local cooperative store) that is almost indistinguishable from a southern supermarket. A number of northern settlements even have their own radio stations and local newspapers. Although many newcomers to the North are disappointed to see that these Inuit communities appear so "southern," they rarely complain when they can spend the night comfortably at a local cooperative hotel which has running water, electricity, comfortable beds, and perhaps a coffee shop or restaurant.

Despite the overwhelming abundance of such southern-manufactured goods and the rapid transition to wage employment and a cash economy, modern Inuit material culture is still oriented toward the demands of hunting, trapping, fishing, and coping with the extreme cold of the arctic climate. To a large extent, traditional skills and knowledge are still relied upon in pursuing time-honored subsistence activities.

Material changes in the hunting complex of Inuit culture have had the greatest impact upon the social and economic organization of northern communities. The Inuit traded fox pelts for the first rifles, traps, knives, stoves, and canned foods that made their way northward. Such outside goods became an integral part of hunting and trapping. As their reliance upon these goods increased, Inuit hunters were forced to devote more time to trapping. The self-reliance of the Inuit was thus gradually undermined, and a radically different way of life began to take its place. Concentration of the population into centralized communities has accelerated this process. Wage employment, a cash economy, mail order catalogs, and improved transportation networks have all increased the Inuit's reliance upon products and services introduced from the South.

The centerpiece of modern hunting is the snowmobile, replacing the slow, albeit dependable, dog team. Snowmobiles were introduced in many regions during the 1960s and 1970s. Until that time, all hunting and trapping activities were still carried out by the dog team. In a period of just a few years, dog teams dropped completely out of use as people opted for the snowmobile as a faster and more efficient mode of travel. Although no longer an integral part of the northern economy and lifestyle, dog teams are still maintained in many settlements for recreation purposes.

The Inuit soon realized that hunting by snowmobile was much easier and more efficient than hunting by dog sled. In the past, an Inuit hunter with dogs would have to anchor his team some distance from the caribou he was stalking and proceed on foot. Today, a hunter on a snowmobile can drive up quickly to a caribou herd and shoot before the herd has time to disperse. If pursuit is required, the hunter can do so much faster on snowmobile than on foot or by dog sled. Although snowmobiles are just as noisy as sled dogs, they have the primary advantage of not smelling like the caribou's most feared predator, the arctic wolf. In addition, use of the snowmobile allows the modern hunter to cover a greater range of territory in search of game.

Although a well-maintained snowmobile is a more effective mode of transportation than a dog team (since the latter must be unhitched, tied down, and fed at the end of each day), the modern snowmobile does lack a number of the advantages provided by dogs. One often-mentioned advantage is that dog teams cannot break down the way snowmobiles do. An individual dog may die on a hunting trip, but it is unlikely that an entire team will be rendered inoperable. The large number of moving parts on a snowmobile, coupled with the abuse that these machines endure by pulling heavy loads and traveling over rough terrain, leads to frequent breakdowns.

When traveling over a previously broken trail, a well-trained lead dog is able to stay on course without the constant attention of the sled driver. This is especially advantageous when traveling in low visibility conditions since dogs can use their acute sense of smell to maintain the proper course.

Finally, the hunter who is stranded out on the land due to bad weather or some other accident can always survive by eating his dogs. Snowmobiles, however, are generally regarded as unpalatable.

Dog team at rest on the sea ice in April. Near
Holman Island, Northwest Territories, Canada.

Theresa Tartak and Pelagie Kubluitok preparing caribou skins in the living room of their modern house.

Supplies are unloaded for the outpost camp at Omingmagiuk, Victoria Island, Canada.

Along with the snowmobile, the *qamutik*, or sled, is another essential item for the contemporary winter hunter. The *qamutik* is pulled behind the snowmobile and is used for carrying supplies and game. The design of today's *qamutik* is similar to the traditional model and may range anywhere from 2 to 4.3 meters (6 to 14 feet) long. These sleds are usually built at home or at a community workshop with imported lumber, rope, and metal strips. The introduction of electricity and power tools has made such work much less tedious than in the past.

Long before the incursion of the snowmobile, the rifle had made an impact upon the Inuit lifestyle. Today, all hunting is done with shotguns and high-powered rifles either bought through the mail or at the local Hudson's Bay Store. Harpoons, spears, and bows and arrows, long the trademark of the Inuit hunter, have fallen completely out of use. Older members of many communities continue to make these traditional items for sale to local cooperatives to be marketed in the South.

In addition to rifles and snowmobiles, the modern Inuit utilizes commercially manufactured boats, outboard motors, gas stoves and lamps, canvas tents, and even CB radios. With few exceptions, major equipment such as snowmobiles, boats, and outboard motors is bought on an installment basis at the local co-op or Hudson's Bay Store.

In spite of the many changes that have been introduced from the outside, the Inuit hunter still utilizes a large number of traditional items such as snowknives, seal hooks, snow probes, open-water boats, ice chisels and scoops, flensing boards, stretching boards, *ulus*, scrapers, and the *qamutik*. The construction of these items has, however, been somewhat modified through the use of such materials as iron, sheet metal, hardwood, canvas, rope, and nails. These materials replace the traditional, locally available materials such as caribou antler, musk-ox horn, whalebone, ivory, and hide rope.

Of all the artifacts of traditional material culture, the *ulu* and snowknife are most readily associated with Inuit culture. The *ulu*, or woman's knife, is a semicircular blade that is still used for a variety of household tasks including skinning, flensing, butchering, slicing meat, and sewing. It may also be used for non-traditional tasks such as cutting up an apple or orange. In the past, *ulus* were made from slate or cold-hammered copper. At present, *ulus* are frequently made from saw blades purchased through the mail or at a local store. One large saw blade may be cut up to make three to five *ulus* of different sizes. Handles for these modern *ulu* blades are made from wood, caribou antler, or musk-ox horn.

Few Inuit hunters travel without a snowknife even though snowhouses are no longer commonly used. Under bad weather conditions, snowknives are used to cut blocks of snow which are placed around the canvas tent to keep it secure in the blowing wind. Modern snowknives are either made from imported saw blades or from large machetes which are ground down to the appropriate size and shape.

Although rifles, snowmobiles, and powered boats have dramatically changed hunting procedures, the knowledge and skills required to be an effective hunter have remained unchanged. The Inuit hunter must still learn how to travel safely over the ocean ice, to track game for miles over hard-packed snow, and to maneuver his boat through treacherous ice floes. He must also remain sensitive to slight changes in wind direction which could send him out to sea atop an ice floe which has broken away from the landfast ice. Such knowledge has come to the modern Inuit hunter from generations of hunters before him. As long as hunting and trapping remain viable components of Inuit life, it is unlikely that this knowledge will pass into oblivion.

Like hunting and trapping, Inuit clothing has undergone dramatic transformations from the skin clothing of the past. Although a few older hunters still insist on using caribou parkas for winter travel, an increasing number of men are buying and wearing store-bought parkas lined with goose down. In addition, snowmobile boots and mitts are becoming common items of apparel throughout the Arctic. Despite the incursion of such clothing styles, Inuit women continue to sew beautiful parkas, mitts, and *kamiks* (boots) out of traditional as well as introduced materials. In addition to being worn by local residents, many of these hand-sewn items are marketed in the South through local cooperatives. Inuit women are renowned for their skill at making brightly colored "visiting" parkas with embroidery and geometric designs (called *kopaking*). Such items command a high price outside the Arctic and constitute one of the major products of the Inuit cottage-craft industry.

Housing

The first government-subsidized housing units were shipped to the North in the late 1950s and early 1960s. These were relatively small, prefabricated units which lacked plumbing and electricity. Water could be stored in large holding tanks and heat was supplied by gravity-fed oil cooking stoves, the oil for which was shipped in by barge. Sewage was dispensed through the use of portable buckets with toilet seat covers, fondly referred to by the local population as "honey buckets."

In subsequent years, the federal government, in conjunction with the provincial and territorial governments of each region, started building larger housing units with more amenities. Between 1966 and 1975, the Northern Rental Housing Program provided over 1,500 three-bedroom houses for Inuit communities, mostly in the Northwest Territories. Housing units built in the late 1970s and early 1980s are equipped with running water, internal sewage systems, electric stoves, and forced-air furnaces. Since it is not possible for water and sewage pipelines to run underground, because of continuous permafrost, these new houses are serviced by sewage disposal trucks and water trucks which are filled at a nearby lake or stream. Some of the larger communities have insulated, external water and sewage pipe systems (called utilodors) which run above ground between housing units. The cost of such utilidors, however, is prohibitive for smaller communities which must rely upon self-contained water and sewage systems.

Despite the large number of modern housing units built in recent years, many of the older units are still occupied by Inuit families. In fact, many people express a preference for these older and simpler units since they require less extensive maintenance and repair.

The interiors of many of the newer housing units are almost indistinguishable from other Canadian households. As more people generate extra income from wage employment, it is increasingly common to see carpets, stuffed chairs and sofas, lamps, tables, radios, stereos, toasters, washing machines, and coffee-makers in Inuit homes. Now that the majority of Inuit communities have television service via satellite, many homes are even equipped with color television sets.

Yet, despite this southern appearance, there are still a number of items which distinguish the Inuit household from the typical southern one. Frequently, a drying rack is placed somewhere in the kitchen and covered with strips of drying caribou meat, duck, or fish. Many households also have a piece of plywood on the kitchen floor upon which are placed raw, frozen, or dried meat and fish which are sliced (usually with an *ulu*) for consumption by household members and visitors.

Because of the very high cost of transporting building supplies and heating oil, all northern housing units must be subsidized by the government. Rents are generally adjusted, on a monthly basis, according to the family's income. Thus, a well-paid wage earner will be expected to pay a higher rent than a trapper whose earning-power is much less.

Springtime in the Inuit community of Holman
Island, Northwest Territories, Canada. Note
the fishing boat in the foreground and
prefabricated houses in the background.

Making a Living

Many researchers and government personnel have espoused the concept of a dual northern economy. According to this view, two distinct economic spheres exist side by side in most arctic settlements: one which is traditional and based upon the exploitation of renewable resources and one, generally consisting of jobs in the service and industrial sectors, which is modern and recently introduced from the South. Often, this notion of duality is simplified into a dichotomy between a "native" economic sector and a "white" economic sector. Unfortunately, this "dualistic" view is overly simplistic and somewhat misleading. Rather than a simple dichotomy, the introduction of southern material culture and economic activities has resulted in a mixing of the two economies. In many settlements, especially those where hunting, trapping, and fishing continue to be of great importance, the extent of overlap is quite pronounced. While trapping remains a viable component of Inuit life in more traditional communities, the spiraling cost of snowmobiles, gas, oil, and other trapping supplies makes it impossible for many trappers to earn a living without additional employment. Supplementary income may be earned through part-time and temporary jobs such as carving, printing, and seasonal construction work. This money can be used to purchase trapping equipment and other supplies.

Fluctuations in both the local fox population and in fur prices also affect the economics of trapping. During a bad year, an individual may decide that trapping is not worthwhile since the overhead for setting and checking traplines may exceed the amount of money generated. Thus, during such a season it is not uncommon for trappers to take on some kind of wage employment.

In discussing the northern economy of today, the concept of flexibility cannot be overemphasized. Flexibility and opportunism have traditionally been essential strategies for the Inuit people. The Inuit hunter had to be prepared to adjust his seasonal wanderings, his search for food, clothing and shelter, and even his social organization to the seemingly capricious availability of resources. This flexibility was also evidenced by his willingness to adopt the new technologies and social practices introduced to the North by outsiders. Many of these elements have become incorporated into the northern economy and are now integral parts of a way of life which the Inuit seek to preserve.

In light of the obvious complexity of contemporary Inuit life, it is perhaps more useful to think of their economy as consisting of four substantially overlapping sectors that are continually evolving and interacting with one another: subsistence hunting, trading of renewable resources, local wage employment, and industrial employment. In many Inuit communities, subsistence hunting remains an essential feature of life. Hunting is not limited to traditional hunters and trappers but is conducted by wage-earners as well. Although wage-earning Inuit must abide by standard work schedules, many will spend holidays, weekends, and time after work hunting seal, caribou, rabbit, musk-ox, and polar bear. Meat can usually be purchased at a local store, but it is always prohibitively expensive and rarely as fresh as local sources of protein. Unfortunately, in larger towns such as Inuvik and Frobisher Bay, the local environment cannot support active hunting by all residents. Thus, there is greater reliance upon imported foodstuffs.

After lashing a freshly killed seal to his sled, a hunter tows his catch home behind his snowmobile. Summer, Umingmaktok, Northwest Territories, Canada.

Hunters skinning caribou on the lake ice. Late October, near Holman Island, Northwest Territories, Canada.

The trading of renewable resources refers primarily to the trapping of fur-bearing animals and the hunting of seals. After being flensed, scraped, and stretched out to dry, the skins of these animals are exchanged for cash or credit either at the local co-op or Hudson's Bay Store. Since maintaining and checking a trapline is becoming increasingly expensive and difficult, fewer young people are becoming full-time trappers.

Despite the younger Inuit's waning interest in trapping, the government of the Northwest Territories has established a special outpost program designed to provide funds to trappers who wish to set up independent camps in isolated areas. Trappers and their families are given grants to purchase lumber, food, gas, oil, and other supplies to aid in the initial establishment of these outpost camps. The only requirement is that the trapper and his family reside at the camp for at least six months out of the year. Generally, these outpost camps are composed of several families which cooperate with one another in building and operating the camp. At present, there are over 50 outpost camps spread throughout the Northwest Territories. The primary advantage of these isolated posts is that they are located at some distance from the nearest settlement, in areas which are less likely to have been subjected to over-hunting or over-trapping. It is perhaps somewhat ironic that the same government which once encouraged the Inuit people to relocate into centralized communities is now aiding many families in returning to the land. By and large, the Inuit response to the outpost program has been favorable, and many families indicate a preference for living out on the land where they are better able to pass on the Inuit heritage to their children.

Lest the reader falsely assume that the Arctic is an isolated region that knows no laws or government regulations, it should be mentioned that all hunting and trapping activities are now regulated by the federal and territorial governments. In addition to a clearly delineated trapping season, there are numerous restrictions on the hunting of caribou, musk-ox, polar bear, and migratory water-fowl. In spite of the fact that all Inuit hold general hunting licenses, there are definite limits to the number of caribou and other wildlife that can be harvested by local hunters. All Inuit communities have hunting and trapping associations which, in cooperation with wildlife officials, assist in the regulation of these activities. Thus, an Inuit hunter who traps out of season or shoots a polar bear without first obtaining the proper license may be levied a fine for violating wildlife regulations.

Unlike the trading of renewable resources, there has been a marked increase in wage employment throughout the Canadian Arctic. Although chronic under-employment and unemployment are endemic, the employment situation today is much better than it was 20 to 30 years ago when wage-employment opportunities were practically non-existent and many families were forced to depend on government assistance. Today, government-sponsored housing construction, educational services, medical care, and general maintenance have led to a rise in both permanent and part-time employment. In most communities, there is a flurry of activity following the yearly arrival of the barge, because houses and roads must be built or repaired before the advent of colder weather. Invariably such time-restricted activities require the employment of large numbers of people, even if only for a short period of time.

In addition to seasonal employment, a limited number of permanent positions are available in law enforcement, public works, housing maintenance, road repair, local government, and the co-ops. In recent years, many individuals have started their own businesses in contracting, recreational facilities, taxi services, tour guiding, and retailing.

The northward expansion of private oil and mineral concerns has resulted in greater numbers of Inuit seeking industrial employment. Such employment has had a much greater impact upon the larger, more-developed communities of Tuktoyaktuk, Resolute, and Frobisher Bay where oil and mineral exploration companies have based their operations. In their attempt to establish better working relations with Inuit communities throughout the Canadian Arctic, many of these firms have created special job-training programs so that young Inuit might have access to the generally higher paying energy-related jobs. Oil exploration in the Beaufort Sea and in Davis Strait, for example, has provided employment, albeit of a seasonal nature, for young and otherwise jobless Inuit. Many of these companies have charter aircraft to pick up individuals from isolated communities where employment prospects are more limited.

While industrial development is providing employment and occupational training for many Inuit, some communities have expressed concern over the nature of this development. Many oil, gas, and mining endeavors are solely oriented towards the extraction of non-renewable resources which are immediately shipped south for refining. Given the severe, restrictive nature of the arctic climate, it is currently unlikely that refineries, pharmaceutical companies, or other industrial operations will be established in the North. The high cost of shipping raw materials and finished products to and from arctic communities effectively prohibits the development of such lasting industries. Many Inuit realize that industries solely involved in the extraction of natural resources could be extremely short-lived. What, for example, will happen to the North and its people when the land is no longer able to provide southern interests with the bounty of its resources? More importantly, will the scars of such development be so great that the northern environment will be irreparably damaged? Such concerns, expressed by Inuit communities and political organizations, do not represent a dogmatic stand against development, but a pragmatic perspective which attempts to balance the positive and negative consequences of arctic industrialization.

The Cooperative Movement

An important social and economic innovation in many arctic communities has been the creation of community-based cooperatives. The impact of the northern cooperative movement has been substantial and the topic probably deserves an entire chapter of its own. Through these cooperatives, the Inuit have both attained a degree of economic self-determination and also learned the rudiments of business administration, retailing, accounting, and marketing.

A special loan fund, established in the 1950s by the Department of Northern Affairs and National Resources, provided financial support for Inuit businesses and cooperatives. In 1959, the first Inuit co-op was established at George River on the eastern coast of Ungava Bay in Northern Quebec. With the help of government development officers and capital borrowed from the Eskimo Loan Fund, the George River Inuit were able to start a small cooperative based upon the fishing of arctic char and the lumbering of black spruce. Soon, other co-ops sprang up throughout the Canadian North. These were primarily produce co-ops that sold prints, carvings, sewn materials, fish, and lumber to southern markets. Some of these co-ops eventually expanded into retailing by importing clothing, food, snowmobiles, household items, and other goods for sale in local stores, often at prices lower than those at the Hudson's Bay Company. Through such retailing, profits are returned to members of the community (in the form of dividends) rather than leaving the community altogether and entering the coffers of the Hudson's Bay Company.

At present, there are approximately 40 active cooperatives, most of which are located in the Northwest Territories; the remaining co-ops are scattered throughout Northern Quebec. In many settlements, co-ops are the largest employer of local Inuit. In addition to operating craft shops which produce prints, silk-screen hangings, placemats, note pads, and other items frequently seen in southern stores, most of these cooperatives encourage an active cottage-craft industry. Co-op members can thus work at home sewing parkas, carving whalebone or soapstone, making replica hunting tools, or drawing pictures which are sold directly to the co-op. The items are subsequently sold either within the immediate community or shipped outside the Arctic to distributors who forward them to the appropriate market.

Perhaps the primary advantage of the community-based cooperative is that Inuit members do not view themselves as working for southerners, as is often the case with government or industrial jobs; rather they view themselves as working for themselves and their communities. Not only are Inuit employed by the local co-op, but, as shareholders, they can help determine its policies and investments by being elected to its board of directors.

Because arctic cooperatives are community-based, they vary widely in management practices and the selection of economic ventures. Some co-ops have limited themselves to manufacturing arts and crafts, while others have expanded into retailing, operating hotels, restaurants, tourist camps, and hunting lodges, as well as into providing vital municipal services such as water delivery, sewage disposal, and oil distribution.

Many Inuit cooperatives have been extremely successful, displaying a vitality to be copied by other co-ops. Others have had difficulty getting off the ground, often requiring substantial government subsidies before turning a profit. Ultimately, many of the problems experienced by these marginal co-ops are due to a lack of sufficient training, poor administration, and extreme isolation, making the importation of supplies and the exportation of native goods prohibitively expensive.

In order to make the cooperative movement a more effective presence in the Canadian North, La Fédération des Co-opératives du Nouveau-Québec was created in 1967. This organization assists already existing cooperatives and aids in the formation of new cooperative ventures in Northern Quebec. In 1972, a similar organization was established for the Inuit and Indian cooperatives of the Northwest Territories. Called the Canadian Arctic Co-operative Federation Limited (CACFL), at present, it plays a primary role in the cooperative movement of the Northwest Territories. Both organizations seek to facilitate communication among member cooperatives, provide marketing and purchasing services, train staff members, audit and inspect accounts, and act as a liaison between northern co-ops and the federal and territorial governments. As a result of the creation of these federations, individual cooperatives no longer have to "go it alone," as was so often the case in the past, but may take advantage of the knowledge and skills developed by other co-ops. CACFL also operates several "Northern Images" retail stores in Yellowknife, Whitehorse, Inuvik, Edmonton, and Churchill which sell art and handicrafts directly to consumers. Both organizations are controlled by a board of directors which consists of elected representatives from member co-ops. The board of directors meets periodically to determine and review federation policy.

Despite problems with the creation of cooperatives in a few communities, the cooperative movement has been successful overall. Today, the movement is growing stronger by providing a viable economic alternative for the isolated and scattered Inuit communities of the Canadian North.

Social Life

As would be expected, Inuit social life has undergone dramatic change as a result of population concentration, the availability of government housing and social assistance, construction of community halls and recreation centers, and the introduction of newspapers, radios, and televisions. Along with these social and economic changes, traditional practices such as infanticide, senilicide, and spouse exchange, which arose as functional social adaptations to the harsh arctic climate, have disappeared. With the increased security of settlement life and all its provisions for food, clothing, housing, and health care, these

A snowhouse-building contest at Holman Island, Northwest Territories, Canada during Easter festivities.

practices have disappeared forever from the northern scene.

Traditionally, the Inuit family has consisted of all blood relatives, in-laws, and adopted children residing in the same household. While small nuclear families are becoming more common in Inuit communities, a large number of modern households still incorporate grandparents, grandchildren, married offspring and their spouses, aunts, uncles, and adopted children. Because kinship networks are extremely flexible and may be traced bilaterally through both parents, Inuit households often display great variety in their size and composition.

In many arctic communities, a lack of adequate housing has significantly affected household composition. In the early 1960s, when government-subsidized housing was first made available, it was not uncommon for several large families to live together in the same dwelling. Newly married couples would have to live with parents for a period of time until a new home was built or an old one vacated. Subsequent construction of housing has eased these crowded conditions. Even in many of today's communities, the building of new houses leads to a slight rearrangement of households as some family members vacate older housing units and take up residence in newer ones.

In the past, the Inuit family was the primary social, economic, and interactional unit. While in winter large numbers of families would gather together on the ocean ice to cooperate in breathing-hole sealing, much of the remainder of the year was spent in relative isolation and self-sufficiency. With the concentration of these previously nomadic and independent family groups into settlements and towns, the Inuit family lost much of its autonomy.

While there was once a loose gathering of households during the winter, today's settlements and towns place families in constant contact with one another at all seasons of the year. Thus, Inuit families today spend more time interacting and cooperating with each other. Children are now exposed to a larger number of age-mates and, consequently, spend greater amounts of time away from the household playing with their peers. Education, once the domain of the small isolated family unit, has been partially transferred to the schools. Here, children often learn more about Euro-Canadian culture than about the Inuit way of life.

Although year-round contact between Inuit families is greater now than in the past, traditional forms of economic cooperation such as meat sharing and cooperative hunting have become less pronounced. In the past, a man who killed a seal was obligated to distribute various parts of the animal to his seal-sharing partners. In this manner, an equitable distribution of food sources was assured for all households. In the modern period, however, the introduction of wage-employment, social assistance, and child allowances has undermined the vital necessity of such economic cooperation.

One positive result of population concentration, at least from the perspective of young people, is the greater availability of friends and potential spouses. The traditional dispersal of Inuit families often made obtaining a suitable spouse a difficult task. Today, however, young people may select from a much larger pool of potential spouses. With increased inter-settlement travel made possible by scheduled air service, many young people carry on courtships between neighboring communities. In the smaller and more isolated settlements, young people often, in fact, express a preference for spouses from other communities.

Weddings in Roman Catholic, Anglican, or Pentecostal churches are now the rule. Nevertheless, many young people live with one another on a trial basis before undergoing a formal marriage ceremony. In this way, young men and women may determine their compatibility before making a final commitment to each other.

In addition to kinship ties, traditional Inuit society allowed for the establishment of special bonds between individuals through various alliances. Paramount among these were dance partnerships, joking relationships, spouse-exchange partnerships, seal-sharing partnerships, wrestling partnerships, trading partnerships, and namesake partnerships. With contemporary social and economic changes, many of these alliances have lost their original functions and, hence, have fallen out of use. Traditional alliances have been replaced by such relationships as personal friendships and trapping partnerships. While motivated primarily by economic and safety concerns, trapping partnerships often reflect close emotional and social bonds between two individuals and their families. Since winter travel on the ocean ice or tundra is always potentially dangerous, few people travel extensively without a partner. In the case of active trappers who may spend days at a time checking lengthy traplines, some up to 320 kilometers (200 miles) long, it is necessary to travel in pairs in the event of a snowmobile breakdown or some other accident. Since trapping partners spend much time out on the land together, economic arrangements also develop into close social ties between the individuals and their families.

Recreation and entertainment are important aspects of social life, especially during the cold and dark winter months. Almost all communities have recreation centers or community halls where adults and children gather to play games, dance, and show movies. Many of the larger settlements and towns have full-time movie houses where the latest films are shown. Others have only community halls and 16mm projectors which are used for viewing older movies. Coffee shops and restaurants also are springing up in even the most isolated settlements and provide a place for local Inuit to socialize and hold meetings.

Since September 1980, many Inuit communities have been dramatically changed by the transmission of radio and television programming through Canada's Anik-B satellite. Most communities, now equipped with satellite-ground receiver stations, are able to view popular programming for at least some portion of the day through the Canadian Broadcasting Corporation's Northern Service. While some of the smaller and more isolated settlements have limited television service on only one station, others have daily service on several different channels for 15 hours or more.

The creation of Taqramiut Nipingat Inc., a non-profit, Inuit-run communications company servicing Northern Quebec, and the Inuit Broadcasting Corporation, which maintains production facilities in Frobisher Bay and Baker Lake, have had an even more important impact on Inuit communities. Both corporations have been founded to develop radio and television programming which is sensitive and responsive to the linguistic, political, and social needs of the Canadian Inuit. Thus, in addition to viewing television programs which are popular in Southern Canada and the United States, Inuit are now able to view pertinent programs in their native language (Inuktitut) as well as English.

Northern Health

Early explorers to the Canadian North encountered a healthy and vigorous population well-adapted to the conditions of arctic living. The extreme cold of the region, relative isolation of the population, and sparse distribution of Inuit groups shielded them from many of the diseases which have perennially afflicted human groups in more populated regions.

Contact with Euro-Canadian culture, however, exposed the Inuit to infectious diseases against which they had developed no natural immunity. With white explorers, missionaries, whalers, and traders came diseases that quickly took their toll among the native population. Whole groups, the most notable of which were the Inuit of Southampton Island and the Mackenzie Delta, suffered total or near total extinction.

More than any other disease, tuberculosis (TB) became the primary chronic affliction throughout the North American Arctic. By 1950, TB had managed to incapacitate 15 to 20 percent of Canada's Inuit. Outbreaks of other infectious diseases such as diphtheria, influenza, and measles became common occurrences as more intense and direct contact was established with the outside world. Even as recently as 1958, an influenza epidemic spread across the Canadian Arctic where it left 16 persons dead in Pelly Bay alone.

A number of factors contributed to the deteriorating health conditions of the Inuit during the immediate post-contact era. First, and perhaps most importantly, the Inuit were exposed to new diseases. Lack of resistence to these diseases was complicated by the extremely crowded and unsanitary housing conditions that became increasingly common as more families moved into settlements of drafty, self-made shelters. Naturally, infectious diseases such as TB and influenza were more likely to thrive and reach epidemic proportions under such circumstances.

Another contributing factor to impaired health was an increase in malnutrition. While starvation and famine were periodic facts of life, the traditional diet of fresh meat and fish, when eaten frozen, raw, or slightly cooked, provided all the necessary nutrients required for proper functioning of the body. In many areas with overhunting and population concentration, there was a gradual depletion of game and, thus, an increased incidence of malnutrition.

As trapping replaced subsistence hunting, the Inuit became more dependent upon store-bought food. Even though nutritious foods were available at the local trading post, Inuit suffered from malnutrition because they were unaware of the kinds of store-bought foods which constituted a balanced diet.

During the first half of the 20th century, outbreaks of infectious diseases and malnutrition had a devastating effect upon the younger members of the population—so much so that, in the mid- to late 1950s the Inuit infant mortality rate was seven times that of the rest of Canada.

In 1945, the Department of National Health and Welfare was organized to attend to the health needs of Canadians. Even though many years would pass before any substantial progress was made in improving the deteriorating health of northern populations, the Northern Health Service branch immediately embarked upon a campaign against TB and other infectious diseases that were devastating the Inuit. The task was a formidable one given the total lack of northern health facilities, the vast population distribution, and the high cost of transporting medical personnel throughout the Arctic. An energetic campaign providing medical examinations, chest X-rays, inoculations, and vaccinations began in the late 1940s. In the Eastern Arctic, the *C.D. Howe*, a government vessel, carried medical equipment, supplies, and personnel to examine and treat the populations of Northern Quebec and Baffin Island. Other medical teams were flown into isolated areas of the Western and Central Arctic. Individuals who were discovered to have TB were often sent immediately to hospitals in Southern Canada for treatment.

Health conditions could not be improved by expanded medical efforts alone. As long as deplorable housing conditions remained prevalent throughout the North, infectious diseases would continue to debilitate and incapacitate the Inuit. This was recognized by government administrators and medical officials, and housing programs were initiated to bring Southern Canadian standards of housing to Inuit communities.

The creation of local nursing and health stations has been instrumental in improving health conditions. At present, Northern Medical Services of Health and Welfare maintains an impressive network of hospitals and nursing stations throughout the Canadian Arctic. While most communities are still too small to warrant the upkeep of hospitals with doctors and nurses, nursing stations, manned by one or more certified nurses, supply vital medical services to even the most isolated communities. Larger population centers such as Frobisher Bay, Inuvik, and Cambridge Bay are able to maintain more extensive medical facilities which have doctors and other medical personnel on call 24 hours a day. In smaller communities, when illnesses cannot be properly treated, patients are flown to the nearest hospital for care.

Local health facilities have also instituted educational and prevention programs to help eliminate the incidence and spread of disease. Such programs encourage proper hygiene, nutrition, and recuperative practices. Each nursing station conducts numerous programs and clinics to monitor the health of the local population. These include the tuberculosis program, chronic disease program, school health program, environmental sanitation program, vitamin program, maternal health program, and preschool program, to name but a few. While most nursing facilities are staffed by highly trained Southern Canadians, local Inuit are receiving limited medical training which enables them to take positions as community health officers.

The overall result of these efforts has been very impressive. There has been a gradual decline in the infant mortality and tuberculosis rates over the past 30 years. In the case of TB, over 100 new, active cases were detected in 1968. This figure has dropped steadily until only seven new active cases were detected in 1978. Similar dramatic declines can be noted for the infant mortality rate.

As with the rest of Canada, medical care dispensed in nursing stations and hospitals is free of charge. In the Northwest Territories, for example, the Territorial Hospital Insurance Services Plan (THIS) and other supplementary health programs pay for the health costs of all territorial residents, whether they are Indians, Inuit, or white.

Even with the positive gains made in northern health and welfare, many health-related problems persist in arctic communities. The Inuit infant mortality rate is still double that of the Canadian national average, and the incidence of rheumatic fever, pneumonia, upper-respiratory infections, and middle-ear disease (otitis media) remains alarmingly high. The consumption of refined sugar products has made dental conditions such as caries and gum disease common among Inuit children. With the widespread availability of liquor in most communities there has been an increase in alcohol use and abuse, predominantly among teenagers and young adults. Because of the many problems caused by excessive alcohol use, many settlements and towns have instituted alcohol restrictions or prohibitions to bring problem drinking under control.

Inuit Education

The history of northern schooling, as with most other topics discussed in this chapter, could easily fill several volumes and still not give an adequate account of the many difficulties in bringing adequate educational programs to the North. Today, Inuit education is a highly complicated and, in some cases, controversial topic, one which involves such issues as bilingual education, Inuit teacher training, and community control over local schools.

Up until the late 1940s, Inuit education had been in the hands of various Roman Catholic and Anglican missions. The missionaries not only nurtured the Inuit's spiritual training but also contributed to their secular education. In the late 1940s, the federal government of Canada through the Department of Northern Affairs and National Resources assumed responsibility for educating the Inuit of Northern Canada. An extensive network of modern schools and luxurious government houses for the teaching staff was built with funds provided by the federal government. In a period of 20 years, over 30 federal schools, some with hostels for students, were constructed in the Northwest Territories and Northern Quebec.

Since many Inuit families continued to spend a great deal of time out on the land in sealing and trapping camps, the tasks of building and staffing these facilities proved to be much easier than that of attracting the young Inuit for whom the schools had been built. During this early phase, such problems as language barriers, cultural differences, and poor attendance plagued northern education. Highly trained southern teachers, many with good intentions, had great difficulty adapting to the unusual circumstances of the North, all of which were exacerbated by the isolation of most communities. For many teachers, the burden was so great that they rarely stayed in the North for more than two years. Unfortunately, by the time many of these teachers became attuned to the special needs of their local communities and the learning styles of Inuit children, it was time for them to leave their teaching posts.

Aggravating the problems of isolation, irregular attendance, and language differences was the use of a curriculum ill-suited to northern culture. The school curriculum used in the Western Arctic was the same as that used by the schools in the province of Alberta; in the Eastern Arctic, the Ontario curriculum was used. In both situations, Inuit children were inundated by a language and way of life with which they were completely unfamiliar.

In some areas, hostels built next to existing federal schools housed Inuit children from communities too small to support their own educational facilities. As a result, many youngsters were taken away from their families, often for years at a time, to attend boarding schools at locations such as Inuvik and Chesterfield Inlet. It was not uncommon for these children to experience difficulties re-adjusting to life in their home communities once their schooling had been completed.

With the movement of the Inuit population into centralized settlements and towns, the federal government built schools in even the most isolated communities. Today, all settlements have educational facilities which offer instruction up to at least grade nine. Children who wish to complete their secondary education after graduating from local schools must attend larger schools at places such as Ottawa, Yellowknife, Fort Smith, and Frobisher Bay.

In the Northwest Territories, control and administration of northern schooling was transferred to the territorial government in 1972. Although most Northwest Territories' schools are still staffed primarily by teachers from Southern Canada, the Department of Education has instituted various programs designed to train local Inuit as teachers and classroom assistants. Northern schools now employ large numbers of local Inuit, usually young women, who work as classroom assistants to certified teachers from Southern Canada. Since these classroom assistants know the language and are intimately familiar with the students, they can be of invaluable assistance

Inuit children attending school at Clyde
River, Baffin Island, Canada, 1972.

in increasing teacher effectiveness. The Classroom Assistant Program, run by the Northwest Territories Department of Education, provides summer training seminars and workshops for classroom assistants who wish to extend their training. A longer and more advanced program, called the Teacher Education Program, is designed to give Inuit more advanced, professional training in the field of education. The Teacher Education Program is open to those who have completed grade ten. The entire training program lasts two years, after which graduates are certified to teach on their own anywhere in the Northwest Territories. The ultimate goal of this project is to train sufficient numbers of Inuit to staff northern schools, thereby eliminating the dependence upon teachers from Southern Canada.

In addition to classroom assistants and certified graduates of the Teacher Education Program, many schools hire local Inuit to offer instruction in more traditional areas of Inuit life including Inuktitut, sewing, carving, and hunting/trapping skills. This gives older and more experienced members of the community an opportunity to impart their knowledge of traditional Inuit skills and lifestyles to Inuit schoolchildren.

All communities in the Northwest Territories have school committees or societies which meet on a regular basis to discuss matters regarding local education. These associations are made up of local Inuit who are elected by the community for two-year terms. Meetings with school staff members are held on a regular basis to enhance local input into the educational needs of each community.

A slightly different form of educational administration exists in Northern Quebec. In 1976, the first completely Inuit-controlled regional school board in Northern Canada was created. The Kativik School Board operates the schools in all Northern Quebec communities, with the exception of Povungnituk and Ivujivik. The mandate of the Kativik School Board is to develop Inuit-oriented curricula for use in local schools as well as to provide training for Inuit teachers so that

they may be certified under the Quebec Department of Education. McGill University has cooperated closely with Kativik's Inuit Teacher Training Program by certifying and accrediting all summer training courses offered in various northern communities.

The Kativik School Board is unique in that it gives local school committees primary responsibility in determining educational policies and selecting teachers (both white and Inuit) to staff local schools. At present, the Kativik School Board offers schooling up to grades nine and ten. As in other areas of the Canadian North, students who wish to pursue their secondary education must attend high schools in Ottawa, Winnipeg, or Montreal.

Bilingual education has been a primary concern in many Inuit communities. It must be noted that there is significant variation in the use of the Eskimo language (Inuktitut) among Inuit settlements and towns. In parts of Labrador and the Western Canadian Arctic which have had longer periods of contact with Euro-Canadian culture, English has arisen as the dominant language, especially among children and young adults. In other parts of Northern Canada, most notably Northern Quebec and the eastern portions of the Northwest Territories, Inuktitut remains an important part of Inuit social life. In both areas, parents have expressed concern that their children may eventually lose their Inuktitut language skills by attending schools which give most or all instruction in English. This has led to the creation of bilingual education programs in many communities. In Labrador, Inuktitut language classes have recently been reintroduced to the Inuit schools. In Northern Quebec, the Kativik School Board provides instruction in Inuktitut as well as in English and French. While each community determines the amount of Inuktitut training to be received and at what grades it is to begin, the child's parents decide whether the second language is to be French or English.

In addition to primary and secondary schooling, numerous vocational

programs in such areas as electrical work, carpentry, plumbing, welding, and heavy-duty equipment operation and maintenance are available to Inuit. In the Northwest Territories, applicants who meet the necessary requirements receive free tuition and accommodations as well as a stipend from the Department of Manpower and Immigration. After attending courses at Fort Smith, students are placed into suitable apprenticeships for additional on-the-job training. Following the apprenticeship, these Inuit may return to their home communities and take up positions previously held by Southern Canadians.

Political Activity

With increased opportunities for education, communication, and economic diversity, the Canadian Inuit have begun to realize that they can no longer live a life apart from the mainstream of Canadian society. The isolation of the Canadian North has been penetrated by oil rigs, bulldozers, pipelines, mines, and huge icebreaking transport vessels. The Inuit have entered the mainstream of Canadian life by organizing themselves into a number of organizations politically active at the national level. Inuit Tapirisat of Canada (ITC), the national Inuit organization, was created in 1971 to represent the economic, environmental, educational, and political interests of all Canadian Inuit. Although initially headquartered in Edmonton, ITC offices were later moved to Ottawa so that representatives could more effectively voice their concerns to the federal government of Canada. The specific aims of ITC include preserving Inuit language and culture, presenting issues affecting Inuit life to the federal government, and helping the Inuit attain full participation in Canadian culture and society.

Since the formation of ITC, a number of regional affiliates have been established to deal with the specific interests and needs of Inuit from different regions of Northern Canada. These include the Committee for Original People's Entitlement (representing the Inuvialuit of

Regional Inuit Associations in Canada.

Key

Regional Associations of the Canadian Inuit
1. *The Committee for Original People's Entitlement*
2. *Kitikmeot Inuit Association*
3. *Keewatin Inuit Association*
4. *Baffin Region Inuit Association*
5. *Makivik Corporation*
6. *Labrador Inuit Association*

the Western Arctic), Makvik Corporation (representing the Inuit of Northern Quebec), Kitikmeot Inuit Association of the Central Arctic, the Labrador Inuit Association, the Baffin Region Inuit Association, and the Keewatin Inuit Association. All of these organizations maintain constant communication with one another regarding political and economic activities in the North.

In addition to these specifically political associations, other organizations have been chartered which also take an active interest in Inuit affairs. The Inuit Cultural Institute, based at Eskimo Point, is particularly involved in matters of Inuit language and culture. It publishes numerous magazines and newsletters dealing with these topics. More economically oriented organizations such as the Canadian Arctic Co-operative Federation and La Fédération des Co-opératives du Nouveau-Québec have been previously discussed. Through these organizations, Inuit involvement and interaction with local and federal governments has been consolidated, thus providing the Inuit with a significant political presence.

Recognition of the common social and economic problems which beseige all North American Inuit has led to the creation of an international Inuit organization. In the summer of 1980, Inuit leaders from Alaska, Canada, and Greenland met in Nuuk (Godthaab), Greenland, to approve a charter for the creation of an international Inuit organization called the Inuit Circumpolar Conference. This organization seeks to strengthen unity among the Inuit of the circumpolar region, to promote sensible management of non-renewable resources in the Arctic region, and to encourage Inuit participation in national and international affairs.

Land Claims
In December of 1971, the Alaska Native Claims Settlement Act (ANCSA) was signed into law. ANCSA was an extremely complicated and ambiguous piece of legislation. Through ANCSA Alaska Natives relinquished claim to over 120,000,000 hectares (300,000,000 acres) in exchange for $962.5 million

and proprietary rights to 16,000,000 hectares (40,000,000 acres) to be held by various village and regional corporations.

Approximately half this amount ($462.5 million) is being paid by congressional allocation over an 11-year period. The remaining sum is being provided under a revenue-sharing scheme from oil and mineral revenues. Since the U.S. government had never signed any treaties with the Indians, Aleuts, and Inuit of Alaska as it had done so many times with the Native American groups of the continental U.S., actual ownership of Alaskan lands had been disputed. The signing of ANCSA was intended to resolve any ambiguity regarding land ownership in Alaska by specifying which lands belonged to the state, the federal government, and village and regional corporations.

Such activity in Alaska stimulated similar land claims negotiations in Northern Canada. In 1975, the Inuit of Northern Quebec, represented at the time by the Northern Quebec Inuit Association, were the first to sign a comprehensive land claims settlement with the province of Quebec and the federal government of Canada. This settlement was called the James Bay and Northern Quebec Agreement. It stated that $225 million would be paid to the Cree and Inuit residents of Quebec, with those funds being allocated to native corporations and organizations according to population proportions. The settlement extinguished all claims to, and interests in, Quebec provincial lands on the part of local Inuit. In exchange, the Inuit were granted exclusive ownership of 8,450 square kilometers (3,250 square miles) of land, a cash settlement, and exclusive access to another 91,000 square kilometers (35,000 square miles) of land for hunting, trapping, and fishing. The Inuit-run Makvik Corporation was created with the cash settlement. This corporation invests funds in such things as construction, shrimp fishing, air transportation, and other activities in order to stimulate economic diversity and growth among the Inuit communities of Northern Quebec.

At present, other Inuit political

organizations are negotiating similar land claims settlements. Because of the complexity of such negotiations and the different communities' range of interests, these land claims discussions may continue for many years before any satisfactory agreements are reached. Inuit Tapirisat of Canada, for example, has recently proposed the creation of a separate territory called Nunavut (Our Land) which would develop political and economic sovereignty similar to that of the Canadian provinces, but would be run by and responsive to the special needs of resident Inuit. While still in the formative stage, the Nunavut proposal has stimulated much debate on the part of federal officials and Inuit representatives. The fundamental rationale of the Nunavut proposal is that the inhabitants of this vast region share not only a common cultural background but similar problems of economic growth and diversity. The ITC believes that only through the formation of a politically autonomous territory will the Inuit have enough control over the development of this region.

Looking to the Future
It is difficult to write a conclusion for a story still in progress. Change has come to the Inuit of the Canadian Arctic, and they have adapted to it with the vigor that one would expect from such remarkable people. This change, however, has not resulted in a total abandonment of traditional values and lifestyles. Inuit hunters will continue to set their traps and hunt caribou in the remote hinterlands of the North, while their children attend school and learn the fundamentals of science, math, history, and the Canadian way of life. Increasingly, northern schools are offering courses in more traditional spheres of Inuit life so that these children will not forget or lose pride in who they are and where they came from. At the same time, by taking advantage of the educational and medical expertise of Euro-Canadian society, these children will be better prepared to direct Inuit participation in the global society of the future.

Footnotes

[1] The term *Inuit*, which is used throughout the text, is the designation that the Eskimos of the Canadian North use to describe themselves in their native language, Inuktitut. In addition to the word *Inuit*, a number of different terms are used to describe the Inuit groups of certain regions: The Inuit of Northern Alaska refer to themselves as *Inupiat*, whereas the Inuit of the Western Canadian Arctic call themselves *Inuvialuit*.

[2] From the Inuit perspective, *southern* refers to that region of North America south of the Arctic. The mainstream culture of Canada and the United States is considered southern culture.

[3] Bureaucratic mismanagement was due, in part, to the Inuit's ambiguous status vis-a-vis the Canadian federal government. Unlike many Indian groups, the Inuit had never signed treaties with the federal government. Without a treaty it was unclear whether the Inuit should be considered wards of the state (as were many Indian groups). Within Parliament, there was long-standing opposition to categorizing these independent (and non-treaty signing) people as wards of the government. Even with the 1939 Supreme Court ruling, it took the government 14 years to decide which of its divisions should manage Inuit affairs.

Reading List

I. Books and Articles:

Berger, Thomas R. *Northern Frontier, Northern Homeland: The Report of the Mackenzie Valley Pipeline Inquiry*, Vol. I., Toronto: James Lorimer and Co., 1977.

Bigjim, Frederick and Ito-Adler. *Letters to Howard: An interpretation of Alaska Native Land Claims.* Anchorage: Methodist University Press, 1974.

Briggs, Jean. *Never in Anger.* Cambridge: Harvard University Press, 1970.

Brice-Bennet, Carol, ed. *Our Footprints Are Everywhere: Inuit Land Use and Occupancy in Labrador.* Nain, Labrador: n.p., 1977.

Brody, Hugh. *The People's Land.* NY: Penguin, 1977.

Burch, E. G., Jr. "The Ethnography of Northern North America: A Guide to Recent Research." *Arctic Anthropology*, no. 16 (1979), 62-146.

Burch, E. S. "Native Claims in Alaska: An Overview." *Etudes/Inuit Studies*, 3 (1980), 7-30.

Carpenter, Edmund. *Eskimo Realities.* NY: Holt, Rinehart, and Winston, 1973.

Cowan, Susan, ed. *We Don't Live in Snowhouses Now: Reflections of Arctic Bay.* Chicago: University of Chicago Press, 1981.

Crowe, Keith. *A History of the Original Peoples of Northern Canada.* Montreal: McGill-Queen's University Press, 1974.

Finkler, H. *Inuit and the Administration of Justice in the Northwest Territories: The Case of Frobisher Bay.* Ottawa: Department of Indian and Northern Affairs, 1975.

Freeman, Milton, ed. *Inuit Land Use and Occupancy Project.* Vol. 1-3. Ottawa: Department of Indian and Northern Affairs, 1975.

Freeman, Minnie A. *Life Among the Qallunaat.* Edmonton: Hurtig Publishers, 1979.

Graburn, Nelson H. H. *Eskimos without Igloos.* Boston: Little-Brown, 1969.

Honigmann, J., and I. Honigmann. *Eskimo Townsmen.* Ottawa: Canadian Research Centre for Anthropology, 1965.

Iglauer, Edith. *Inuit Journey.* Seattle: University of Washington Press, 1979.

Jenness, Diamond. *Eskimo Administration: II. Canada.* Arctic Institute of North America Technical Paper No. 14. Washington: Arctic Institute of North America, 1964.

Paine, Robert, ed. *The White Arctic: Anthropological Essays on Tutelage and Ethnicity.* St. John's: Memorial University, 1977.

Pitseolak, Peter, and D. Eber. *People from Our Side.* Edmonton: Hurtig Publishers, 1975.

II. Scientific and technical journals:

Arctic
The Arctic Institute of North America
University Library Tower
University of Calgary
Calgary, Alberta T2N 1N4

Arctic Anthropology
Department of Anthropology
University of Arkansas
Fayetteville, AR 72701

Etudes/Inuit Studies
Department of Anthropology
Laval University
Quebec City, Quebec G1K 7P4

The Muskox
Institute for Northern Studies
University of Saskatchewan
Saskatoon, Saskatchewan S7N 0W0

III. Magazines and Newsletters:

Arjungnagimmat
Inuit Cultural Institute
Eskimo Point,
Northwest Territories X0C 0E0

The Beaver
Hudson's Bay House
77 Main St.
Winnipeg, Manitoba R3C 2R1

Inuit Today
Inuit Tapirisat of Canada
176 Gloucester St.
Ottawa, Ontario K2P 0A6

Inuktitut Magazine
Department of Indian and Northern Affairs
10 Wellington St.
Ottawa, Ontario K1A 0H4

North/Nord
Publishing Centre
Supply and Services Canada
270 Albert St.
Ottawa, Ontario K1A 059

Here, a daring sculpture has been carved out of a single block of soapstone.

Carving of Hunter, Woman, and Musk-ox
by Luke Airut (Igloolik, Northwest Territories, Canada). Soapstone, ivory; 1970s; 56 cm long. CMNH #31581-165.

Inuit Art

Nelson H.H. Graburn, Department of Anthropology,
University of California, Berkeley, California

Introduction: The Prehistoric Background

Eskimo artistic expression changed considerably as the result of European contact and trade. This was not the first or only such dramatic change, however. The various prehistoric Eskimo cultures were characterized by distinctively different artistic traditions that reflected different economic conditions, settlement patterns, and spiritual concerns. Unfortunately, we have no way of tracing what were probably the most important, though ephemeral, forms of artistic expression of these long-dead peoples: Their songs, dances, and stories are, for the most part, lost to us. Also, the difficult struggle for life was time-consuming, and the need for mobility and flexibility, paramount. The early Eskimos, therefore, left no imposing monuments and had little time to devote to elaborate religious paraphernalia. They simply decorated the weapons, household utensils, and clothes they needed for survival; and when they carved amulets for their own protection or toys for their children's amusement, they carved them small and portable.

Within these general requirements, artistic variation has been great, both in the quantity of recovered artifacts and in the quality of workmanship. For example, the tiny, finely worked, vividly colored flint and chert tools of the Arctic Small Tool tradition display a single-minded attention toward the hunt, but with an eye to beauty of material and precision in manufacture. The Dorset culture that followed also displayed a highly developed carving skill, which was turned toward the design of objects for spiritual comfort and physical safety. Naturalistic human and animal figurines of bone and ivory were ominously slit and pierced with wood slivers. Other artifacts also bespeak a preoccupation with supernatural appeals: tiny ivory masquettes, wooden face masks, hanging pendants, and antlers carved into a crowd of faces oriented in many directions. The preponderance of such items over materially utilitarian objects has led some analysts to infer an intensified fear on the part of the Dorset. This fear may have been due perhaps to Thule hunters attacking from the North, or to the uncertainties of hunting the largest of the sea mammals. In any case, the exquisite carvings of Dorset hunters and shamans represent a highly developed art form in both religious and utilitarian objects.

In the West, the Arctic Small Tool tradition developed into several different cultures, each having a recognizably distinctive artistic emphasis. Although the Norton culture of Central and Southwest coastal Alaska produced little decorative carving, its people were the best of Eskimo potters. Ipiutak hunters of Northern Alaska and Siberia produced no pottery but lavishly decorated their harpoon heads and carved an elaborate array of grave art: chains, swivels, fantastic animals, and ivory burial masks with jet inlaid eyes.

The Old Bering Sea or Okvik culture of the Bering Strait Islands and Chukchi Peninsula resembled the Ipiutak culture in many ways but had a more complex harpoon technology. Okvik seal hunters carved representational designs into their harpoons and made rather crude pottery. Though they carved countless small figurines of ivory, their art, like the Arctic Small Tool tradition, was primarily tool-related.

This trend was further exemplified by the Punuk culture, which developed around A.D. 500 from the Okvik on St. Lawrence Island. As the Punuk settlements grew larger, their pottery grew heavier, and ivory carving became relatively more consigned to the decoration of tools.

In all three of these cultures, there are hints of Asian artistic influence. Nucleated circle motifs used to mark the hip and shoulder joints of animal figurines recall the Seytho-Siberian animal styles of Central Asia as do the jet eye insets in Ipiutak burial masks.

Punuk settlements in Western Alaska were probably directly ancestral to the Thule culture. With their umiaks and specialized whaling technology, the hardy Thule people spread rapidly eastward into the Canadian Arctic, eventually supplanting the Eastern Dorset people. Thule success and their art had much to do with an elaborate technology devoted to sea-mammal harvest. Their pottery was crude, their flintworking and tool decoration, minimal. Other than the interesting exception of decorated women's tools (combs, belt toggles, clothing) and some human figurine toys, the Thule discharged their creative energies on an exceptionally elaborate hunting toolkit.

It should be clear at this point that there was no single "prehistoric Eskimo art." There was, in fact, no separate category set aside as artistic or artful. In the Arctic Small Tool, Okvik, and Thule traditions, the lives of hunters stressed the making of beautiful, functional tools, as the lives of their wives and daughters included the sewing of beautiful clothing. Ipiutak and Dorset hunters and shamans stressed the appeasement and manipulation of supernatural forces. In either case, though,

artistic effort was intrinsically interwoven into the social and economic necessities of difficult circumstance.

As European traders entered their lands, circumstances for the Eskimo became, in many ways, even more difficult. At this point, the flexibility and adaptability for which Eskimo peoples are rightfully admired allowed them to turn their extraordinarily developed skills for making things out of the scarce materials at hand into profitable exchange.

The Souvenir Trade
Ever since the Europeans first penetrated the world inhabited by the Eskimos, there has been trade in material items. Though many of the early contacts were marked by hostility, especially when the Eskimos saw the opportunity to gain some of the white man's coveted materials without exchange, the impulse to trade came from both sides. The ships' crews of the early explorers and traders were fascinated by the Eskimos' exotic cultural items and willingly exchanged beads, nails, knives, and other metal objects wanted by the Eskimos for items of clothing, hunting equipment, ivory tusks, and sometimes food. By the 18th century the Eskimos had become used to these summer visitors and started to make miniature models of the desired items for the increasingly regular trade. Nonetheless, few of these materials could be called "art" in Western terms. At that time, the Thule Eskimos had remarkably little in the way of non-utilitarian items for trade, even though many of their tools, clothes, and utensils were artfully decorated and beautifully made.

By the 19th century, explorers and traders became more frequent. Each year fleets of whaling ships visited both Alaska and Eastern Canada and some even set up bases where they could winter-over in the Arctic. The Canadian and American governments also established meteorological, police, and other stations within the true Arctic.

The souvenir trade was greatly increased by this regular contact with the Eskimo inhabitants. With the exception of those groups isolated

in the Central Arctic, this trade, along with other forms of employment, provided a regular form of income for the Eskimos. In turn, the Eskimos sought such items of white manufacture as metal for hunting equipment and knives, guns and powder and shot, portable stoves and cooking utensils, textiles for making clothes and tents, and some exotic items for consumption such as tobacco, tea, and some foodstuffs. As a consequence, the trade in models expanded from the manufacture of miniatures of traditional Eskimo items to new forms. These included ivory, stone, and wood carvings of both people and objects of Eskimo material culture as well as models of men with guns, chairs, accordians, wooden boats, and other items reflecting the white man's culture. Ironically, most of the latter kind of models rarely appeared in the post-1949 traditions of Eskimo art as we know it. Along with models manufactured for white consumption, the Eskimos continued to make small models (called *pinguak*) such as toys, gambling chips, and occasionally amulets, for their own use.

In the first two decades of the present century, whaling declined due to the fall in demand for baleen, leaving resident traders as the primary white contacts. With the rise in demand for white fox furs, the Hudson's Bay Company and other trading companies established permanent posts within the Eskimo lands. Souvenirs including models of such things as men, birds, and other animals continued to be sought by these traders. In Alaska and Canada, inspired by the whalers, some Inuit perfected the art of scrimshaw, and, consequently, an export trade in carved and engraved ivory developed in both areas. Such scrimshaw items, mainly smoothly carved realistic models in Alaska and decorated walrus tusks and cribbage boards in Canada, were exported for sale in the United States.

The outlet for handicrafts grew with the establishment of other white institutions such as the Royal Canadian Mounted Police (RCMP), Anglican and Catholic missionaries, medical facilities, and schools. By the 1930s when the Depression had

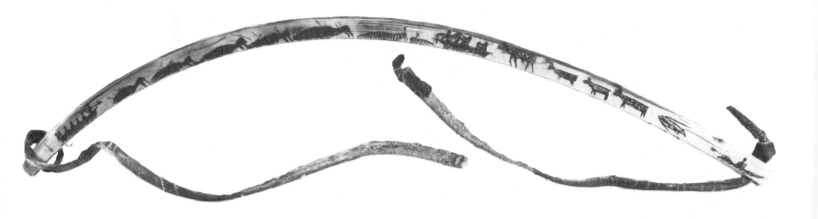

Scenes of animals and traditional hunting practices are incised on the ivory bow drill. The art style is typical of the late Thule culture.

Bow Drill (Provenience unknown). Ivory, hide; 35.5 cm long. CMNH #23102-15519.

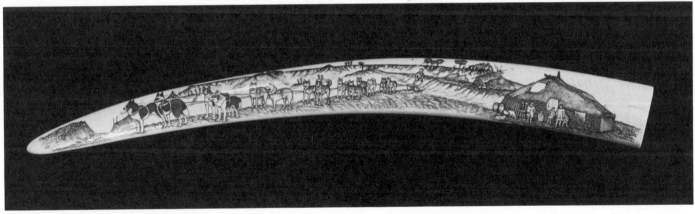

This tusk is incised with a typical Eskimo village scene. Happy Jack, the carver, was a renowned Eskimo artist who learned his skills from his association with whalers in the early 20th century.

Carving by Happy Jack (Nome, Alaska, U.S.A.). Walrus tusk, early 20th century, 63 cm long. CMNH #23102-15445.

lowered the prices for fox pelts and the Inuit were dependent on regular trade for imported items, there were attempts to increase the scope and scale of the handicraft "industry." The Hudson's Bay Company and the missionaries, with the encouragement of the Canadian Handicrafts Guild, held some exhibits of both men's and women's crafts with an eye to increasing export sales. Very little came of these sales, and World War II, with the accompanying irregularity of shipping, lack of interest and money, and temporary increase on fur prices, halted the activity, if not the ideas, about the craft export industry in Canada.

The Successful Promotion of the Commercial Arts

After World War II, the price of fox pelts and other Inuit products again fell, and the people of many areas were subject to privations. In 1948 a young Canadian artist, James Houston, travelled to James Bay and then on to Port Harrison to sketch and paint the arctic scenery and the people. While there, he became fascinated by the *pinguak* (miniature) models and souvenirs, collected them, and encouraged the local Inuit to make more for him. He took his collection back to Montreal, where the Canadian Handicrafts Guild persuaded him to exhibit them.

The reactions were so positive that the Guild requested his return to the east coast of Hudson Bay in 1949 to encourage the production for export of more of these delightful pieces. Houston travelled to Port Harrison and then north to Povungnituk and Cape Smith, asking the Inuit to make more stone and ivory carvings for sale. While some were confused at this sudden burst of interest, Houston encouraged them by offering credit at the Hudson's Bay Company stores, exchanging their art for his sketches, and assuring them of the worth of their creative efforts. He returned South where the Guild held a very successful sale in the autumn of that year and promised to take a steady flow of Inuit works to be bought through and shipped out by the Hudson's Bay Company store managers.

The federal government of Canada heard of this venture and, being concerned about the Inuit financial straits and the amount of welfare payments at that time, negotiated with the Guild to pay for Houston's 1949 trip and for him to travel more extensively in the North the following year. Thus, Houston became unofficial roving crafts officer in the Canadian Arctic, continuing his successful encouragement of the budding artists in many Eskimo settlements. Arrangements were made with the Hudson's Bay Company for their managers to extend credit to the artists and to ship out their productions annually for sale, both through their own retail stores and through the stores of the Canadian Handicrafts Guild and other outlets. The volume of arts and handicrafts grew tenfold each year. Sculptures made from the soapstone and serpentine deposits common throughout most of the Arctic soon replaced the miniature models as the most popular items.

Though the federal government thought at first that the initial subsidy of Houston's efforts would put the crafts industry on a self-sustaining or profit-making basis within a year or two, events made the whole phenomenon far more complicated, and, in many ways, more successful than anyone ever dreamed. What Houston had done was to encourage the manufacture of bold stone sculptures that set the tradition in the direction of art rather than handicrafts and the replication of items of material culture. This sculpture appealed to a different and infinitely more expandable market than had the little models and souvenirs of the previous era.

By 1951 the volume of sculpture produced had grown so large that the Canadian Handicrafts Guild could not handle it, and Houston called upon his friend Eugene Power of Michigan to help export the works to the United States. A successful businessman, Power bought a large quantity of sculpture and became wholesaler for the United States. This, along with publicity through *Time* magazine and the Smithsonian Institution, helped to create a favorable market within the United States.

At the same time, the Canadian federal government saw the financial possibilities and the nationalistic importance of the trade and agreed to subsidize Houston and to help expand sculpture production into other areas of the North. Houston travelled to most settlements in the Arctic, promoting commercial art production. In time, he was based at Cape Dorset on Baffin Island where he encouraged some very successful artists and eventually developed Inuit printmaking.

In the meantime, other white visitors and residents encouraged the new art forms. Hearing of the possibilities for monetary gain in settlements where there were no white agents, Eskimos sold their works to ships' crews and local whites. Houston and other government employees wrote a large number of articles about the new "discoveries" which were published in journals around the world. Through the National Museum, exhibitions were mounted, and publicity material was produced for wide distribution. When Princess Elizabeth visited Canada, she was given an Inuit sculpture and, in 1953 at the time of her Coronation, a major exhibition was held at the Gimpel Fils Art Gallery in London. Publicity from the Smithsonian Institution, as well as articles and reviews in journals and newspapers across the world, all helped to increase the demand and the prices for "Inuit Art." The increased public attention and demand also encouraged further production on the part of the Inuit.

Not all, however, was smooth going. The Hudson's Bay Company, which by the mid-1950s was responsible for the bulk of the purchasing throughout the North, found that many items were unsalable and that some regions' or artists' works were worth much less than others. The company also found that, at times, the production of art drew men away from what they considered to be the more lucrative occupation of providing pelts for sale. There was a general fear that the market, so well started, would collapse. Hudson's Bay Company managers stopped buying from some settlements, thus throwing the now even more dependent Inuit back on welfare rations.

During this period the federal government was establishing day schools, administrative offices, and nursing stations throughout the Arctic, thereby providing more resident customers for the Inuit artists. In some places the local administrators told the Inuit to carve for sale rather than go on welfare. Government agents, thus, began to buy the arts and handicrafts in competition with, or in place of, the Hudson's Bay Company, shipping them out to be sold through the Canadian Handicrafts Guild or other retail stores. This further government involvement led eventually to the creation of a government-backed corporation, Canadian Arctic Producers, that is now the major outlet for Canadian Inuit arts of all genres. Further publicity was in order and was provided through the production and wide distribution of two films by the governmental Canadian Film Board: *The Living Stone* and *Kenojuak —Eskimo Artist*. These attractively made films are about stone sculpture and print-making respectively.

During the 1960s further government involvement came in a number of forms. Publicity and exhibitions continued in Canada and abroad, and Canadian Inuit art became almost a "totemic" national symbol. The government encouraged its Northern agents to start producers' cooperatives in many Inuit settlements, which, though run by local people, received much subsidized assistance in management and marketing. For a while, the Inuit cooperatives in various areas of the Arctic were under the aegis of different governmental bodies— whether provincial, territorial, or federal. In all cases, however, the form and function of these cooperatives grew throughout the North. Though most of them began in order to sell art products to Southern Canada and other parts of North America, many of them also added consumers' cooperatives in the form of general stores that competed with the Hudson's Bay Company. By 1967 a Federation of Cooperatives was

started in Northern Quebec to coordinate both purchasing and selling efforts in that area; a similar federation was established soon thereafter in the Northwest Territories.

At most of these cooperatives, experiments in further kinds of commercial art and handicraft manufacture have been undertaken through the guidance of artists and technical experts from the federal, provincial, and territorial governments. Most of these experiments have been successful. The introduction of further print-making centers, appliqué and embroidery production, the making of dolls, souvenirs, silk-screen textiles and cards, and the sewing of wall hangings and high quality clothing have been among the successful ventures. Other ventures have not met with the same success. For example, some early attempts at clothing manufacture, batik production, the manufacture of *Ookpik* dolls, and pottery making have since been discontinued. Some of these unsuccessful ventures were temporary successes but then faded due to such factors as lack of demand, overly expensive production costs, and bad administration.

The major art forms—stone sculpture, bone sculpture, and print-making—have had their ups and downs. Prices to the producers-artists have risen so enormously that retail sales have often fallen off as collectors stop buying. Massive publicity has, however, accompanied huge travelling international exhibitions such as *Sculpture Inuit: Masterworks of the Canadian Arctic* (1971-73) and *The Inuit Print/L'Estampe Inuit* (1977-1980) as well as other Canadian exhibits. Because of this publicity, the demand and price level have held up, and these arts have retained their place among the most exciting and best known of all the art traditions extant in the world today. Thus, as the oldest artists who were there at the beginnings of the recent traditions grow old and die, a younger generation, born long after Houston first visited the Canadian Arctic, has come to see art production as a viable occupational avenue. With the influx of young talent, new styles and themes continue to emerge and excite

the connoisseurs, collectors, and the interested public.

Change and Differentiation within the Commercial Arts

When Houston visited the Canadian Arctic soon after World War II, most of the Eskimos still lived a traditional style of camp life, modified to include winter fox-trapping and the use of imported guns, boats, and textile clothing. Missionary activity had long since converted them to Christianity, but, for the most part, they ran the "churches" themselves. The missions and the Royal Canadian Mounted Police had been fairly successful in banning some of the more extreme traditional customs such as infanticide, senilicide, wife exchange, and polygyny. Though they were materially dependent on the outside world, the Canadian Inuit basically ran their own lives, and most lived in homogeneous, monolingual social environments. The models and souvenirs they made were not an important part of their lives, and their major artistic expressions still included the making of clothing, drumming and singing, dancing, and the telling of traditional stories.

It is fortunate that Houston was both an artist with a feel for and connections in the white art world and an artist attracted to the Inuit minor arts and sympathetic to their material conditions. When he bought the little souvenirs and miniature models, he always encouraged the Inuit to make more items for sale. At that time, many were not used to making souvenir models and did not understand why he would want more and more. Houston's encouragement as well as that from governmental agencies, however, led the artists to believe they could improve their work. Though the sculptural style was based on the traditional and 19th century miniature models, attitudes of both the Inuit and the white world led to great changes within the first decade or so of the fledgling industry.

Ivory was the preferred medium, as it was for traditional Inuit culture, but it imposed limitations on the expansion of production and stylistic change: First, ivory comes in relatively

179

This model igloo scene is reminiscent of the souvenir models of earlier times. After World War II, however, distributors discouraged pieces with detachable parts that could become broken or lost. The Inuit, nevertheless, like the contrasting colors and textures of various parts.

Carving of Snowhouse *by Moosones (Coppermine, Northwest Territories, Canada). Soapstone, ivory, fur, leather, copper; 1960s; 15 cm long, 8.5 cm wide. CMNH #31581-131.*

In the early 1950s, Inuit sculptors were encouraged to produce large, bold, realistic pieces such as this one to satisfy the demands of the Western art market.

Hunter with Harpoon and Seal *by Lazarusie (Port Harrison, Quebec, Canada). Soapstone, 1950s, 34 cm high. CMNH #31591-1.*

small sizes (walrus tusks and whales' teeth) and amounts (there was a limited number of these sea mammals to kill). It is also a hard medium that slows production and imposes limitations on the final artistic output. Finally, ivory is brittle, especially when not "cured" for a year or two, and can crack and split in warm environments.

Soapstone, on the other hand, is found in large quantities throughout most of the North. Through their traditional manufacture of cooking pots (*ukusik*) and oil-burning lamps (*qullik*), the Inuit know most of the workable sites where soapstone is found. The veins are large enough that, given the right tools, they impose little limitation on the size of the resultant artworks. Furthermore, even within a particular region, the quality, texture, and color of the stone varies, giving a variety of media to suit different artists.

The first pieces made for Houston were generally small (5 to 10 centimeters long, 2 to 4 inches long), rather rough models of common animal species and, occasionally, man. A few were representations of the Inuit spirit world; such subject matter was encouraged by Houston and many other buyers, even though it had previously been suppressed by missionary activity.

The Inuit soon learned that they could get more praise and money by making their sculptures larger, better finished, and more realistic. Within two or three years, sculptures of 15 to 25 centimeters (6 to 9 inches) with good polish and considerable detail began to emerge. The uniformity of the perceived market demand, however, did not result in uniform stylistic developments throughout the North, nor did absolute realism become dominant save in a few areas. The Inuit soon learned that, though their art was getting "better," it was not supposed to "look like the white man's art" (of which they had little familiarity anyhow); nor was it supposed to represent the known world around them, the familiar world of the 1950s. On the contrary, they were encouraged to feel, and soon did, that their art—their messages to the appreciative outside world—should represent what was truly Eskimo, i.e., their past traditions, many of which had already disappeared or were fast fading. Unlike the souvenir art of the previous 100 years, attempts to portray store-bought or textile clothing, wooden canoes, guns, saws, houses, and so on were discouraged. As their traditions rapidly disappeared, many Inuit consciously thought they should portray what it used to be like "to be Eskimos," not only for the white market but also for their own younger generations.

But it is not only the strictures of the buyers and advisors that have influenced the directions in Canadian Inuit sculpture. The artists and their local critics have their own definite ideas of aesthetics and technical success. The rock with which they work, varying widely in color, hardness, and brittleness, likewise presents an enormous range of possibilities.

During the 1950s the size of the average sculptures continued to increase as the Eskimos realized that many store managers (who bought most of the arts then) priced "by the inch," and, thus, there was less "effort per dollar" in making large rather than small pieces. Furthermore, very small pieces, if they are detailed, require very finicky work that often stretches the patience, eyesight, and skills of many of the artists. In some areas the buyers gave fairly definite instructions as to what subject matter or style was wanted, whereas in others the Inuit remained somewhat confused and either experimented with a large variety of types or interpreted for themselves "what the white man wants."

Within the first 10 years several specific trends were visible. In addition to sheer size, many of the sculptures became bolder, with specific emphasis on bulky curves and "monumentality." Many Inuit enjoyed putting in such detail as characteristic faces, weapons and equipment, and the folds and nuances of skin clothing. Bone and ivory faces, harpoon parts, boots, hands, and eyes became popular, and the small, white appurtenances set against the massive stone sculptural background were very attractive.

Boldness was also displayed in other ways. The artists delighted in making more complex figures. Sometimes scenes of many figures were carved on a single base or very detailed single figures, people, or animals were daringly carved out of one piece of stone. Though the buyers often discouraged such pieces because they might break in transit, in many areas the Inuit continued to produce them.

As the ability to display detail and realism developed, the expression of movement and humor also became common and much admired. Individual artists began to experiment within their regional styles, and many of them developed certain formal or content or stylistic characteristics (*nalunaikutanga*, "that which helps one to know") by which their pieces could be recognized by other Inuit of their community. This trend towards individualism was encouraged at another level by the agents of the white art market, who requested that all artists sign their names on the bottom of their sculpture; most artists did so in syllabics. The agents also began to recognize individual styles and to promote individual artists by holding one-man shows and by inviting them to visit galleries and exhibitions in Southern Canada.

The differentiation of artists within a particular community exacerbated the Inuit's typically competitive spirit and directed it toward art production. The Inuit began to recognize who were the "leaders" in each settlement, enabling them to rank the best artists and accord prestige to the most admired and the most successful. The new prestige accorded artists indicated that art production had come to take the place of hunting prowess as a major feature of relative status, especially among the men. Art production had moved from an ancillary occupation, practiced when bad weather or surfeit of food made hunting undesirable, to the center stage of Inuit life. It became a major source of livelihood for the support of whole families. Nevertheless, most Inuit men and women would have preferred to be able to make their livelihoods from hunting and trapping or from secure wage labor. Even though hunting and trapping are risky, for the Eskimo they represented a traditional lifestyle that provided good food. Wage labor, although not common, provided a steadier income than art production and required less effort. In fact, when a large number of Inuit were interviewed during the 1960s and 1970s, most indicated that they only produced art works *inurutiksaktuariraku*, "because it is the only way I have of making a livelihood." Interviews indicated that in each community artistic leaders emerged, and their styles and subject matter were often emulated by the less successful. Many artists, however, pointed out that they did not have the talent to do as daring or detailed works as the leaders, so they felt contained to do less ambitious, and often smaller and less realistic, pieces than those whom they admired. Women and old people whose strength and eyesight were failing also typically declared themselves unable to do as well as the most successful men.

Individual talent aside, the major factor that has differentiated the art work of the various regions has been the different kinds of rock available. Throughout the Arctic, rock ranges from the very soft steatite (soapstone) through the harder forms of serpentine to the very hardest fieldstones such as granite and gneiss. In addition to hardness, texture varies considerably. The very soft rocks are very evenly grained, whereas brittle rocks are very granular and veined and thus prone to splitting while being worked. Rock also varies in color from the creamy white oolite limestone, through various shades of grey, to the light and dark green serpentines and various brown and black stones. Within this color range some are evenly colored while others are speckled with blue or even red. Many of the rocks even change color from their natural shade to a darker, more evenly intense shade when wet or polished.

The limitations of the medium combined with the leadership of the most skilled artists and the demands and suggestions of specific local buyers have been responsible for the development of regional styles. Found only in relatively small pieces, the stone from the Belcher Islands and Great Whale River, for instance, is very fine grained and smooth with longitudinal striations. Thus, the people from this area are constrained to make small figurines and often adapt the rock to elongated birds and other creatures, using the colored grain as part of the final pattern. In their works, detail is well developed, but a high polish is not usually possible.

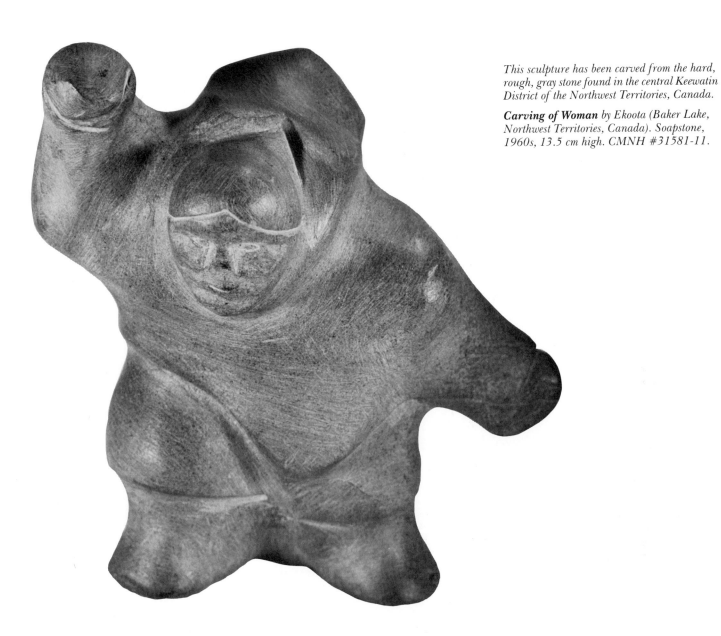

This sculpture has been carved from the hard, rough, gray stone found in the central Keewatin District of the Northwest Territories, Canada.

Carving of Woman by Ekoota (Baker Lake, Northwest Territories, Canada). Soapstone, 1960s, 13.5 cm high. CMNH #31581-11.

The smooth, fine-grained stone used for this piece is characteristic of that found in the Belcher Islands.

Carving of Loon by Shoapik (Belcher Islands, Northwest Territories, Canada). Soapstone, 1960s, 19 cm long. CMNH #31581-16.

Sculptor George Arlook of Baker Lake (Northwest Territories, Canada) uses a hacksaw to cut soapstone, 1982.

The softish grey rock of the Povungnituk, Ivujivik, and Sugluk area is also fine grained but not so strong. This rock allows the artist maximum freedom to produce any kind of shape, but fine parts and projections are very brittle. The grey rock is rather unattractive in itself but takes a high black polish which is then further incised for the light grey contrasting details of faces, fingers, and clothing decoration.

The grey stone available in the Rankin Inlet and Baker Lake area is hard but very brittle and is best used for "lumpy" carvings with few thin parts or projections. It does not take any polish, and the majority of the pieces are oiled, often by the buyers, to produce a shiny black surface.

Lake Harbour and nearby Frobisher Bay often use a mottled light green serpentine of great beauty. Though hard, it is of even texture and allows for fine parts and detail, though it does not polish as well as some others.

The areas which encompass a variety of attractive rock types are perhaps the most enduringly successful carving communities. These include Cape Dorset and Repulse Bay, both of which have a number of different colored serpentines (green, bluish, grey, and black) which are eminently suitable for sculptures. Most of the stone takes a good polish, is not too brittle, and looks very well when combined with ivory and bone accessories. The Inuit themselves prize the rocks of the Belcher Islands and Lake Harbour for their absence of brittleness. The sculptors of these areas are envied by those inhabiting less well-endowed settlements.

The Inuit know the characteristics of all these rocks, and their most intense interest focuses on the material and its possibilities rather than on the final form. When starting a sculpture, the artist turns the lump of stone over and over, trying to imagine what might "fit" into it. Having made a decision, he or she starts to tap or cut the rock with a primary tool such as an axe, hacksaw, or rough file, hoping that the stone is workable. If it is, the rough shape is formed quickly with these tools, and the artist constantly checks the form from different angles. The next stage involves using a different set of tools for more detailed work; files, pocketknives, and chisels are employed until the near-final form is reached. If the stone cracks or breaks in the process, the artist again turns the stone over and tries to see how it could be modified into another image without wasting the work done. The final stage involves surface and detail work. Shiny surfaces are much admired, and most stone will take a polish that may be applied with wet sandpaper or emory paper. Occasionally, the piece may be polished by rubbing with the hand or some kind of oil. Surface detail is finally applied by cutting through the polish with fine tools and using the natural color of the rock as relief. The artist's name is then inscribed, usually in syllabic script, on the base of the piece. More recently, the name of the settlement, a © for copyright, and the company or co-op's stock number are also inscribed on the bottom. Because many sculptures portray mythological or other culturally meaningful scenes, the artist may also attempt to write the story on the base, though very few of the purchasers or even dealers can read the script and translate and understand the scene.

The three carvings show different stages in the sculpting process, from roughing out to final polish.

Walrus Carvings *by Kakasalala Kasudluak (Pangnirtung, Northwest Territories, Canada). Soapstone, ivory; 1970s; 18 cm, 23 cm, and 18 cm long. CMNH #31581-119m, o, p.*

Print-Making

James Houston became government administrator in Cape Dorset on Southwest Baffin Island in 1955. Cape Dorset served as the commercial and governmental center for the 450 or so Inuit, called *Sikusuilamiut* ("the people in the place without thin ice"), who lived mainly in hunting camps stretched out along the coastline between the Foxe Basin and Markham Bay. As a result of Houston's prior visits, Cape Dorset was already known for its fine production of green serpentine sculptures. At that time the Hudson's Bay Company was buying sculptures for export and the few other local white residents and visitors also bought the attractive green carvings for their own collections.

Although Houston was the government administrator, he spent much of his time developing the Inuit arts. He encouraged the sculptors, praised them, and paid them well for their efforts. Other means of making a cash livelihood were also sought for the Inuit, who had begun to settle in ever greater numbers around the white institutions. Even though Houston thought of many possibilities for the "craft industry," none came to success except print-making. According to Houston, this started when he was trying to explain to an Inuk how the white man printed the same little picture on cigarette packages. Houston then proceeded to demonstrate the process by inking an engraved ivory tusk and pressing it onto paper. The Inuk artist became enthusiastic about the idea, and, under Houston's direction, he and other artists experimented with all sorts of print media including ivory, stone, linoleum, and sealskin stencils. However, given the paucity of materials in the North and the extreme difficulties with shipping, none of these media were practical except stone blocks quarried from local sources.

Houston encouraged the local sculptors to carve images in stone blocks, which were then inked and printed, using materials that had to be imported from Southern Canada. Most of the original printmakers were men and most of their subjects were animals, hunting scenes, and men and women in traditional dress. Mrs. Alma Houston also encouraged women, who had been sewing crafts for sales, to try their hand at print-making. The women claimed that they were not strong or skillful enough to cut the stone block, so they were given paper and pencil (later colored crayons) to produce drawings that were translated into print blocks by men. Thus, a core of specialized blockcutters was formed, and this artistic division of labor soon characterized all of Cape Dorset's work.

The Hudson's Bay Company sold a set of the experimental prints in 1958, and in 1959 there was a successful exhibition and sale of the previous year's prints at the Shakespeare Festival at Stratford, Ontario. Since that time, annual editions of Cape Dorset prints have been exhibited and sold every autumn, with increasing demand from dealers and collectors all over the world. Every year the manager of the West Baffin Island Cooperative buys drawings from the artists. Of the hundreds or thousands of drawings bought every year, a small percentage is selected for potential inclusion in that year's collection. These are transferred onto large, flat stone blocks as follows: The drawing is first transferred onto tracing paper and then onto the print block by the artist. Secondly, one of the five or six trained Inuit block cutters chisels around the carbon image until only the raised black image remains on the rock. Thirdly, one of these same Inuit men inks the image with colored inks and places print paper on top of the image. The ink is then transferred onto the paper by slow and careful rubbing, and the print is eventually pulled off the block and hung up to dry. Each print is titled and stamped with an anagram of the artist's and the printer's name. Two proof prints are drawn and sent to the Eskimo Art Council in Ottawa where it is approved for the year's collection or rejected. A catalogue of all approved prints is published every year. If a print is approved by the Eskimo Art Council, 50 more copies are then produced and sent to dealers in Southern Canada for exhibition and distribution.

Not all the Cape Dorset prints are produced by the stone-cut block method. In 1961 copper plate engraving was introduced, and since then a few such prints have appeared in the annual collections. Copper plate engraving involves a different socio-artistic organization, because the artist directly makes the plate from which the final paper print is drawn.

Engraving a copper plate is rather like engraving ivory, archaeologically and historically an important part of Inuit art traditions. A burin, a sharp pointed tool, is used to cut on a hard, nearly flat surface. There is no tolerance for error, and the final image consists of very fine lines or speckled surfaces.

The sealskin stencil print-making technique has been likened to traditional boot and garment-making techniques. However, use of this technique has been a failure. A stencil pattern is cut from the seal skin and then inked, but the images become messy at the cut edge of the skin after three or four images have been printed. Since 1958, however, cardboard-type stencils have been substituted for the sealskin technique. Cardboard stencils are cut following the outline of the artists' drawings. These have resulted in some very famous prints.

Since the early 1970s, prints have been made by a combination of techniques, especially using stone cut and stencil to produce different parts and textures in the same image. In the same period, one further technique, drawing with a grease pencil on a lithography plate, has become important. This technique, as with engraving, usually requires that the artist's drawing be transferred directly from the plate onto the print paper. However, unlike engraving, the texture of the image may be much softer and more varied; for such prints, complex polychrome designs are the norm.

Other Arctic communities soon emulated the success of Cape Dorset. Povungnituk, which had already established an art-producing cooperative in 1958-61 under the guidance

The artist Aiola is inking a print block in the Cape Dorset (Baffin Island, Canada) print shop, 1968. Note the copper plate printing press at the rear and the proofs hanging on the wall.

of Father A.P. Steinmann, hired an artist to teach the Inuit how to make prints in 1961. After a year of experimentation with many techniques, another artist spent two years training Inuit in stone block cutting and print-making. The first annual collection was published and sold in 1962, and collections have appeared in most subsequent years.

Unlike the Cape Dorset techniques, the artists of Povungnituk usually carve their own print blocks directly. Images are sketched on paper and then carved on the block or drawn directly on the block. The block is then sold to the cooperative where the trained print-makers produce the proofs and the final images for the collection.

The socio-artistic print-making organization at Povungnituk differs from Cape Dorset in several ways. Each artist is able to produce very few images for sale each year and, thus, the co-op amasses up to a few hundred blocks rather than the thousands collected each year at Cape Dorset. As a consequence, a far higher proportion must be selected for the annual collection. Although fewer mistakes and corrections are tolerable with this method, the final image is a more faithful reproduction of what the artist originally drew. Unlike Cape Dorset, the intermediary role of specially trained block cutters is eliminated. With the drawing composed by the artist and cut directly onto the stone, the uncut parts are often left as a border; the direct influence of the stone medium itself is, thus, much more overt.

Povungnituk has also differed from Cape Dorset in having few, if any, white advisors present in the community. While some think that this has resulted in a generally lower quality of art (by white standards), others believe that Povungnituk prints are a more direct expression of genuine Inuit aesthetic ideas. In the past decade, more advisors have been present and the range of techniques has been expanded to match more nearly those found at Cape Dorset.

At the other end of the Canadian Arctic, the community at Holman Island began experimenting with print-making in the early 1960s. The first collection for sale appeared in 1965. Both stone block and stencil techniques have been used, but the prints and resulting images have been kept simpler than those of most other communities. As in Cape Dorset, artists have submitted drawings. In the first few years, the image was transferred by cutting through the drawing directly onto the fine-grained stone block, and, thus, destroying it. Plastic stencils have been made for each portion of the original drawing that is to be printed in a different color. The production of the final image is consequently complicated and time-consuming.

In the Central Arctic, the inland people at the community of Baker Lake have been involved with print-making for almost as long as the other groups. It was not, however, until the arrival of the artist-advisor Jack Butler in 1969 that print-making took off. That fall an experienced Cape Dorset artist and block-cutter, Aiola, came as an advisor, and by the next summer the first annual collection was approved for sale. The people of Baker Lake use both stone cut and stencil, as at Cape Dorset. Though some of the images of the oldest artists are simple, even "primitive," Baker Lake is particularly known for the complexity of color and design. In some cases, each print is composed of many superimposed stonecut and stencil images; for each of these prints it may take as long as two years to produce one series of 50 images.

In the 1970s another community, the large village of Pangnirtung on Baffin Island, became a print-making center under the direction of James Houston's son, John Houston. Using both stonecut and stencil, the artists have stayed with fairly simple, often pastel colored images that often portrayed the early history of the Pangnirtung area and its involvement with the whalers of the 19th century.

Most recently, Clyde River, another village on the east coast of Baffin Island, has joined the print-makers; its first series was accepted by the Eskimo Art Council in 1981. These images, again fairly simple but in bolder colors, have so far concentrated on simple images of traditional life, somewhat similar to those common in the earlier Povungnituk prints.

Modern Canadian Inuit print-making is an "assimilated art form." Its format and techniques have been derived from the mainstream Western culture that now dominates almost all of Eskimo life. Although there has been some modification of the Western materials and tools used, print-making derives from Western art traditions and is judged and made for sale in the Western art world, where it is remarkably successful both aesthetically and commercially. Nonetheless, the formal organization and the content of this art form do not resemble that of other North American print-makers with whom the Inuit are in competition.

The content of Inuit prints, like that of their sculptures, is related to traditional Inuit life for two reasons. First, the Inuit, especially the older ones, are more familiar with their own culture and environment than they are with that of the white man; so far, most of them do not feel competent to portray things outside of their background milieu. Secondly, they have often been told by their art advisors and customers not to do things that look as though they could have been done by the white man. These two reinforcing rationales allow the Inuit to portray things which are specifically "theirs," things of which they can be proud and which form part of their emerging self-conscious ethnic heritage.

A basic theme, found in many media, is that of the land and the animals and their relation to Inuit as hunters. Other aspects of their traditional culture such as igloos and tents, domestic activities, mothers with children in their parkas, forms of play, and games are also portrayed.

Another theme is that of imagination and spiritual beings. Before literacy and books, the supernatural world of shamans and spirits—good and evil—was very much part of everyone's imagination. Each person had his own mental image of the spirits and souls of people and animals. These powerful representations are now emerging in the fantastic representations that print-making, with its fluidity and colors, allows the artist to portray. The choice of subject matter seems to vary according to the sex of the artist. Eskimo men tend to portray the "real" world, the environment and animals. On the other hand, some of the women who have led a more sedentary, circumscribed life have given rein to their imaginations in portraying the fantastic and unreal.

Print-making is an individual art form that within the bounds of the medium, the guidance of the art advisors, and the selective judgments of the Eskimo Art Council, allows a tremendous range of creativity and personal and regional variety. Individual artists stand out for the style and content of their works, ranging from the very realistic and detailed images of natural species and traditional scenes by Kananginak, to the whimsical portrayal of imaginary birds by Lucy, and the strongly design-oriented, symmetrical works of Oonak and Qirnuajuak. Even with such variety, one may make some generalizations about Inuit prints.

Most importantly, we should remember that Inuit art is not done from life or from models. Thus, the graphic tradition is a "mental" art, much like that of most non-Western aboriginal peoples. This fact alone has powerful consequences: It detaches the artist from the need to make images of his or her immediate surroundings. A large proportion of the works are either "memory" art, recalling long-past days of traditional scenes and events or fantasy, portraying mental images for which there is no prototype. Freed from the need to portray "accuracy," the artists can concentrate on key symbols or on aspects of color and design. Thus, there is no attempt to portray perspective, and horizon lines are rarely included. Figures may be portrayed as visually frontal or, as is often the case in the work of older artists, from other angles such as above, or from multiple, simultaneous angles. Background may not be included and many scenes seem to "float" on the white paper.

As noted earlier, there is a tendency for men to portray scenes of traditional hunting and figures of animal species. Women may portray domestic scenes, images of fantasy creatures, and patterns of colors. In the traditional activity of making skin boots and clothing, women have often cleverly juxtaposed light and dark furs creating abstract patterns. Women's prints often reflect this tradition in their strong emphasis on symmetry, design elements, and repetition, often building around a central "realistic" image. Both men's and women's art eschews the straight line; whereas men may emphasize rugged lines, women employ intricate and billowing curves.

The Inuit believe that they have been instructed to avoid showing anything of the white man's world in which they now are immersed. Thus, the vast majority of prints portray little if anything of the modern, lived-in world of the contemporary Inuit. Since the late 1970s, however, a few such images have begun to appear, both because the Inuit wish to portray aspects of their familiar, known world and because the Eskimo Arts Council has accepted some of these portrayals as part of the yearly print series.

Over the past 20 years, there have been some general changes in Inuit prints. Major trends include print-makers' increasing technical sophistication and mastery of a greater number of print-making techniques. This has allowed for ever more complex images as the Inuit experiment and extend the limits of their mastery over the medium. Very few

Inuit have received any formal training outside of their Northern villages, but within the past 10 years the government has supported an increasing number of technical workshops for print-makers. It is probable that some of the younger artists may wish to break away from accepted styles and techniques and experiment within the full range of traditions and genres of the Western art world.

Since their beginnings in the late 1950s, the graphic arts have become "big business" both for the Northern settlements and the entire Canadian art world. Each of the print-making centers is situated within a cooperative. Although the cooperatives often include other activities, profits from art sales may sustain the parent organization. Cape Dorset's West Baffin Eskimo cooperative, the most successful example, has had graphic sales in excess of $1,000,000 per year. The annual sales of graphics generate millions of dollars in revenue both to the Inuit and their cooperatives and to the extensive distribution network. Additional income is generated through the sale of reproduction rights for calendars, postage stamps, illustrations, and special commissions. Exhibitions, catalogs, books, television programs, and artists' travels also help to maintain and promote Inuit arts.

Some of the cooperatives have started to sell graphic arts other than prints. Selected drawings from the vast stocks collected but not made into prints may be sold individually or in the form of expensive sets of reproductions. In some cases, artists may have become famous since the drawings were originally made, or a famous artist may have died. Thus, the value of the backlog of graphic materials continues to increase and may be a source of artistic, historical, and commercial value for years to come.

A few Inuit have become professional artists outside of the cooperative-controlled, print-making arena. Some have moved to Southern Canada where they work as illustrators of books and magazines. Such individuals may also produce graphics for exhibition, often using media not

commonly available in the North.

A few artists living in the Arctic have become famous for their watercolor, oil, and acrylic paintings. These individuals have usually acquired non-traditional materials through a close relationship with whites who may be artists themselves. These paintings are not usually exported through the usual commercial channels but are bought by local residents for themselves or for export. They are frequently commissioned for display in local governmental institutions such as schools and offices. So far most of these artists are men, and the styles are usually conventional and depictive. Though the mastery of the technique has improved, the paintings do not show the scope and imagination characteristic of the well-guided, cooperatively run print-shops.

Other Art Forms
Stone sculpture and print-making have constituted the major forms of commercial art. Other media and techniques have also evolved in the past 40 years. This section provides a brief description of the many forms of commercial art that supplement stone sculpture and print-making. Within regional contexts, other art and craft forms—both old and new—have flourished.

In some areas, although there was interest in carving, suitable stone was either poor or entirely absent. Other hard media were, thus, used for carving. In the Northwest Territories' Pelly Bay and Baker Lake, caribou antler was adapted to make small sculptures of people, birds, and equipment. Independently, Inuit in various settlements have invented the idea of using antlers as "trees" with small sculptures of birds, or even seals, sitting on the tips!

With ivory hard to obtain, antler, like bone, is also often used for accessories in stone carvings or in multi-media figures. Around Hudson Strait and Foxe Basin where walrus abound, the penis bone of the walrus (dense and up to 60 centimeters [two feet] long) is a favored medium as a substitute for whole ivory tusks. Like the ivory cribbage boards carved prior to the 1950s, these bones are mounted on short legs and sometimes incised with many small soapstone sculptures or even a complex scene mounted on top.

A major sculptural genre which emerged in the 1960s has been carvings made from fossil whalebone. The Arctic abounds with the archaeological sites of the Inuit's Thule ancestors who, like the Northwest Alaskan Eskimos of today, were mainly whale hunters. They lived in semisubterranean dwellings with whalebone roofs rather than in igloos. The collapsed remains of these dwellings are favorite sources of whale ribs and vertebrae. This bone, which varies from hard, elongated pieces to large masses which are cellular and friable, is an ideal material for innovative sculptures. In the 1960s, residents of communities with a poor supply of stone, such as Pangnirtung on Baffin Island and Spence Bay and Coppermine in the Northwest Territories, mined the sites of their ancestors, despite the objections of archaeologists and the Canadian government. The large imaginative sculptures they created have made clever use of the shapes of the bones themselves. These pieces were created when large sculptures were becoming acceptable and fashionable in the commercial Inuit art market. During the 1970s when the United States banned whaling and the importation of the products of whaling, these sculptures were, ironically, barred by U.S. Customs, and, consequently, the rate of demolition of archaeological sites dropped off considerably.

Jewelry is another art-craft form which has enjoyed a long popularity. For decades the Inuit have made small ivory finger-rings for sale and export. Often these rings are carved in relief with the figure of a man, whale, or something else that is recognizably "Eskimo." Since the 1960s additional detail has been added to the tiny figures carved on the rings. In the mid-1970s, the Canadian government encouraged other kinds of jewelry-making through an educational crafts program and an Arctic-wide competition. The artists of Cape Dorset have been most successful at jewelry making and little sustained interest in this craft has emerged elsewhere.

The graphic arts of the Canadian Inuit have centered on print-making, using stone-cut blocks, stencils, copper-plates, and lithographic engraving. Other two-dimensional arts in a variety of media have also shown continuous development. The major artistic skill of the traditional women was the sewing of clothing and boots from caribou and sea-mammal skins. Thus, clothing has not merely been utilitarian, but its creation has involved the juxtaposition of light- and dark-colored skins in striking and intricate geometric patterns.

During the 1950s, as the production of commercial stone sculpture got underway, Inuit women were encouraged to use their needlework skills in sewing depictive scenes for wall hangings. These rectangular pictures of traditional life were usually made of attractive sealskins. Caribou skin is too long-haired and brittle for this purpose. The wall hangings were sold to local residents as well as being exported to Southern Canada. Some women became very good at this rather time-consuming activity, and, as the price of sealskin rose dramatically, they substituted other materials.

With the increased price of sealskin, a true appliqué technique has evolved. Rectangles of colored blanket or duffle cloth have been overlaid with cut-out figures in other colors to create elaborate scenes. This new art form has avoided the problems of the availability, price, and unpleasant smell of sealskin. The textile wall-hangings grew both in size and popularity, and embroidery with colored wools has become an additional form of decoration. Huge hangings have been commissioned for the decoration of government and other buildings. This art form is now practiced by many famous women artists, particularly those who have also been successful designers of prints. A few men, particularly those whose design sense has made them famous print artists, have also created famous pieces in this genre.

Other textile arts have been produced under government programs. Batik-making was unsuccessfully taught in Povungnituk in the 1960s. True loom weaving has been introduced with more success in Baker Lake and other areas. Decorated clothing, made from textiles imported from other parts of Canada and the United States, has been introduced as an export commodity. Some women sew clothing in their own houses, whereas others work in factories where the cutting and sewing are done with the aid of machines.

Although originating from the souvenir trade, the production of dolls has evolved and flourished over the years. The first dolls were minimal human representations with a hard body-head of wood or bone that was wrapped in skin or cloth clothing. With commercial demand the dolls became more elaborate; stuffed, soft bodies and detailed textile clothing have been substituted, although in some areas the head may be a stone sculpture. These dolls are usually made by women in their homes, but, on Holman Island and other places with specialized craft shops, they are made in the central workshop to predetermined patterns. Though most of the figures are human, stuffed animals and birds have also been made.

In 1963 Jeanie Snowball, a woman from Fort Chimo on the Labrador Peninsula, made a truncated owl figure that caught the fancy of Canadian officials with its whimsical appearance and ability to stand up. Rush orders were received for more of these sealskin covered *Ookpik* (owl) figures, but the women of the community could not keep up with the demand. The Canadian government and the Fort Chimo Cooperative, therefore, entered into an agreement with two companies for large scale manufacture of this owl in different sizes and price-levels. For a while the sales flourished, the profits returned to the Co-op, and the inventor became nationally famous.

Another craft, coiled basketry, has been produced both in Alaska and in the Canadian Arctic, in a small area along the east coast of Hudson Bay, from the Great Whale River to

First invented in 1963 by Jeanie Snowball of Fort Chimo, Labrador Peninsula, ookpik dolls are still popular and are now manufactured throughout the Northwest Territories.

Ookpik *(owl) doll by unknown artist (Holman Island, Northwest Territories, Canada). Sealskin, felt, leather, cotton; 1970s; 16 cm high. CMNH #32142-19.*

Central Canadian Eskimo women living along the east coast of Hudson Bay traditionally wove coiled baskets. Made from dried grasses, these baskets were usually cylindrical and lidded. After 1949, women were encouraged to produce baskets for sale.

Basket and Lid *by Malaya Tookalak (Great Whale River, Quebec, Canada). Grass, soapstone; 1960s; 13.5 cm wide. CMNH #31581-51.*

Povungnituk. Although some baskets were collected in the pre-Houston era, it was not until after 1949 that Inuit women were encouraged to make them specifically for sale. Made from dried local grasses, these cylindrical, lidded, loosely coiled baskets were easily adapted to the consumer market. Though traditionally plain, commercialization was enhanced by weaving geometrical patterns into the vertical sides, either by dyeing grasses with chemical colors or by weaving with strips of dark sealskin. Often a small soapstone sculpture was added to the lid as a handle, thus making the basket more usable and relating the craft to the known tradition of Inuit soapstone sculpture. At a few hundred per year, the volume of commercial basketry has never been large; it is a time-consuming process that is not very lucrative, and relatively few women known how to weave well.

This listing does not exhaust the range of arts and crafts that have been made for sale in the past 40 years. Models and miniatures of traditional crafts are still popular, and large items such as kayaks and harpoons can be made to order. Inuit ingenuity, stimulated by the government-sponsored crafts programs and the local crafts officers, has resulted in experimentation with many forms and media, each with varying degrees of commercial success. As long as easier, high-paying employment opportunities are not available, the Inuit will continue to produce innovative materials designed to capture a segment of the market. Some of the avenues explored thus far have been miniaturization, gigantism, exoticism, humor, and scatological material. Some Inuit consciously create the "studiedly primitive" to appeal to some sections of the market, whereas others wish to innovate with the wildest of colors and fantasies to get away from the stereotypic images of tradition. A new generation has been born since the early successes of the commercial arts, and, unlike their forebears, they have gone to regular schools and learned English and become familiar with the outside world. Television and comic books

abound in the North, stimulating not only new images, but new perceptions of "what the white man wants." A few young Inuit have been trained in art schools outside the North and have produced remarkable new synthetic art forms that have found a place in the mainstream arts of the world.

Conclusion
In the past few decades the visual arts have emerged as an important source of livelihood for the Canadian Inuit, fitting well between self-employment through hunting and trapping and the increasingly dominant salaried forms of institutional employment. Indeed, beyond paying the artists, the art industry has generated employment opportunities through the running of the cooperative institutions, the heart of many communities. In spite of the strains of a new sedentary lifestyle, compulsory education, unemployment, and rapid cultural change, the Canadian Inuit have become particularly proud of their place in the world. Local and national exhibitions, books, journal articles, visits by dignitaries, public adulation, and various prizes and medals have impressed upon the Inuit the prominence of "Eskimo arts." Increasingly, the Inuit see the production of their visual arts as an opportunity to make statements or to "send messages" about what it means to be Inuit. It is seen as an opportunity to impress the rest of the world and to give expression to memories of a distinctive but fading past. Some Inuit also view their arts as a chance to illustrate to their own children and to posterity "what it was like to be Inuit," because the younger generation has never known the world of nomadism, struggles for survival, and sociocultural autonomy. This didactic function will increase in importance as the Inuit are seen as recorders of their own history. However, to date, very few Inuit keep their arts for their own purpose; the vast majority make them only to sell.

While the outburst of creativity and illustrative materials of the past generation has thrust the visual arts to the center stage of Inuit life and

created new forms and genres, other forms of artistic expression have been suppressed. Other than small carvings and utilitarian forms of decoration, traditional art consisted of the manufacture of skin clothing and the vocal forms of singing, storytelling, and drum dancing. The ephemeral vocal art forms have undergone great transformation since World War II. The singing of personal and traditional songs, including the peculiar "throat singing" of women, has almost died out in the Canadian Arctic. Drum dancing has completely disappeared from the Eastern Canadian Arctic, though it has retained its status as a minor and somewhat self-conscious art similar to the role played by traditional singing in the Western Arctic and parts of Alaska. In some areas, the interests of white people, self-conscious "ethnic gatherings," and the making of tape-recordings and records have, however, temporarily revived these art forms. But the vocal traditions have moved totally away from the household and community context, as other forms of entertainment such as the radio, modern dance, movies, and television have come to dominate.

Inuit visual arts have done much for Canada. Since World War II, governmental organizations, commercial companies, and countless individuals have promoted the arts of the Inuit, the most famous of the native peoples of Canada. One reason for the promotion has been to provide an income for these indigenous peoples whose former lives of hunting and trapping have become less and less rewarding. "Carving instead of welfare" was at times one of the official rationales for supporting the Inuit art industry.

On the other hand, the degree of support and pride goes well beyond temporary relief measures and economic rationales. Part of the answer lies in the post-World War II international stress on ethnic arts and on the fates of enclave minority peoples.

Another reason for the support lies in the nature of Canadian culture itself. Canada, though vitally concerned with the arts, has not been known as a leader in the world of visual arts. For a long time Canada has faced serious identity and cultural problems. The need for art forms that are unique and ethnically characteristic of Canada has, therefore, frequently been voiced. Compared with the United States, which is well known for its Indians but less well known for its Alaskan Eskimo arts, Canada has been able to place its "Eskimos" as an emblem or symbol on the national and international scene. The Eskimos as a symbol of Canada demonstrate the country's artistic taste, its separateness from the United States, and its paternalistic generosity towards a minority people who carry a favorable image. For their part, the Canadian Inuit have, in comparison with their cultural relatives in Alaska and Greenland, used the opportunity to innovate and create exciting new genres that provide as much continuity with their traditional means of existence as does the subject matter of the art forms themselves.

Reading List

Artscanada, 162-163 (1971-72). (Special issue on the Eskimo world.)

Blodgett, Jean. *Port Harrison/Inoucdjouac.* Winnepeg: Winnepeg Art Gallery, 1977.

Blodgett, Jean. *The Coming and Going of the Shaman: Shamanism and Eskimo Art.* Winnepeg: Winnepeg Art Gallery, 1978.

Boas, Franz. *The Central Eskimo.* 1888; rpt. Lincoln: Univ. of Nebraska Press, 1964.

Carpenter, Edmund. *Eskimo.* Toronto: Univ. of Toronto Press, 1959.

Carpenter, Edmund. "Artists of the North." *Natural History*, Feb. 1962, pp. 8-15.

Carpenter, Edmund. *Oh! What a Blow that Phantom Gave Me.* NY: Holt, Rinehart, and Co., 1973.

Carpenter, Edmund. *Eskimo Realities.* NY: Holt, Rinehart, and Co., 1973.

Collins, Henry B., ed. *The Far North: 2,000 Years of Eskimo and Indian Art.* Washington, DC: National Gallery of Art, 1973.

Dumont, D.E. *The Eskimos and Aleuts.* London: Thames and Hudson, 1977.

Goetz, Helga, ed. *The Inuit Print/L'estampe Inuit.* Ottawa: National Museum of Man, 1978.

Graburn, N.H.H. "The Eskimos and 'Airport Art.'" *Trans-Action*, 4, No. 10 (1967), 28-33.

Graburn, N.H.H. *Eskimos without Igloos.* Boston: Little, Brown, 1969.

Graburn, N.H.H. "Art and Acculturative Processes." *International Social Science Journal* (UNESCO), 21, No. 3 (1969), 457-468.

Graburn, N.H.H. "A Preliminary Analysis of Symbolism in Eskimo Art and Culture." *Proceedings of the XXXX International Congress of Americanists*, Rome (1972), 2 (1974), 165-170.

Graburn, N.H.H. "Some Problems in the Understanding of Contemporary Inuit Art." *Western Canadian Journal of Anthropology*, 4, No. 3 (1975), 63-72.

Graburn, N.H.H., ed. *Ethnic and Tourist Arts: Cultural Expressions from the Fourth World.* Berkeley: Univ. of California Press, 1976.

Graburn, N.H.H. "*Nalunaikutanga*: Signs and Symbols in Canadian Inuit Art and Culture." *Polarforschung*, 46, No. 1 (1977), 1-11.

Graburn, N.H.H. "I Like Things to Look More Different than that Stuff Was: An Experiment in Cross-Cultural Art Appreciation." In *Art in Society.* Ed. M. Greenhalgh and V. Megaw. London: Duckworth, 1978.

Graburn, N.H.H. "*Inuit Pivalliajut*: the Cultural and Identity Consequences of the Commercialization of Canadian Inuit Art." In *The Consequences of Economic Change in Circum-Polar Regions.* Ed. G. Muller-Wille, P. Pelto, et al. Boreal Institute Occ. Paper No. 14. Edmonton: Boreal Institute, 1978.

Graburn, N.H.H., and B. Stephen Strong. *Circumpolar Peoples: An Anthropological Perspective.* Pacific Palisades, CA: Goodyear, 1973.

Houston, J.A. "Eskimo Sculptors." *Beaver*, 282 (1951), 34-39.

Houston, J.A. "In Search of Contemporary Eskimo Art." *Canadian Art*, 9 (1953), 99-104.

Houston, J.A. *Eskimo Prints.* Barre, MA: Barre Publishers, 1967.

Hudson's Bay Company. Special Issue on Canadian Eskimo Arts. *Beaver*, 298 (1967).

Larmour, W. *Inunnit—The Art of the Canadian Eskimo.* Ottawa: Queen's Printer, 1968.

Martijn, C. "Canadian Eskimo Carving in Historical Perspective." *Anthropos*, 59 (1964), 546-596.

Meldgard, J. *Eskimo Sculpture.* London: Methuen, 1960.

National Museums of Canada. *Sculpture/Inuit: Masterworks of the Canadian Arctic.* Toronto: Univ. of Toronto Press, 1971.

Nungak, Z., and E. Arima. *Eskimo Stories—Unikkaatuat.* National Museums Bulletin, No. 235. Ottawa: National Museums of Canada, 1969.

Pisteolak, Peter. *The People from Our Side.* Edmonton: Hurtig Press, 1975.

Ray, Dorothy Jean. *Artists of the Tundra and the Sea.* Seattle: Univ. of Washington Press, 1961.

Ray, Dorothy Jean. *Eskimo Masks: Art and Ceremony.* Seattle: Univ. of Washington Press, 1967.

Ray, Dorothy Jean. *Eskimo Art: Tradition and Innovation in North Alaska.* Seattle: Univ. of Washington Press, 1977.

Ray, Dorothy Jean. *Aleut and Eskimo Art: Tradition and Innovation in South Alaska.* Seattle: Univ. of Washington Press, 1981.

Routledge, Marie. *Inuit Art in the 1970's.* Kingston, Ontario: Agnes Etherington Art Centre, 1979.

Roch, E., ed. *Arts of the Eskimos: Prints.* Barre, MA: Barre Publishers, 1975.

Saladin d'Anglure, Bernard. *La Parole Changee en Pierre: Vie et Oeuvre de Davidialuk Alasuak.* Cahiers du Patrimoine, No. 11. Quebec: Ministry of Cultural Affairs, 1977.

Swinton, George. *Eskimo Sculpture.* Toronto: McLelland and Stewart, 1965.

Swinton, George. *Sculpture of the Eskimo.* Toronto: McLelland and Stewart, 1972.

Swinton, George. *Eskimo Fantastic Art.* Winnepeg: Univ. of Manitoba Gallery, 1972.

Swinton, George. "Touch and the Real: Contemporary Inuit Aesthetics—Theory, Usage, and Relevance." In *Art in Society.* Eds. M. Greenhalgh and V. Megaw. London: Duckworth, 1978.

Tagoona, Armand. *Shadows.* Ottawa: Oberton Press, 1975.

Williamson, R.G. "The Spirit of Keewatin." *Beaver*, 297 (1965), 4-13.

Watt, Virginia, ed. *The Permanent Collection: Inuit Arts and Crafts.* Montreal: Canadian Guild of Crafts, 1980.

*Fifteen Eskimo women were photographed in
the early 20th century on board a ship at Cape
Fullerton, Hudson Bay, Canada. Two of the
women carry children in the hoods of their
parkas. During this period Eskimos wintered
near whaling ships and government vessels
and supplied the ships' crew with clothing and
meat. In exchange for the food and clothing
the Westerners provided the Eskimos with
guns, boats, and other items.*

Epilogue: Living in Two Worlds*

Minnie Aodla Freeman, Writer and Film Producer,
Edmonton, Alberta

I am Inuit. Throughout my lifetime I have seen many changes. *Qallunaat* ways have had a great impact on Inuit life. Just as Inuit have done for the past 4,500 years, over my lifetime I have learned to adapt to these changes while still maintaining my own Inuit sense of identity.

For many years my people have been called Eskimos—a name originally given to us by the Cree Indians. Today we prefer to be called *Inuit*, our own name for ourselves. The use of this term, meaning "the people," is but one indication of my people's continued sense of identity and vitality.

Inuit Culture

Traditionally, the Inuit have taken their cultural values for granted. Why? Because, traditionally, Inuit did not have any other culture with which to compare their own. This does not mean that Inuit have not appreciated their culture. For, if today I were a very old Inuk (person), I would ask myself: "Without the values of my own system, who am I?" Our values evolve around our environment, our traditional religion, and our psychological teachings from birth until we die. We could not have survived for 4,500 years if these cultural values were not practiced or kept intact. If only I could be sitting in front of you to try and explain my culture; I could not explain it all in one sitting. Having been born in the traditional system of the Inuit and living today with contemporary changes, I will say that I have been born twice.

In explaining my traditional culture, I hope I speak for all Inuit. Long before I was born, preparations were made to teach me the values of the Inuit system. The teachings had already been prepared by my elders.

Everybody who would be involved with my birth and future development had already been chosen: There was that person who would put on my first clothing, that person who would be my namesake, that person who would shape my mind as I grew up, that person who would choose my future husband. All these people have had responsibility for my up-bringing as well as the values I have learned regarding animals, the land, sea, weather, sun, moon, and all of my surroundings. I have had to become aware of everything around me to become aware of myself.

Wrong Interpretations of Inuit Culture by Non-Inuit

If I had remained solely in the tracks of my traditional culture, I would not speak of the wrong interpretation of Inuit culture by the non-Inuit, for I would know only of the Inuit values. With today's changes, and as an Inuk involved in contemporary life, I want to express my feelings.

The most widely held misinterpretations of Inuit culture need to be corrected. For instance, there is the notion that Inuit rub noses; Inuit do not rub noses, they caress with their noses, just as non-Inuit caress with their lips.

Likewise, we Inuit do not always eat raw meat. We sun-dry and, otherwise, age meat as well as boil and, of course, with modern equipment today, we fry it.

Another famous misinterpretation is that Inuit never get cold. The Arctic does not always have a winter climate. However short they may be in some areas of the Arctic, we do get summers. In some areas we even experience a definite spring. The Inuit express the seasons of the Arctic in this way: "Geese flying, the spring has come." "Rivers flowing and sounds of water, summer has come." "Lakes drying, fall is upon us." "Hunters honing winter gear, mother sewing furs and skins, winter has come again."

Inuit do get cold. We have human skins. We feel severe changes of our environment, but we have learned how to keep warm. We will stay warm so long as we follow our system of hunting.

* Much of this chapter has been drawn from A Century of Canada's Arctic Islands: 1880-1980, *Proc. of the 23rd Symposium of The Royal Society of Canada, 11-13 Aug. 1980 (Ottawa: The Royal Society of Canada, 1981).*

A Copper Eskimo tent is pictured at Bathurst Inlet (Northwest Territories, Canada) in 1916; a sledge and kayak frame can be seen in the foreground. During the spring, summer, and fall such caribou skin tents provided shelter as the Eskimos continuously shifted camp in search of food.

Oral History

I want to tell of events that happened to some Inuit in some Arctic Islands. These are not fantasy stories.

The oral history I have heard since I was a child goes way back. When I say "way back," I mean before my time, and I am pretty old. The descriptions and stories that I heard are of funny boats that used to be seen traveling around at a distance. Because it was not known who they really were and where they came from, Inuit called them *arnasiutiit* "women kidnappers." They were described as being tall people, with long blonde hair, who smoked white pipes. Their boats used to be described in detail: They were shaped like old, worn-out boots, the front coming inwards like a turned-up nose. They had paddles that were long. Why I remember these stories is because I used to get scared to go very far from our settlement by myself.

Oral history has always been very strong in Inuit culture. You could imagine how old this history could be. I cannot date it myself, but I know that the telling of those first *qallunaat* arriving to the Arctic were not fantasy stories, but they are old, nevertheless.

However old the stories are, those *arnasiutiit* had a tendency to kidnap women and, if anyone touched them, even so much as in shaking hands, the person who was touched usually died not long after the event. Anyone who saw them close enough described them as covered with an impetigo-like infection all over their hands.

Those oral histories are alive today, mingled with other Inuit oral histories. How long ago it began, I do not know. But I believe that the stories capture the arrival of *qallunaat* in the Arctic.

Though Inuit that long ago did not change much from their early ancestors, Inuit knew that a different culture was looming amongst them. They were cautious because the strangers did not communicate. My grandfather used to predict that one day Inuit lands would be full of *qallunaat*, *qallunaat*-language and *qallunaat*-equipment, and that if Inuit did not show their own ways they would be covered all over with *qallunaat* ways. He was not wrong!

Changes in Inuit Culture

It is not my intention to be prejudiced or sarcastic, nor to be unaccepting of the history that has happened on these Inuit Islands. I did not grow up to panic while sitting on cracking ice. If I do not seem to be speaking for all Inuit throughout all these islands, then I would like to speak as a person who is involved during this history-making in Canada, to express my views how on our native side (the other side of the coin, so to speak) changes have affected Inuit.

Most of you, and I too, are aware that twenty-some years ago the government of Canada did have good intentions to care for Inuit. That was the first mistake the government made. Why do I think that it was a mistake? Because every culture has different eyes, different ways of looking at things, situations, and events.

Now that I have lived among *qallunaat* for the last 26 years, I understand that Inuit, upon being first seen by the early *qallunaat* arrivals, looked destitute, helpless, and were smiling too much. The first *qallunaat* arrivals did not understand our ways, our culture, which is entangled so much with psychological beliefs.

Probably the first thing that came to their minds was to look after Inuit the way they would with welfare-needy people in the South. I also understand now that *qallunaat* culture is very based upon material possessions. Can you picture a *qallunaat* seeing Inuit in furs, with skin tents, fur bedding, and stone utensils? To some *qallunaat* that is enough for them to run back South and tell the government that there are people living very poorly.

In some ways, they were a lot like my grandmother who, upon first being sold a cotton jacket down on the beach at her settlement, tried it on, took it off as fast as she put it on, and said, "How useless, the wind goes right through this!" It was a mistake. It was a mistake, at least the way Inuit understood the intentions on the part of the *qallunaat*. For Inuit people, my grandparents and my parents, understood that the government of Canada committed themselves to look after the Inuit for the rest of their lives, and they still believe that.

I have heard how much progress has been made here in the Arctic. I think any good change is always welcome to any kind of culture. Inuit have always looked for better ways, for useful things to aid survival. For instance, the *uluk (ulu)*, the woman's knife, went through several changes —and always to so-called progress. I could imagine that at one time it was made out of ordinary stone, and for those archaeologists who are familiar with these objects from their diggings all over these islands, I am sure they have seen the changes the *uluk* went through. But I do not think changes that happen within the culture itself hurt as bad as the changes that have occurred during the last 100 years. How many of us can go from extreme hot to cold conditions within a few minutes? There is bound to be some very painful change within our body. The changes the Inuit have gone through are similar to that example.

While Inuit have been here more that 100 years, the changes that began 100 years ago within our culture are not all bad, but as my grandmother always used to say, "It is human nature to learn the bad things first." Maybe it is not necessary for me to mention the lack of information Inuit have had with drastic changes. Who would have known that excessive drinking was bad? Who would know that garbage from the *qallunaat* world is not the same as garbage we had, which was all natural and therefore did not pollute the land? Who would know that not eating properly with *qallunaat* food is unhealthy? Who would know that irregular sleeping habits when one has to work and go to school in *qallunaat* style are bad? What are bad and good manners in *qallunaat* style? Inuit have had all kinds of examples.

The changes are here to stay. That we realize very much. It is up to you *qallunaat* to show Inuit not only *what*, but also *why* some things are good or bad, to adopt. If I were to reverse the situation and Inuit had the dominant culture, would any of you decide to walk on the ice in the middle of May? Would you eat the liver of polar bear? Would you keep traveling when overtaken by a blizzard-storm? Would you take a walk to the next mountain (when you don't know that the distance is deceiving)? Would you behave differently in front of children who might be in their baby ways, *makutuk* ways (soft age) or *imummariit* way? Would you know the cause of social behavior at any given different situation? There are *qallunaat* ways I am readily willing to adopt and there are things I do not—or cannot—understand. Quite a few years ago I finally learned to separate the two cultures. I became two people—my manners, speech and behavior at any time during social scenes changed—because both the *qallunaat* and Inuit ways demand different behavior.

Missionaries

The first arrivals of missionaries were quite scary to some Inuit. They affected a lot of fears and even caused killings. First of all, mission-aries considered Inuit primitive, and we Inuit considered their teachings very primitive. Everything was "thou shalt not"—when the very traditional laws and beliefs of old Inuit were "thou shall." "Thou shall," for the benefit of learning. I mean, we Inuit survived these harsh lands through testing and trying new ways. There were so many things we did that the missionaries did not like. I don't know if they ever stopped to look at our old religion. For instance, they stopped our traditional trial marriages, which to Inuit were very vital in order to make successful marriages—as a result of which there were no separations or divorces, or children separated from parents. They stopped Inuit men from having more than one wife. Their rules from the book were so important to pass on, that they did not see the necessary reasons for some Inuit men to have a couple of wives. Missionaries saw it as a big sin, whereas Inuit practiced it because of the importance of family life—to maintain the unity of family life. For often a man took a widowed woman in order to help her raise her many children. Plural marriage was practiced not as a sin, but for the sake of strengthening family life in Inuit society.

I realize that at this moment I would not have learned to speak the *qallunaat* language if it were not for missionaries. I went to their schools and lived with them ten months out of the year. But they did not allow me to speak my own language in their schools, so that I began to think that there was something wrong with my language. At that time, I used to feel that I was in two hells: one while I was in school, the second when I went home, because my grandmother would not hear any other language spoken in her presence in our house.

One of the strangest things that affected family life was the separation caused by *qallunaat* religion, as when the Catholics managed to convert a brother while his sister remained Protestant. Really, it's a farce when today, the church tells us that the family that prays together stays together.

The Hudson's Bay Company

I think I can say that since 1670, the Hudson's Bay Company made Inuit lives easier. They were in my home area of James Bay long before I was born, fur trading with my ancestors. Inuit have always traded amongst themselves either for short periods or long perods of time. Inuit understood the trading systems of the Hudson's Bay Company. I think one of the reasons why Inuit welcomed the Hudson's Bay Company was the fact that the company never tried to change Inuit ways of behaving or thinking.

Yes, they changed our equipment —to better steel knives, steel saws, steel nails, steel axes, and manufactured cloth. Inuit understood it was the furs that the Hudson's Bay Company were after. Inuit hunters had employment through the Hudson's Bay Company. It was a familiar type of job which Inuit enjoyed. We still hear older Inuit today saying that the Hudson's Bay Company is most useful in Inuit lands. They did not interfere with the lifestyles of Inuit.

A 1938 Carnegie Museum field party and their Eskimo guides are shown preparing camp for the night at Hudson Bay, Canada. The group has built a snowhouse on the sea ice.

The Royal Canadian Mounted Police (RCMP)

The RCMP were known to Inuit as a very humane people. In James Bay when their yearly ship arrived, they visited individual homes either to count the household inhabitants to see how many of us were left or how many of us were born. Mind you, they never called us by our names; instead, they always wanted to see our disc numbers. I know now the RCMP were doing Inuit statistics, giving out family allowances, and registering births.

I was involved as a translator in the 1950s when the Department of Northern Affairs was taking over the welfare role of the RCMP. It was painful to watch and hear some RCMP and welfare workers arguing and fighting over files. At the same time, it was funny to observe that one was trying to find work to do, and the other trying to stay on the job. In those days there were no criminals, no thieves, no drunks, and at the time Inuit were still obeying their own community laws. Today, the RCMP probably have the longest lasting job in the Arctic.

Scientists

There were many Inuit natural scientists who acquired their knowledge from their own observations and by purely wanting to understand their total surroundings, whether animals, snow and ice, people, or land. Today, to me, it is questionable if those Inuit scientists are still around. Probably, not many are, because for the last 20 years or so Inuit have not really passed on their knowledge to their children. This knowledge has not been intentionally ignored, but how can you be aware of your own environment if you are working from 9 to 5? Also, the qallunaat system of education has interfered a great deal with the development of knowledge of our surroundings.

There are some communities now that are filming Inuit ways and interviewing knowledgeable Inuit. I know that scientists from the South have been working in the Arctic for a long time, but only a few have made some Southerners understand Inuit culture.

Over the years scientists have always been very welcome in Inuit communities. Some have been adopted by Inuit—in fact, I adopted one permanently. It has been said that the ideal family in the Arctic consists of a husband and wife, four children, and an anthropologist. As scientists are often willing to admit, Inuit have clothed them, fed them, and taken them to wherever they wanted to go to do their studies. Often Inuit have taken chances in matters of life and death, because they felt responsible for a particular scientist.

We Inuit have met many different kinds of scientists, both in terms of personality and in terms of what they wanted to study. We have studied them while they studied us.

There are some communities now that have begun to screen scientists before they get to the community. One of the reasons for this was because in some places scientists who came to study a community stayed in a hostel, hotel, or in a qallunaat house. They got their information from qallunaat who had never really been involved themselves with Inuit households. Then these scientists went back South and wrote their reports based on hearsay. Inuit consider these scientists not only dishonest with the Inuit, but also dishonest to their superiors in the South.

Personally, I have been involved with scientists since I was born. But that doesn't mean I have to like everything scientists do. For instance, I know that scientists, when preparing to go into the field, have to find financial support. I am wondering when scientists are going to start to include in their budgets funds to have the information gathered translated into Inuktitut and sent back North?

The Future

What is happening to Inuit over the next 100 years? Will Inuit be just as involved in Canadian affairs or more so during the next 100 years? I hear, I listen, I observe, I investigate, and I formulate my own opinion of what is happening to Inuit today. Old Inuit have always believed that nothing is ever solved with bitter emotions. We of this and the next generation have a heavy load to bear. Will we remain without bitterness? The old Inuit did have a hard life, but their burdens were familiar and there were no drastic changes during their lifetimes.

I am not saying that we of this generation do not welcome the changes. But without background information and proper resources, we cannot weigh options and make decisions. Inuit never went out into the ocean without testing their kayak first, Inuit never put up their igloo without examining the location, Inuit did not go into action without weighing the total situation first. Yet, the plane arrives, the government or industry officials step out, and out comes a new situation. Even today, there are often no letters, no phone calls, no information. Are qallunaat always so unthinking, unfeeling, and so rash?

At the present, Inuit are working very hard to find meaningful ways to have a say about their land. I cannot pre-judge these plans and make rash statements by myself. It is not fair to other Inuit that I should anticipate their wishes. But starting today, no one should take Inuit land claims lightly, for that is where fairness and equality begin for the native people of Canada.

Here ends me.

Reading List

Briggs, Jean L. *Never in Anger: Portrait of an Eskimo Family*. Cambridge: Harvard Univ. Press, 1970.

Freeman, Minnie Aodla. *Life among the Qallunaat*. Edmonton: Hurtig Publishers, 1978.

French, Alice. *My Name is Masak*. Winnipeg: Peguis Publishers, 1976.

Gedalof, Robin and Alootook Ipellie, eds. *Paper Stays Put: A Collection of Inuit Writings*. Edmonton: Hurtig Publishers, 1980.

Lewis, Richard, ed. *I Breathe a New Song: Poems of the Eskimo*. NY: Simon and Schuster, 1971.

Metayer, Maurice, trans. *I, Nuligak.*
Toronto: Peter Martin Associates, 1966.

Metayer, Maurice, ed. and trans. *Tales
from the Igloo.* Edmonton: Hurtig Publishers, 1972.

Steltzer, Ulli. *Inuit: The North in Transition.*
Vancouver: Douglas and McIntyre;
Seattle: Univ. of Washington Press, 1982.

Tagoona, Armand. *Shadows.* n.p.: Oberon
Press, 1975.

*A modern Inuit family is pictured at Rankin
Inlet (Northwest Territories, Canada). Their
dress reflects some of the changes that have
occurred in Inuit culture.*

Index

Author Biographies

Richard G. Condon is a Post-Doctoral Fellow at the Peabody Museum of Archaeology and Ethnology, Harvard University. His research interests include behavioral ecology, demography, and human development. Since 1978 Dr. Condon has spent a total of 28 months conducting field research with the Copper Inuit of Holman Island in the Central Canadian Arctic. His book dealing with Inuit behavior and seasonal change is currently in press, and he is writing a monograph on Inuit adolescent development. Dr. Condon received his Ph.D. from the University of Pittsburgh in 1981.

David Damas is Professor of Anthropology at McMaster University. Begun in 1960, his fieldwork in the Canadian Arctic has concentrated upon the social structure and ecology of the Central Canadian Eskimo tribes. Dr. Damas is the author of *Iglulimuit Kinship and Local Groupings: A Structural Approach*, and he is currently the editor and the author of a number of chapters for *The Arctic*, a volume in the *Handbook of North American Indians*. Since receiving his Ph.D. from the University of Chicago in 1962, he has worked as an ethnologist for the National Museum of Man, National Museums of Canada and has taught at McMaster University.

Mary R. Dawson is Curator, Section of Vertebrate Paleontology and Chairman, Earth Sciences Division, Carnegie Museum of Natural History. Since receiving her Ph.D. from the University of Kansas in 1957, she has had extensive paleontological field experience in the western United States, Sardinia, Sicily, and France. Her several field trips to the Canadian High Arctic from 1973 on have resulted in the discovery of the first Tertiary land vertebrates within the Arctic Circle. She is interested in interpreting Tertiary climates in the Arctic as well as in understanding vertebrate relationships.

Minnie Aodla Freeman was born in 1936 on Cape Hope Island in James Bay. She was trained as a nurse at Ste. Therese School in Fort George and, in 1957, went to Ottawa to accept a position as a translator with the Department of Northern Affairs and Resources. She served as Manager of the Inuit Broadcasting Corporation from 1981 to 1982 and is deeply committed to dealing with the problems facing her people — the Inuit of Canada. Mrs. Freeman is a poet, writer, and translator and is the author of the play *Survival in the South* and the book *Life among the Qallunaat*. She was an advisor for the Carnegie Museum of Natural History exhibit, "Polar World: Wyckoff Hall of Arctic Life."

Nelson H. H. Graburn is Professor of Anthropology, University of California, Berkeley. His special interests are social structure and kinship, ethnic arts, and tourism. His fieldwork in the Arctic has focused on the art of its indigenous inhabitants. Dr. Graburn is the author of *Eskimos Without Igloos* and *Hunters and Artists: The Commercial Arts of the Canadian Inuit*. Since receiving his Ph.D. from the University of Chicago in 1963, he has worked as a Research Anthropologist for the Northern Coordination and Research Centre of the Government of Canada and has taught at the University of California, Berkeley.

Robert McGhee is Head of the Research Section at the Archaeological Survey of Canada, National Museum of Man, National Museums of Canada. Dr. McGhee is a specialist in the archaeology of the Canadian Arctic where he has undertaken extensive fieldwork. He is the author of *Canadian Arctic Prehistory* and *Beluga Hunters: An Archaeological Reconstruction of the Mackenzie Delta Kittegaryumiut*. Dr. McGhee received his Ph.D. from the University of Calgary in 1968.

Joseph F. Merritt is Director of Powdermill Nature Reserve, the biological research station of Carnegie Museum of Natural History. He received a Ph.D. from the University of Colorado in 1976. A mammalogist specializing in physiological ecology, Dr. Merritt has written laboratory manuals in mammalogy and ornithology and published widely in the field of ecology of mammals inhabiting montane environments of North America. In 1982, Dr. Merritt participated in a field expedition to Rankin Inlet in the Central Candian Arctic during which materials were collected for the Carnegie Museum of Natural History exhibit, "Polar World: Wyckoff Hall of Arctic Life."

James B. Richardson III is Chief Curator, Section of Anthropology at Carnegie Museum of Natural History. A specialist in maritime adaptations, he has done extensive field research in both Peru and New England. Since receiving his Ph.D. from the University of Illinois in 1969, he has taught at the University of Pittsburgh and was Chairman of the Department of Anthropology there from 1977 to 1980. Dr. Richardson became Chief Curator of Carnegie Museum of Natural History's Section of Anthropology in 1978; he was Project Director for the development of the exhibit, "Polar World: Wyckoff Hall of Arctic Life."

Frederick H. Utech is Associate
Curator in Charge, Section of Botany,
Carnegie Museum of Natural History.
Since receiving his Ph.D. from
Washington University (St. Louis)
in 1973, he has done worldwide
botanical field work on plant system-
atics and evolution, particularly on
the family Liliaceae. In 1982 he
participated in a Carnegie Museum
of Natural History field trip to
Rankin Inlet where he surveyed the
flora and collected some 5,000 specimens for the Museum's herbarium,
the "Polar World: Wyckoff Hall
Arctic Life" exhibit, and for
exchange with other institutions.

James W. VanStone is Curator of
North American Archaeology and
Ethnology at the Field Museum of
Natural History. His research interests include the archaeology, ethnography, and ethnohistory of Arctic
America, especially Alaska, where he
continues to carry out field research.
Dr. VanStone received his Ph.D. from
the University of Pennsylvania in
1954 and has taught at the University
of Alaska and the University of
Toronto. He is the author of numerous monographs and scientific articles
on Alaskan Eskimos and was a
consultant for Carnegie Museum of
Natural History's "Polar World:
Wyckoff Hall of Arctic Life" exhibit.

Co-editor, Martina M. Jacobs is
Program Specialist, Division of
Education. Since receiving her Ph.D.
in 1977 from the University of
Pittsburgh, Dr. Jacobs has been
involved in writing, editing, research,
and exhibit development at Carnegie
Museum of Natural History. She is
the author of *Kachina Ceremonies and
Kachina Dolls* and an editor of
Carnegie's Dinosaurs and *Guidebook,
Carnegie Museum of Natural History,
Carnegie Institute*.